Wow! This book is a must-read. These principles will help anyone make it through the shift. Whether new to real estate or a seasoned veteran, this book gets to the core of what it takes to succeed. Thank you, Gary, for sharing your experiences and stories of how to look for the opportunities in a shifting market.

RICK AND TERI BRENKUS, Las Vegas, Nevada

Sales Volume: $97 Million

After reading this book, we realized that we have been through five shifts in our market over 21 years of selling. We survived, we thrived, and we became better because of the experience. Shifts are a little like childbirth: you don't want to remember going through it, but you sure love the gift that comes from it.

KURT AND DARLA BUEHLER, Dallas, Texas

Sales Volume: $71 Million

Don't let this title fool you. While SHIFT certainly is profound and timely for the market most of us are experiencing right now, this book also works for you in any market. The savvy agent will put it right next to The Millionaire Real Estate Agent *for back-to-back reference.*

TODD BUTZER, Minneapolis, Minnesota

Real Estate Company Regional Director

Wow! They have done it again. This book is amazing. I feel like I have just had the best real estate conversation of my life with my three best friends. At the same time, I feel like I have been hit over the head with a two-by-four! This is a powerful survival handbook for this market ... or any market. Pick it up, read it, change your outlook, and your future.

DORIS CARLIN, Joplin, Missouri

Sales Volume: $24 Million

Sunday, August 26, 2007 4:15 PM

From: **Gary Keller**

To: KWU Course Writers

the market has created a need for timely and tightly focused courses that agents can dig into quickly for answers on what to do **RIGHT NOW.**

the 12 topics they struggle with RIGHT NOW are:

1. **seller pricing strategies** (pricing right, price reductions, pricing lower than market to create multiple offers,etc...)
2. **seller staging strategies** (getting the home in it's best condition and then presenting the home in it's best light)
3. **transaction issues and how to resolve** (with this market lots of issues show up that weren't there before once a property is sold)
4. **creative financing** (as credit tightens or rates rise this becomes a huge issue)
5. name/number capturing and **converting to an appointment** (another huge issue. with less leads - the ones you get become more precious)
6. name/number capturing and converting to an appointment - **internet leads** (this is THE issue on the internet and thus deserves it's own course)
7. how to run lean and mean (when sales drop - **expense management:** what to spend on/ what to cut becomes a real issue)
8. **getting the most from your staff and sales team** (when sales drop - our people must be more effective)
9. **creating urgency for buyers** (when the market becomes a buyer's market, the buyer's seem to lose urgency to take action)
10. **short sales** (when the market shifts, foreclosures go up. this course needs to be reexamined and updated for this exact market)
11. **lead generation** in a shifting market (agents need clarity about how to focus their lead generation tightly with appropriate source, message and script)
12. **a positive mindset** and an understanding that it is all hands on deck time right now. keeping a tight focus on what matters and spending more time on those tasks. jay, dave and i would be happy to sit down and brainstorm these with you to help you lay these out.

onward...... gk

WHAT AGENTS ARE SAYING ABOUT *SHIFT*

I have been in real estate for a long time and have survived many ups and throughout my career—but I wish I'd had this book. It's a great tool that I cou *used a long time ago.*

Sylvie Bégin, Ottawa, Ontario Canada

Sales Volume: $22 Million

SHIFT *is a true wake-up call. Gary hits the nail on the head when he says c easy yet long-term success requires it. The concepts should resonate deeply w serious about having a thriving real estate business.*

Martin Bouma, Ann Arbor, Michigan

Sales Volume: $50 Million

I love this book. You've blended both importance and inspiration into tool for real estate agents everywhere. Encouraging us to remember how m agents employ a simpler business approach, you've shared the key fundam can insulate us from the staggering market shifts and get us through the. faster, with the least collateral damage.

Rick Brash, Calgary, Alberta Canada

Sales Volume: $24 Million

Gary and his team have hit the nail on the head... once again! Your twelve tactics are right on. I have been a student of The Millionaire Real Estate Agent *since day one—thanks for truly changing my life. Keep writing your books—I can't get enough! The more I read them, the better my business and life become.*

JANA CAUDILL, Crown Point, Indiana
Sales Volume: $93 Million

Real estate is a simple business that's often overcomplicated in its application. SHIFT *is a book that gets to the heart of what makes a real estate business work and work well, no matter the market. Read it over and over again, and keep implementing the basics of this powerful tool.*

TONY DiCELLO, Austin, Texas
National Real Estate Sales Trainer and Coach

Knowledge is power and Gary has once again given us this power by taking us step by step through the reality of today's market. SHIFT *has clarified for me what to do and, more importantly, how to think. I see what is possible for me and my business right now.*

JOHN FURBER, Toronto, Ontario Canada
Real Estate Company Regional Director

This isn't the first shift nor is it going to be the last, but it has been devastating in its effect on the unprepared. Finally, we have a guide to preparing for, adjusting to, and thriving through this shift and any others! This sets the tone for sustained success and profitability throughout your real estate career.

RICK GEHA, Fremont, California
Sales Volume: $34 Million

This is the first buyers' market I've experienced, and frankly, I wasn't prepared. With SHIFT in hand, I've made a few quick changes and am back on the right track.

BRANDON GREEN, Washington, DC

Sales Volume: $27 Million

Gary's training had prepared me and my team for the shift. Gary's proactive approach convinced me to scale back spending, build reserves, and gain market share. The changes we made have increased our market share in our target market from 19 percent to 28 percent and allowed us to remain profitable.

BOB GUEST, Austin, Texas

Sales Volume: $32 Million

This book is both timeless and well-timed. A shift to a buyers' market requires us to be doing the things we should have been doing all the time. Agents would be well-advised to keep this book at hand at all times.

DAN HARKER, Dallas, Texas

Sales Volume: $24 Million

Where was SHIFT when we found ourselves in this situation last time? All who read, internalize, and implement the principles of this authoritative guide will change lives, not only those of your buyers and sellers, but also of yourself and your family! Get the principles down, work smart, and you will not only survive, but thrive!

MARY HARKER, Dallas, Texas

Sales Volume: $36 Million

Gary and his team have outdone themselves again. This book allows agents to stay on the cutting edge of this changing market and well ahead of their competition. It's the pinnacle of what each new or seasoned agent needs to read again and again.

CHRIS HELLER, Encinitas, California

Sales Volume: $60 Million

Succinct, direct, instructive, and with a road map to success. Reliably researched and right on the mark, as always. Gary, thanks for your intense passion for supporting the industry in a powerful way.

JUDY JOHNS, Overland Park, Kansas

Sales Volume: $41 Million

Many agents have never experienced a buyers' market and therefore continue to perform the same tasks, the same way, only trying harder. Gary Keller and his team understand the shift in the real estate business at a level no one else does. I know because the agents we coach are using the strategies and activities in this book and are currently producing at a level higher than they were before the shift.

DIANNA KOKOSZKA, Austin, Texas

National Real Estate Sales Trainer and Coach

Gary's new book is packed with hope, knowledge, and a real plan for success. It reminds us to control our fears and think about the opportunity that all markets bring. Thank you, Gary!

LINDA MCKISSACK, Flower Mound, Texas

Sales Volume: $58 Million

Gary, I cannot thank you enough for this book! I felt like you were speaking directly to me. I built my business by following the models from The Millionaire Real Estate Agent *and I plan on improving my business with the models in* SHIFT. *This is a must-read for every agent desiring a great career not just a great year!*

MELONEE PIPERI, Houston, Texas
Sales Volume: $64 Million

Like all of Gary Keller's books, SHIFT *is more than just a book. It is a timely, straightforward, instructional manual for success. I predict that the income of real estate professionals will be directly proportional to how well they master the 12 tactics outlined in this book. Gary Keller is, without question, "The Wizard of Aha's!"*

SHAUN RAWLS, Atlanta, Georgia
National Real Estate Sales Trainer and Multi-Office Owner

Shifts happen! This book is a lifeline for continued success as a real estate professional. Thanks to Gary Keller's insight, SHIFT *helped me identify deficiencies and apply the tools to master them.*

BRAD REESER, Edmond, Oklahoma
Sales Volume: $35 Million

It's called a "shift," not the "end." The game was here, now it's there. You need to remember that everyone goes to bed at night somewhere, and that they can either own it or rent it, but someone sold it to the owner. If you get back to what really works in all markets, that sale can and will be done by you. Read this book, get your head on straight, and get back to what works in all markets—and you will own your market!

GENE RIVERS, Tallahassee, Florida
Sales Volume: $57 Million

If this book doesn't light you on fire, check for a pulse. As always, Gary has found the unifying principles on which survival in a shift are based. This should be mandatory reading for any agent whether old or new. Having survived a shift or two, we still found it eye-opening, informative, and insightful. You can survive and thrive. This book will be your manual.

RUSSELL AND WENDY SHAW, Phoenix, Arizona

Sales Volume: $104 Million

The information in SHIFT is so basic and so true! We have seen many large producers fall by the wayside in this market because they had not built their business on the fundamentals of lead generating, expense accountability, talented support staff, and a commitment to continual learning. We have discovered and corrected some of our own weaknesses using the concepts in this book.

STEVE AND DEBBIE TUFTS, Atlanta, Georgia

Sales Volume: $52 Million

After 22 years in the business I thought I understood the trends, but SHIFT made it crystal clear. After reading the book, I knew without question what I needed to be doing in this type of market. If you're serious about staying in this business, now and in the years to come, then this is your guide.

DEBBIE ZOIS, Las Vegas, Nevada

Sales Volume: $40 Million

HOW TOP REAL ESTATE AGENTS
TACKLE TOUGH TIMES

SHIFT

GARY KELLER

WITH DAVE JENKS AND JAY PAPASAN

NEW YORK   CHICAGO   SAN FRANCISCO   LISBON   LONDON   MADRID   MEXICO CITY
MILAN   NEW DELHI   SAN JUAN   SEOUL   SINGAPORE   SYDNEY   TORONTO

ISBN: 978-0-07-173938-2
MHID: 0-07-173938-6

This publication is designed to provide accurate and authoritative information in regard to the subject matter covered. It is sold with the understanding that neither the author nor the publisher is engaged in rendering legal, accounting, or other professional service. If legal advice or other expert assistance is required, the services of a competent professional person should be sought.
  —From a Declaration of Principles jointly adopted by a Committee of the American Bar
    Association and a Committee of Publishers.

McGraw-Hill books are available at special quantity discounts to use as premiums and sales promotions, or for use in corporate training programs. To contact a representative, please e-mail us at bulksales@ mcgraw-hill.com.

This book is printed on acid-free paper. The authors and McGraw-Hill are committed to sustainable publishing practices, which include the use of recycled and acid-free paper whenever available.

This book is dedicated to sales professionals everywhere
who are committed not just to having a great day, month, or year,
but to a great real estate career. To those who understand
that the foundational skills demanded during the most difficult
times will sustain their careers through all times.

ACKNOWLEDGMENTS

ON BEHALF OF MY COAUTHORS, Dave and Jay, I want to give grateful recognition to all those who helped make this book possible. I'd like to extend a heartfelt thanks to the thousands of top real estate agents across North America who continue to accompany us on this journey. They actively partake in our mastermind sessions, training programs, and focus groups. They often allow us to serve as their coaches and consultants. In truth, we have actually been their students, learning from their real-life experiences and capturing their best practices. They have taught us well.

MEGA AGENT MASTERMIND GROUP 1 FROM SPRING 2008 MASTERMINDS
Back Row Jodi Boxer, Andy Hodes, Jackie Ellis, David Kupfer, Darla Buehler, Kurt Buehler, Denton Aguam, Michael C. Williamson, Jeff Kucic, Chris Minteer, Marion Franke, Linda Alexander, Donna Grissom Middle Row Stamie Karakasidis, Pat Sankey, Johnette Pyron, Spalding Pyron, Quito Keutla, Shawn Lepp, Mary Harker, Steve Shepherd, Patti Siebold Front Row Josh Buxbaum, Suzette Teague, David Fogg, Katria Weyl, Lesley Thomas, Dan Harker, Gary Leogrande, Mike Hansen, Larry Bartow

MEGA AGENT MASTERMIND GROUP 2 FROM SPRING 2008 MASTERMINDS

Back Row Margaret (Maggee) Miggins, Chris Carter, Kristina Arias, Jim Fischetti, Bud Cortner, Patrick W. Woods, Kelly Hagglund, Seychelle Van Poole, Barbara Van Poole, Dave VanDermyden, Ed Hunnicutt, Cathy Hunnicutt, Jo-Anne LaBuda, Nikki Ubaldini, Barry Slaton, Michelle Edwards Middle Row Betty Bezemer, Robin Siino, Mindy DeMain, Linda Carter, John Veytia, Cesi Pagano, Peg Braxton, Christine Ricci, Peggy Sloan Front Row Mike Mendoza, Fran Johnson, Tim Thompson, Joe Charters, Mary Charters, Sherrie Puffer, Brad McKissack, Holly Perry, Doris Carlin

MEGA AGENT MASTERMIND GROUP 3 FROM SPRING 2008 MASTERMINDS

Back Row Keri Ricci, Bruce Kink, Debbie Knox, Tom Guajardo Jr., Lisa Healey, Sean Healey, Gabey Giblin, Ben All, Tim Nystrom, Ben Kinney, Michael Shoffner, Rick VanDermyden Middle Row Leesa Nuttall, Debbie Zois, Jeff Pantanella, Rae Wayne, Linda Bishop, Carol Young, Carolyn Capalbo, Brad Puffer, Debbie W. Romero Front Row Helen Guajardo, Melissa Scagliola, Mary Harker, Chris Cormack, Lisa Jalufka

MEGA AGENT MASTERMIND GROUP 4 FROM SPRING 2008 MASTERMINDS
Back Row Sue Long, Ron Young, Larry Baumgartner, Bill Knox, Bernie Christian, Phil Buoscio,
Jayne Parsons, Matt Fetick, Tom Yeatts, Skip Tebo, Rick Southwick, Laura Kittleman Yeatts,
Don Ubaldini Front Row Scott Smith, James Biedenharn, Jim Eason, Steve Johns, Bernadette Hurley,
Christopher Hurley, Sue Adler, Diane Kink, Martin Bouma

In addition to the Mastermind attendees from our spring 2008 sessions, we want to recognize the contributions of those top agents who were with us at our Mastermind sessions in 2006 and 2007. It was during those intensely focused meetings that we truly connected with what was happening in the shifting real estate market. The agents helped us get clear on the issues and brainstorm the strategies and tactics for surviving and thriving. They willingly and passionately shared their clearest thinking, their most instructive experiences, and their best practices.

To all of our Mastermind participants we owe heartfelt thanks— you are clearly among the very best at what you do: Camille Abbott, Bob Andrews, Gene Arant, Antonio Atacan, Cindy Baglietto, Mark Baglietto, Doug Balog, Alicia Barnes, Linda Bartlett, Tom Brandt, Rick Brash, Rick

Brenkus, Teri Brenkus, David Brownell, Jessica Bruehl, Jim Buff, Chad Burnett, Nate Butcher, Jana Caudill, Andy Clark, Robert Coalla, Steven Cohen, Greg Cooper, Judy Copple, Mike Cusimano, Roxanne Deberry, Bonnie Dillon, Matt Dimmick, Rick Dittemore, Kevin Elliott, Bobby Faulk, Janet Faulk, Tricia Fox, Sherry Francis, Elaine Garner, Rick Geha, Gary Gentry, Mel Gentry, Martin Gibbs, Chad Goldwasser, Tara Goldwasser, Jason Gorman, Leslie Gowin, Brandon Green, Chris Hake, Don Hamilton, Sharon Hamilton, Bruce Hardie, Erick Harpole, Sandy Hartmann, Chris Heller, Paul Herrick, Kathy Hewitt, Pat Hiban, James Hightower, Michael Hilgenberg, Marie Hoffman, Barbara Hogoboom, Alex Jauregui, Judy Johns, Matt Keller, Linda Kepple, Sharon Ketko, Pam Kiker, Cheryl Krone, Aaron Lancaster, Lorraine Leonard, Jay Liebe, Sue Lusk-Gleich, Karen Marshall, Maria Martinez, Ryan McCarty, Miles McCormick, Jennifer McKenna, Timothy McKenna, Jim McKissack, Linda McKissack, Josh Mendoza, Jude Mendoza, Vikki Middlebrook, Susan Murphy, Kathy Muscatell, Dave Neal, Mike Netzel, Marc Nicholson, George Philbeck, Melonee Piperi, Nancy Poss, John Prescott, David Raesz, Russell Rhodes, Jan Richey, Gene Rivers, Rebekah Rivers, D'Arce Rotta, Carol Royse, Louis Rugolo, Gary Segal, Roberto Sexias, Russell Shaw, Wendy Shaw, Judy Sheller, Sylvia Smith, Michael Soares, Zee Spezzano, Ida Terbet, Marybeth Tiemeyer, Debbie Tufts, Steve Tufts, Gary Ubaldini, Gitta Urbainczyk, Vicki Wagner, Larry Wall, Laurie Wall, John Werkmeister, Kathy Werkmeister, Ron Wexler, James Willoughby, Mark Worley, Karen Wunderlick, Robert Yoder, Don Zeleznak, and Ryan Zeleznak.

This publishing journey began in the 1990s with our coursework on "The Remarkable Real Estate Sales Business Game" and culminated in 2003 with the publication of *The Millionaire Real Estate Agent* and, two years later, the publication of *The Millionaire Real Estate Investor*. The ups and downs of the market during the last 30 years made us realize the significant need to focus on the unique issues of a shifting market.

Reflecting on my historical roots, I want to thank my original partner, Joe Williams. Without his initial investment in the business and in me, I'm not sure where I'd be. I also want to acknowledge my business partners Mo Anderson, Mark Willis, and Mary Tennant. Mo's spiritual integrity, commitment to standards, and unstoppable work ethic are incredible. Mark's amazing energy, tactical tenacity, and strength under pressure are legendary. Mary's unwavering commitment to all things agent, persistence through adversity, and win-win attitude are inspiring.

I'd also like to thank a number of others on our greater team who informed this book directly or indirectly through their work: Chris Buckelew, Michaelann Byerly, Brooke Caldwell, Doris Carlin, Linda Cooke, Mona Covey, Tony DiCello and Dianna Kokoszka, Dick Dillingham, Bryon Ellington, Julie Fantechi, Michael Flemming, Rick Geha, Bruce Hardie, Roger Higle, Dr. Rebecca John, Bruce Keith, Bob Kilinski, Brad Korn, Mike Kranz, Brandi Lauve, Cheiri Lowry, Mary Mann, Alice Nguyen, Linda McKissack, Jack Miller, Suman Olney, John Prescott, Shaun Rawls, David Reed, Gene Rivers, Dawn Sroka, Stacia Thompson, Toni Tolerico, Nikki Ubaldini, Linda Warren, Mary Weaver, and Paul Wylie.

Also, we appreciate and acknowledge the contribution from the best real estate instructors, authors, and coaches in the business, who work so hard to help so many: Bill Barrett, Dave Beson, Howard Brinton,

Brian Buffini, Darryl Davis, Mike Ferry, Michael Gerber, Ken Goodfellow, Allen F. Hainge, Mark Victor Hansen, Gregg Herder, Don Hobbs, Tommy Hopkins, Carol Johnson, Johnnie Johnson, Danielle Kennedy, Robert T. Kiyosaki, David Knox, Linda McLean, Laurie Moore-Moore, Steve Murray, Craig Proctor, Jerry Rossi, Steve Shull, Joe Stumpf, Rick Willis, Floyd Wickman, Tim Wood, and Pat Zaby.

I want to especially acknowledge the can-do team that directly supports our writing and publishing. Our partners at McGraw-Hill saw the need for this book and helped publish it with all deliberate speed. Thank you Mary Glenn, Seth Morris, and Peter McCurdy. Thanks also to Ellen Marks, Annie Switt, Jill Dwyer, Michael Balistreri, and Skipper Chong Warson, and to Julie Savasky, whose design contributions brought a clarity and accessibility to the layout. High fives to Jim Talbot, Brett Decker, Tamara Hurwitz, Jeff Ryder, Maryanne Jordan, Mary Sallee, Mary Keith Trawick, and Katie Nelms who helped complete the circle from raw manuscript to finished book to agent bookshelves and training rooms. Thanks to agent Doug Holaday, whose wisdom and well-designed graphs greatly enhanced our treatment of pricing. And special thanks to editor Jonas Koffler who quarterbacked numerous projects related to this book, coordinated the efforts of many of those listed above, and also offered detailed editorial feedback throughout. Jonas, you rock!

Over the past five years, we have come to rely on some very special people. They are our personal support team and they provide us exceptional leverage—allowing us to stay focused and on-task with confidence that all else is being taken care of with diligence, skill, and finesse. To Valerie Vogler-Stipe, Allison Odom, Jeannine Abbott, Mindy Hager, and Teresa Metcalf, thanks for all you do, so that we can do all we do!

I never tire of thanking my coauthors, Dave Jenks and Jay Papasan. We are a synergistic team, making our own unique contributions to a unified goal—to share timeless truths in compelling ways that create impact on our readers and change in their lives. We each bring our unique God-given gifts to the venture. I couldn't do this without them.

With deep gratitude we thank our families and our loved ones. They provide us with the motivation to do what we do and the support that sustains us through. My parents, Lew and Minnie Keller, were always there when I needed them the most. My wife Mary, Jay's wife Wendy, and Dave's life partner Laurie are the love-forces in our lives. My son John, Jay's children Gus and Veronica, and Dave's three children and nine grandchildren are really the ones for whom we are writing the books. They are our legacy and the reason we care so deeply about how all this turns out. And thanks to God from whom all things come.

To you, our reader, we give our most enthusiastic thanks. We are grateful for your investment of time to read this book and your faith in the opportunities it promises. Good luck and Godspeed.

GARY KELLER
Austin, Texas

For more information about us, free tools, and resources,
visit us at www.MillionaireSystems.com.

CONTENTS

FOREWORD TO THE LIMITED EDITION

*You cannot control what happens to you, but you
can control your attitude toward what happens
to you, and in that, you will be mastering change
rather than allowing it to master you.*

BRIAN TRACY

NO CHALLENGE, NO SUCCESS

I THINK ABOUT SUCCESS A LOT. I think about it in regards to my life, but I think about it in regards to your life too. I think about what it means and what it doesn't mean. I think about achieving it and not achieving it. I ponder the possibilities, I evaluate the odds, I imagine the outcomes, I consider the consequences, and I visualize the victories. Clearly, I think success matters enough to, well, think about it.

In our business we actually refer to success quite often, and I sometimes wonder if we're completely in touch with what we're even talking about. We'll repeatedly hear someone say that success isn't easy and quickly nod our heads in agreement. But I must say that I'm not so sure that it's hard either. I actually view it in a more practical and straightforward way that sidesteps the very concepts of hard or easy—I think of success simply as the end result of a challenge accepted and achieved. In fact, I'm convinced that's why challenge, achievement, and success are all linked together. Success is achieved when we meet a challenge we set out for ourselves. No challenge, no achievement, no success.

Without a doubt, achieving success takes more than just wanting it or visualizing it. Success takes action. And sometimes those actions will be hard and sometimes they'll be easy. Keep challenging yourself long enough and you'll experience both. Everyone who is successful has this in common—they accept a challenge, take action, and sometimes encounter circumstances that are tough and other times that aren't so tough. And this is where the possible and the probable part. In the real estate business, success is possible for all, but only probable for those who take action.

Successful, achievement-oriented action means getting up and flat out running toward what you want. Some people take action because they're running toward something, while others take action because they're running from something. Both can serve as effective catalysts, because either way—you're running. And the running is what matters. The only difference is merely in the motivation. A lot of people say there are many ways to be successful. And yet I think what they really mean is that there are often a lot of reasons why people are successful. From all my research, I'm continually reminded that while the reasons for wanting success may vary, the most successful people tend to be doing the same things. The motivations differ, but the means don't. Gather together a great number of successful real estate agents and ask them how they do what they do, and you'll hear very similar strategies and tactics. Why? Because successful people run in the same direction with similar approaches. Their reasons are varied and personal, but their actions are comparable and their language incredibly alike. They are doing and saying the same basic things. And those who aren't succeeding? They're not.

You could have picked this book up for a lot of reasons. But regardless of your reasons, hopefully the outcome you seek is to become the best you can professionally be in the real estate business by running with the best and doing what the best do. If that's true, this book was written for you.

LIVING TO THE RIGHT OF MIDDLE

During his junior year in high school, my son, John, and I were having a father and son one-on-one about achievement. I had asked him to do something and he quickly informed me that he didn't want to do it. When I asked him why, he simply replied, "I just don't want to." Of course, my initial reaction was to say, "I didn't ask you if you wanted to," but then I got mentally parental and said, "let me share something with you."

"John, a lot of people make decisions about what they will or won't do based on whether they want or don't want to do it. But I'm not sure if they fully understand the corner they may be painting themselves into with this approach. Their response has everything to do with success and achievement, but probably not in the way they think."

I drew a line on a sheet of paper, and continued. "I want you to think of the far right of this line as complete success and the far left as complete failure. It's my personal belief that all of us live our lives somewhere in between these two points. Now, I want you to know that I've never ever met anyone who is a complete success or, for that matter, anyone who is a complete failure. In fact, John, I believe most people simply live their lives in the middle—they're average. What I think happens is that, as we go about our lives, most of us miscalculate what it takes to succeed at a high level, and as a result we end up getting unceremoniously caught at the midpoint of achievement. Not going any further and not really knowing why we're not. No matter the motivation for more, no matter the desire of our dreams, the results tend to hover right around the middle of the line. Now, why do you suppose people get stuck there?"

I paused to let him absorb all of this and then I very quietly answered my own question. "They get there by making decisions based on whether or not they *want* to do something, rather than whether or not they *should* do something. You see, John, the road to average is paved with 'I don't want to's.'"

HOW DO YOU GET OUT OF BEING STUCK IN THE MIDDLE?

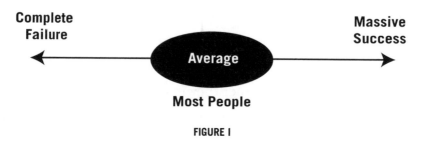

FIGURE I

I said, "In order to get to the middle of life at anything, all you have to do is what you like to do. But if you want to live on the right side of average at anything that really matters to you, you must move past doing only what you want to do and do some things you don't want to do. And the more you can conquer this and do what you need to do but don't like to do, the farther to the right of middle you get to live. In other words, the measure of your success in life is in direct proportion to what you're willing to do when you don't want to do it."

Now, I'm not sure it's fair to expect a seventeen-year-old to absorb this all at once. But I'm certain John got the essence of what I was saying. Average is doing only what you want to do. Success is doing what you must.

Frankly, I don't know of any job where anyone loves 100 percent of all it entails. There's no goal worth having that doesn't require your doing some undesirable tasks to attain it. Everything you desire will come with some undesirables. Likes come with dislikes. Wants come with unwanteds. There just doesn't seem to be any desired outcome you can't resist where you also can't resist doing all the tasks or functions required to achieve it. It's why most people miss out on the seemingly irresistible in life. Their effort stops in the middle—and so does their success.

The fly guide loves to fish, but doesn't love hauling the boat in and out of the water. The musician loves to perform, but doesn't love dragging equipment around from show to show.* My point to my son, and my point to you, is that there will always be things we don't like to do on the way to achieving what we want to achieve. You have to drag the amp on stage before you can play. You have to drag the boat in the water before you can fish. You have to lead generate and get appoint-

---

* A fun classic rock story: Because Eric Clapton hated dragging around his beloved Marshall amp head and speaker cabinet so much, he asked Jim Marshall to combine the two for him into one amplifier. Jim did and the celebrated Marshall "blues breaker" combo amp was born!

ments before you can actually work with a buyer or seller. You gotta do what you gotta do to get what you want when you want it. The formula for success doesn't get any clearer than that.

THE ERA OF EXTRA EFFORT

After spending more than a year traveling across the United States and Canada teaching *SHIFT* and interacting with top agents who have read and implemented its tactics, I'm more convinced than ever of this inescapable truth: We're in the era of extra effort.

When a shift occurs, people lose jobs. It's that devastatingly straightforward. You read the headlines or listen to the news and the overriding concern of almost everyone is "will I lose my job?" I say almost everyone because there is one group that isn't concerned. You guessed it. It's the people living to the right of the middle. A shift becomes the era of opportunity for those who are willing to do what others won't.

There is no escaping this certainty; there is only dealing with it. In a shift, the effort that got you where you are isn't going to keep you there. If you just came from the era of average effort, then most likely you noticed that "getting by" effort returned "getting by" results. Average effort meant you got to keep your job. In the era of extra effort, average effort could very well cost you your job.

THE BAR OF THE PAST

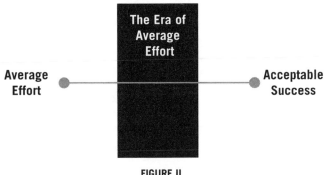

FIGURE II

Look at it this way. In the era of average effort, it was easier to attain an acceptable level of success. You could do little and still get enough and maybe even get a lot. A market shift changes the achievement formula by raising the bar of required effort and lowering the results for average effort. All of a sudden, what you did in the past no longer delivers an acceptable level of success.

THE BAR HAS BEEN RAISED

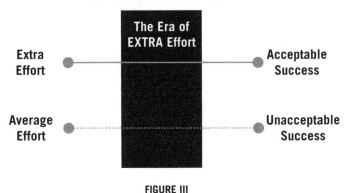

FIGURE III

To bring this point home, in the fall of 2008, in one of the toughest hit markets in the country, Tallahassee, Florida, top agent and successful businessman Gene Rivers worked with a group of agents who tracked their efforts and results over an eight-week period. They were participating in a class called Success Series, where each week the students set out to make a certain number of contacts and record their outcomes. Here's what they found out: On average, for every 34 contacts an agent made with prospective buyers and sellers, they netted 1 closed transaction. Plainly put, that's a 34:1 contact-to-close ratio.

SUCCESS SERIES EIGHT-WEEK STUDY

Category	Goal	Actual	%
Contacts	1,155	846	73.2%
Seller Leads	530	276	52.1%
Buyer Leads	402	229	57.0%
Listings Taken	107	66	61.7%
Buyer Agreements	143	60	42.0%
Contracts	89	44	49.4%
Closings	43	25	58.1%

FIGURE IV

What makes that number notable is that past studies have shown an average contact-to-close ratio of around 24:1. At first blush, ten additional contacts per transaction may not feel like a lot more, but you must realize this means you'd have to increase your efforts by a very challenging 42 percent just to get the same results. If you kept giving the same "past market" 24:1 effort, your business would likely drop off by a hard-hitting 30 percent or more.

And Gene's experience wasn't unique. Top agents across the continent have all discovered this adjusted reality of business life—you must jump to a higher gear to hit any goal you set during a shifted year. Courtney Yates of Murfreesboro, Tennessee, who has always tracked the numbers that drive her business, shared with me that "during this market, for every 43 showings I'd get a contract. It used to be 10, then it was 17, then it was 43." For Courtney, "extra effort" translated to 33 additional showings for every sale—a 330 percent increase in effort from one market to the shifted one. Florida agent Pilar Moscoso discovered she needed to make an additional ten contacts every day just to stay on track. She reported that, for her, connecting with ten people required an average of twenty-five additional calls each day. All across the United States and Canada, it adds up to the same blueprint for achievement.

That's why top productivity coaches Dianna Kokoszka and Tony DiCello say, "When the market reinvents itself, you must reinvent yourself." You simply need to pick the results you want and match the effort those results require. It will take extra effort, whoever you are and wherever you may be.

One condition of consistent success that can trip us all up is understanding that what works for one market situation rarely works as well for another. What isn't obvious is that while bad habits can still lead to good results in a good market, when the market slows, those same bad habits can now lead to some awfully bad results. Altered economics call for adjusted actions. You must drop the bad habits of a good market and adopt the good habits of a bad market.

Allan Domb of Philadelphia, one of the top real estate professionals in the world, gets this better than most. A lot of agents will spend less than an hour marketing an open house and then go sit in an "empty" house for up to four hours on a Sunday. Allan just flips this approach around by spending up to four hours aggressively marketing an open house, and then when he holds it open, it's packed and can last less than an hour. He says that it's more than just extra effort; it's about putting the extra effort where it belongs. And he's right. It's both. It's extra effort on the things that matter most.

THE ONE THING

So, what matters most? If we step back and look at our business, we can see that there are actually six competencies at the core of what we do as real estate professionals. First, we lead generate, capture, and convert leads to appointments. Second, we present to potential buyers and sellers and get representation agreements signed. Third, we show our buyers and market our sellers. Fourth, we write and negotiate purchase contracts. Fifth, we coordinate our resulting sales to closing. And sixth, we manage all the money that flows through our business. We actually discuss all six on page 38 as they relate to leverage and delegation, but I'd also like to give you a slightly different perspective.

These six core competencies are really an outline of our basic sales job description—the areas that must be done from beginning to end for any real estate transaction. And although they're all important and none can be left undone, they're very different in two key ways: which one matters most and which ones can and can't be successfully delegated. Areas two through six can be effectively delegated with a high degree of success and at a predictable cost. We know this because top agents do it all the time with tremendous results. Plus, we also know what we have to pay for people to do two through six for us, for it has been well documented.

Presenting, showing, writing, negotiating, coordinating closings and managing money are all activities that, to a certain degree, can be delegated successfully.[†] However, it is extremely difficult to effectively delegate number one: lead generation and conversion to an appointment. Why? The skill level it takes to generate a lead, capture the appropriate information, and then convert that lead to an appointment is a distinct skill set that takes extensive practice over time to develop to a high level. And it's where the money is! We've observed that when top agents delegate lead generation and appointment setting, their conversion rate usually falls from upward of 80 percent to much less than 10 percent. When there are lots of leads to burn through, this isn't as big a problem as when there are few to be found. In a shift where every single lead is essential to hitting your minimum goals, lead generation can't be delegated. It's a dirty job and the someone who has to do it is you.

So, when you leave the house each morning and say, "honey, I'm going to work," here is the all-important question for you: Are you going to do number one or something else? It's a great question and gets to the very heart of achievement and success in our business. How you answer will go a long way toward determining your ultimate success—in any market.

[†]Research and experience show that although you can delegate contract writing, negotiating, and also money management, you must still stay involved to some extent.

WORK VERSUS PLAY

I once asked Garry Peterson, the legendary drummer of The Guess Who and coauthor of the mammoth classic rock hit "American Woman," whether he was working or playing whenever he performed. His answer was insightful. He said "playing." I then asked him, "When do you work?" And he said, "When I practice, I'm working. When I perform, I'm playing. And how hard I work when I'm practicing not only determines how often I play, but also my pay." I've since asked many other successful musicians and all of them have given me essentially the same response. It reminds me that success always leaves clues and this is a gigantic one no one can afford to ignore. A lot of real estate agents want to go straight to playing without ever putting in the work and practice beforehand. And to top that, they then have the expectation that they'll also earn a great deal. The poorest performing agents want to get paid a lot to play a lot before they've earned the right by working a lot. It's faulty thinking that when played out never pays out.

While on a fly-fishing trip, John, Jay, Tony, and I wandered into a vacant retail space where we discovered celebrated artist Pat Matthews—painting one of his famous aspen scenes. Without missing a stroke, he began to tell us about the canvas he was working on and about life. At one point I asked him how he became so good at what he does that he could carry on a conversation with four total strangers while creating incredible art. Pat gave us a one-word answer: practice. He'd always imagined that if he were a pool player and practiced 4 to 5 hours a day for 6 to 7 years, he'd become a really good pool player. He told us that he took that concept and just applied it to painting, while adding two additional disciplines. First, that he will finish at least one painting every day and, second, that he will strive to only touch the canvas with single strokes and no touch-ups. To help develop his talent and further this discipline, Pat said that sometimes he even set a timer to finish a painting within a set amount of time, often two hours. Amazing. To be honest, some of his work requires weeks and even months of his attention. But for me his mastery is apparent in his ability to paint a canvas in two hours that looks as if it took two years. His work and focus on a few core disciplines have allowed him to rise up and become a truly extraordinary and renowned artist who today commands tremendous artistic respect, critical acclaim, and financial appreciation.

For incredible artists like Garry Peterson and Pat Matthews, the world is thrilled to pay them to play because they work so hard each and every day.

A MODEL BUSINESS

Ever since *SHIFT* was published, I get repeatedly asked if the four models in *The Millionaire Real Estate Agent* still apply. The answer is yes. The only change is in the numbers you have to plug in. The twelve tactics presented in *SHIFT* sit on top of the four models as the actions you take to implement them. Nothing's changed. Everything is still fundamentally the same. The tactics of *SHIFT* are an extension of *The Millionaire Real Estate Agent*. *The Millionaire Real Estate Agent* focuses you on models. *SHIFT* focuses you on tactics.

No matter the market, you must still have an Economic Model to tell you the numbers you have to hit to reach your financial goals. The chain of events between you and your income is still contacts to appointments to signed agreements to accepted contracts to closings. Knowing your numbers is what informs your specific actions. And only purposeful action rewards you with the production you desire.

**THE FOUR BUSINESS MODELS
OF THE MILLIONAIRE REAL ESTATE AGENT**

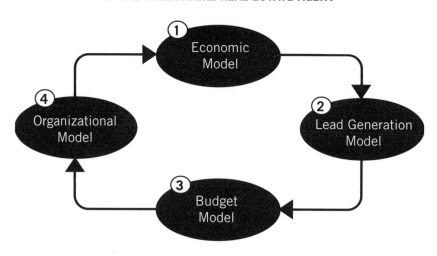

FIGURE V

Informed by your Economic Model, you now know the number of leads you must generate from your Lead Generation Model. Armed with this objective, your singular assignment becomes putting in four or more time-blocked hours a day focused on achieving it. And your activities will have to be prospecting based and marketing enhanced. At the time of our early research for *The Millionaire Real Estate Agent*, due to the market, this was flipped. Now, we're all quite certain of the order, never to retreat from it. And to have a business worth owning over time, once a contact is made, the name is fed into your database for you to systematically touch.

Once you start spending money, you begin to realize the importance of having a basic Budget Model that establishes the expenses you can afford. Without a financial plan, it's easy for your overhead to put you underwater. Although every agent's personal experience is unique, the 30-30-40 formula (30 percent Cost of Sale, 30 percent Operating Expenses, and 40 percent Profit) is still attainable, but in a shift it takes extraordinary effort to accomplish it.

Finally, when you've done all you can do by yourself, you hire help by implementing the Organizational Model. The progression never changes. It's still hire administrative assistance first, buyer assistance second, and listing assistance last. The secret of successful hiring is to let your support needs grow based on one result: having too many leads to handle. Always allow someone to prove themselves as an assistant before they're awarded the top position for their area. So, you hire an executive assistant who can become an assistant executive. You hire a showing assistant who can become a buyer specialist. And you hire a listing assistant who can become a listing specialist. Never violate the basic concept of making good hires prove they're great and earn the right to move up the ladder to the key leadership role for their area.

DRIVE THROUGH TO BREAK THROUGH

If you want to run through a wall, don't judge your effort based on the wall. Let the wall judge your effort and deal with it. The wall isn't your issue, your effort is. If you want a breakthrough during a shift, you're going to have to drive right through your target. Professional golf instructors will tell you to imagine a point just in front of the ball when you are preparing to swing—the idea is to drive your stroke through the target, not to the target. Golfers who don't get this never achieve their optimal success. And it's the same in karate. The sensei teaches to imagine a point at the back of an opponent's head as the target. When you aim for the nose, your strike falls at the end of your punch. But when you plow beyond the point of contact and put your whack at the center of your wallop, you're at your maximum power. Again, your power comes from driving through a target. It's a graphic illustration, but a potent one. When you aim past obstacles they may slow you down, but you'll still have breakthroughs.

Laserlike focus and relentless effort. It's an incredible formula for achievement. When this is your blueprint for action, the market informs your present but doesn't determine your future. Should you wake up one day and feel like you're in a crisis, just remember that CRISIS stands for Circumstances Requiring an Immediate Shift In Strategy. So should you decide to shift, the twelve tactics in this book will get you up and running and successfully guide you to your goals.

Onward ...

GARY KELLER
Austin, Texas
December 10, 2009

> *And finally, I want to acknowledge that making changes in your life is never an easy task. The key, however, is not to get caught up in the distance you have to go to get to where you want to be. Nor should you despair over the amount of control you have over your circumstances. Progress is made in the small, intentional steps, and chances are, you have more power than you think. By focusing on little steps you can take every day, the progress you make will motivate you to continue your journey, and eventually, you can go wherever you want to go. The important thing is simply to begin.*
>
> STEPHEN CHERNISKE, MS

INTRODUCTION

The worst that happens to you can be the best
thing for you, if you don't let it get the best of you.
UNKNOWN

THE REAL ESTATE MARKET has shifted drastically and dramatically. Sales volume and the number of transactions have dropped significantly. Inventory has reached an all-time high. Buyers have never been more reluctant. Fear is rampant, anxiety is high, and people are getting out of the business left and right. Sound familiar? Sure it does. The year was 1979 and that's what was happening all around me.

I was 22 years old, new to the industry, and new to Austin. I basically knew nothing and no one and still I sold six houses my first month in the business, five of which closed. Then the market collapsed—interest rates soared to over 18 percent, the marketplace fell into chaos, and I didn't close a sale for five straight months. By Christmas I was six months into my real estate career and broke.

My dad offered to help. Based on my growing database and the business I had in the pipeline, he loaned me $500 to keep me going. The very next day my dad's faith in me was validated and I wrote a contract on a home for Jack and Dorothy Saul. Ultimately my hard work paid off and I ended my first twelve months hitting all my financial goals.

EIGHT YEARS LATER

Fast forward to 1987 and it happened again. This time the government changed tax laws, which had a disastrous effect: the market shifted. Seemingly overnight, the listing inventory went through the roof, sales transactions fell to the floor and our local real estate board went from over 5,000 members to below 2,000. Panic and confusion reigned. It felt like everybody was running helter skelter, looking for shelter but finding no place to hide. There was no escaping the shift.

By this time in my career I'd started my own company and we had become the tenth largest in the market. My competitors were going bankrupt all around me and the number of agents in my office abruptly dropped from more than seventy to below forty. To make matters worse, in the midst of getting my feet back under me and reestablishing my profit margin, a new competitor entered the picture. Five of my top ten associates and my entire administrative staff walked out the door. My business world was being assaulted from all sides. As bad as my first market shift experience was as an agent, it was even more devastating as an owner.

In the end I found my way through this shift just as I had before. And once again, I not only survived, I thrived and ultimately emerged stronger, more capable than ever. Less than two years after the shift, our company became number one in our market—a position never to be relinquished.

Are you facing a shift? If you are, you shouldn't be surprised. History repeats itself. This is not the first time real estate professionals have been in this position. What's happening to you today has happened before and is destined to happen again. Real estate markets shift. They always have and always will. And the business goes on. As bleak as things can look during shifts, when I look back I believe they've served as the genesis for everything I've become and the catalyst for all that I've achieved. In fact, I've come to see them as opportunities. So can you.

PART ONE

THE MARKET SHIFTS

SHIFTS HAPPEN

REAL ESTATE IS A CYCLICAL BUSINESS. What goes up must come down. And what is down won't stay there. Shifts are never unexpected but rarely predictable. You know one is coming. You just don't know when. They are, in fact, inevitable—shifts happen.

But we forget. Each time a shift occurs, we act surprised, as if it had never happened before. Once the shift is over, we act as if it'll never happen again. It's like we have amnesia. And that's odd since we deal with something similar every year. It's called seasonality—the seasonal cycle of sales that repeats each and every year. From month-to-month there is an ebb and flow to the real estate business. Within each year, there is a time to make money and a time to save money. It is so natural most simply take it in stride.

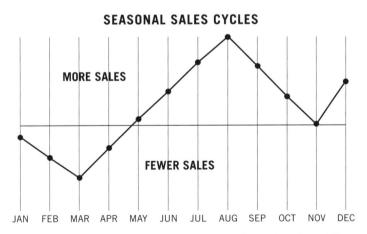

SEASONAL SALES CYCLES

FIGURE 1 The monthly ratio of listings sold to listings taken. The midline represents an equal number of listings sold and listings taken. [1]

[1] Based on a study of more than a million closed transactions over a five-year period.

There is a natural buildup of listing inventory from January through April and an offsetting decline in inventory from May through October, with an up tick in sales at the end of the year. This seasonal cycle of sales causes a corresponding seasonal cycle of income.

SEASONAL INCOME CYCLE

FIGURE 2 The percent of annual income that is closed in each month. The midline represents 8.3 percent of total annual income. [2]

For real estate agents, these graphs are a heads-up and give meaning to the phrase "make hay while the sun shines." The fact is, every year, real estate agents have to deal with the seasonal sales cycle and its impact on their cash flow.

While seasonal cycles occur within a single year, economic shifts happen over several years. Seasonal market cycles are month-to-month and economic market shifts are year-to-year. Just as the seasonal cycles dictate a rise and fall to your income over a period of months, the larger economic shifts create a rise and fall to your income over a period of years. Seasonal cycles feel predictable, short-term, and manageable. Economic shifts feel unpredictable, indefi-

[2] Based on a study of more than a million closed transactions over a five-year period.

nite, and overwhelming. One feels like business as usual and the other feels, well, downright scary.

The real estate industry has learned to live with regular seasonal cycles, but it is always challenged by irregular economic shifts.

THE ANATOMY OF A SHIFT

Shifts are easy to understand. They occur whenever supply and demand move out of balance. When seller supply exceeds buyer demand, it's a buyers' market. When buyer demand exceeds seller supply, it's a sellers' market. A shift occurs when the market moves from one to the other. Think of it this way. If over time more listings are selling, you're moving toward a sellers' market. If over time fewer listings are selling, you're moving toward a buyers' market.

THE THREE TYPES OF REAL ESTATE MARKETS

1. BUYERS' MARKET More than 7 months of inventory

2. BALANCED MARKET From 5 to 7 months of inventory

3. SELLERS' MARKET Less than 5 months of inventory

Balanced markets occur during the transition between markets and rarely last for long.

FIGURE 3 Inventory defines the state of your market. At the current pace of sales, how many months of housing inventory do you have?

Why does the shift to a buyers' market create pain? Two reasons. First it leads to fewer sales and less available sales income in your market. Second it tends to be abrupt and precipitous. The misleading aspect of an economic shift is that it seems relatively natural and gradual when looked at nationally. When experienced locally it is usually dramatic and fast.

NATIONAL SHIFTS HAPPEN GRADUALLY

FIGURE 4 On a national level the mid-90s shift from a buyers' market to a sellers' market took more than four years. The shift back took about three.

LOCAL SHIFTS HAPPEN FAST!

FIGURE 5 The above is a composite look at existing home sales in five large metro areas (Sacramento, San Diego, Las Vegas, Orlando, and New York City). Beginning in the fall of 2005, several years of market growth were erased in less than 18 months.

The national perspective rarely, if ever, matches the local experience. The hard truth is local market shifts are seldom slow and local landings are almost never soft. It's a lot like a pendulum or a golf swing, beginning relatively slowly but accelerating very quickly through the middle. Some local shifts can actually take your breath away.

LOCAL MARKET TRANSITIONS DON'T LAST LONG

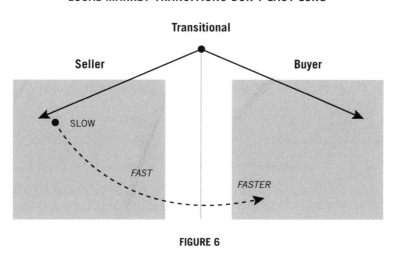

FIGURE 6

Several factors can cause an economic shift. Currency exchange rates and political climate are the primary global factors. On a national level it's interest rates and inflation. Population, jobs, and household income take center stage at the city level. And at the most local level, it's neighborhood dynamics and housing prices. All of this simply boils down to buyer demand, which is driven by affordability and perception—how many buyers can afford to buy and how many think it's a good time to buy.

So are shifts bad? Well, it depends. For the real estate industry in a particular market, it certainly can be—the available income for everyone in that market has dropped. For any single individual in their local market, it doesn't have to be—there is still enough available income for them to achieve their goals. The challenge for individual agents? Fear and how they will respond to it.

When shifts occur, fear runs rampant, although not everyone responds in the same way. Some individuals, though they do feel the fear, also know they are in an equal opportunity, unequal reward business. It's really the 80/20 rule at work—20 percent of the people will do 80 percent of the business in any entrepreneurial endeavor. Those who understand this know that they must be better than average to earn the better than average rewards. If individuals understand a shift or have actually experienced one, they know they have to push past the fear and face two tests—first to survive and then to thrive. They have to hang tough until the Law of Equilibrium reasserts itself. Then it's opportunity time.

THE LAW OF EQUILIBRIUM

THE LAW OF EQUILIBRIUM is as old as the real estate industry itself. It is simple and straightforward. The law states that the available income in a market determines the number of agents in that market. As the number of transactions rises, so does the number of agents. Conversely, when the number of available transactions falls, so does the number of agents. People are attracted to the industry by the perceived income opportunity and driven out by the reality of the competition for it.

Since perception tends to trail behind reality, two lag periods show up in every economic shift—the down-lag and the up-lag. The down-lag occurs because the number of agents doesn't decline until the number of transactions has already been dropping for some time. The low point of income opportunity then occurs when the most agents are chasing the least amount of income. The up-lag works in reverse when the transactions increase. The high-income opportunity point occurs on the way up when the fewest agents are chasing the most amount of income.

With relatively few barriers to entry the real estate industry can become flooded with practitioners during a prolonged sellers' market (an upshift). Larger and larger numbers of agents are attracted to the industry and this increases the competition for the existing business. When the amount of business then declines (a downshift) the competition becomes untenable. There are more people but less business and fewer deals. Fewer deals mean less money and less money means lower income for everyone—and eventually it means fewer people doing business. If you can ride out (survive) this initial lag period as more and more people get out of the business you can find yourself in a less competitive market. There is now more business relative to the number of people working to get it. This is the time to thrive.

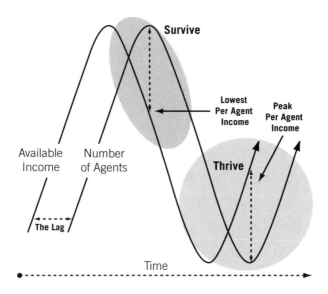

FIGURE 7 Conceptually you can see it this way. For the historical graphs, see Figure 64 and Figure 65 in the appendix.

How long it takes to get from survive to thrive can vary greatly from time to time and from person to person. There is the market's shift and its lag time, and then there is your shift and your lag time. If you don't shift fast, your lag time will parallel the market and you may be at risk. To thrive in the upshift you must first survive the downshift.

Let's be clear here—there is nothing that says that an agent cannot thrive before the market upshifts. In fact, we have known and worked with many agents who had their best years in a "down market." This book is based on the lessons learned from those agents who have actually accomplished this.

Here's the truth: not everyone will, but anyone can.

THE RESILIENCE FACTOR

Even though you know that history repeats itself, in order to profit from it, you have to remember it. You must carry the lessons of the past into the present. The past has taught us that "this too shall pass" and that success comes to the resilient. Here is a tangible way to look at it: if your career goes three steps forward then the market drives you four back, you're essentially below zero and out of the game. If it's three steps forward and three back all you've done is survive. But, if you've taken three steps forward and the market only drives you two steps back, you're just absorbing the hit. You're still in the game and you are more than just surviving.

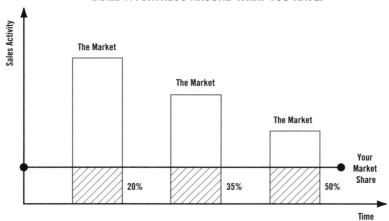

BUILD A FORTRESS AROUND WHAT YOU HAVE!

FIGURE 8 As the market falls, hold your numbers steady and your share of the market will grow.

The key is to be resilient and on your toes—take the hit, but don't get knocked out. This is the survival strategy—adapt to the realities of the new (downshifted) market quickly. Change what you need to change, do what you need to do. Build a fortress around what you have. At the very least, this means maintaining your number of sales while the market declines. The net effect will actually be an increase in your market share.

When the natural lag plays out, you will be positioned to take advantage of the inevitable rebound. You can then ride the wave of increasing transactions and available commission income by simply holding the new level of market share you've gained. If you do, your number of sales will increase dramatically and you will thrive.

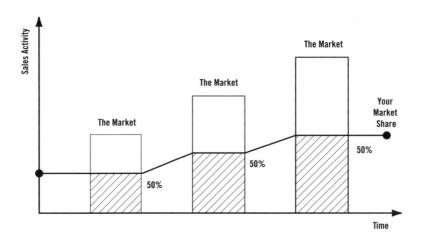

FIGURE 9 When the next upshift happens, your market share will hold steady but your numbers will explode!

In order to survive and then thrive, you'll need to shift gears. Can you put it in another gear? Most people fear a shift because they don't understand the Law of Equilibrium. They can't shift their thinking, so they don't shift their tactics. If you can shift gears— shifting both your thinking and your tactics—you will accelerate ahead of the rest.

So how do you shift gears? It's actually a very straightforward and pragmatic process. Our research has identified the twelve tactics you must deploy. These issues aren't special, unique, or new—they're the basic components of any successful real estate career. And when business gets tight they become the critical factors that determine the difference between success or failure. These tactics represent the gear shifts that respond to the market shifts. Are you ready? Are you willing? Let's get after it!

PART TWO

YOU SHIFT

TWELVE TACTICS
FOR TOUGH TIMES

1) Get Real, Get Right – Mindset and Action

2) Re-Margin Your Business – Expense Management

3) Do More with Less – Leverage

4) Find the Motivated – Lead Generation

5) Get to the Table – Lead Conversion

6) Catch People in Your Web – Internet Lead Conversion

7) Price Ahead of the Market – Seller Pricing Strategies

8) Stand Out from the Competition – Seller Staging Strategies

9) Create Urgency – Overcoming Buyer Reluctance

10) Expand the Options – Creative Financing

11) Master the Market of the Moment – Short Sales, Foreclosures, and REOs

12) Bulletproof the Transaction – Issues and Solutions

TACTIC #1
GET REAL, GET RIGHT—
MINDSET AND ACTION

Decide what your priorities are and how much time
you'll spend. If you don't, someone else will.

HARVEY MACKAY

IN *THE TRAVELER'S GIFT,* Andy Andrews passes on the wisdom that "our lives are fashioned by choice. First we make choices. Then our choices make us." I wholeheartedly agree. We are what we decide we will be, and we do what we decide we will do. We become our choices. The twelve issues you face in a shifting market are really an opportunity. An opportunity to make the twelve most important choices that will directly impact your career and power you through any shift. Of these twelve choices the first and most significant will be to get real about your situation and get right about what you're doing.

When a shift occurs confusion follows. Not only in the marketplace but also in the mind and body. What to think and what to do becomes fuzzy because what once worked is no longer working and you may not know why. Don't let yourself panic. Keep fear at bay. When a market shifts there is only one thing to do—shift with it. In truth, there are two shifts you must make. A mental shift and an action shift.

THE MENTAL SHIFT

I believe that your life will be either about your problems or your opportunities. You'll either be running away from something or running toward something. It's your call. To survive a shift you must first make the mental shift to run towards what you most want and avoid the temptation of running away from what you most fear. One approach lifts you up and the other drags you down. You must keep both eyes on your target and not the ever-moving market. Remember that success is never about the chosen few, but always about the few who choose. You get to choose and your life builds from there.

Agents must rethink, restructure, refresh, reenergize, and reinvent every aspect of their business. The ostrich approach guarantees extinction.

Linda Alexander, Portland, OR

There are three types of people who emerge when a market shifts. First, those that fearfully predict the worst and are unnecessarily pessimistic; second, those who hopefully wish for the best, believe they can't fail, and are unrealistically positive; and, third, those who respect the fact that they might fail, actively prepare for the worst, and strive for the best. These are the resourcefully realistic and are always the timely triumphant. They are matter-of-fact about the market and sensible about their situation. They see things as they are and openly acknowledge how they're doing. At the same time they stay optimistic about their opportunities. As my friend Zig Ziglar says "they do a checkup from the neck up" and make sure that even though the market is reshaping itself it isn't reshaping their attitude.

You can't control the market but you can control your outlook and your response to the market. Remain resolute. Know that while everyone won't succeed in a shift, some will and anyone can. You must be an "anyone can." This is not just a short-term attitude you adopt, but a life-long posture you take. It's a journey you embark on led by the mental choices you make. Be certain of this—your mindset matters.

Most people lead a "flow with the tides" life. Their careers and their fortunes seem to rise and fall with the tides of the market. When things are going well anything and everything works—their boats float. What they fail to realize is that literally all boats float at high tide and no captain gets credit for that! When times get tough and the tide goes out, all of a sudden not everything works. Their boats don't float. Those quick to adjust will have a floating boat. On the rocks or out at sea—the choice is yours.

Be a low-tider—always be prepared for low tide. Know that it is always a good time to be in the real estate market when you take a long-term view of the market instead of getting caught up in its short-term volatility. Know that there is always enough business for you to survive with a minimum income while striving for your maximum. Keep your perspective. Judge your suc-

I've had to get much deeper into my business. I have stepped back in and I am in much more contact with my sellers.

Martin Bouma, Ann Arbor, MI

cess over the length of your career not the high or low of any single year. Know that growth comes from clarity, priorities, and focused action. The first two are how you think and the last is what you do. To make a strong mental shift be clear about your situation and what it is you want. Write down and prioritize the necessary steps you must take to achieve your goals. Now you're focused on what you want, you know what you need to do, and you know what comes first. So what are you waiting for?

THE ACTION SHIFT

Once you've gotten real, you've got to get right—right into action and into the right action. For all the necessity of knowing what to do, taking the right action now is just as necessary. Once you know then it's not about more knowing—it's about doing. The difference between a career worth having and a career worth heaving is the amount of focused action you take every day. It's about knowing what to do and then doing it. Keller Williams CEO Mark Willis often shares that his inspirational and energetic mother, Rachael Willis, always taught him to "Do right—Fear not." When you do the right things you leave fear behind.

When you know what to do it's time to move from inspiration to perspiration. So the straightforward question that jumps right at you in a shift is a simple one. "What do I do right now?" Actually, this is a two-part question that first asks "what must be done right?" and then "what must be done now?" The answer to that two-part question becomes your focus and yours alone. Understand what worked yesterday probably won't work today and what matters now probably didn't then. When the market shifts, new strategies are required and new actions are critical.

You need to double your efforts to grow. That doesn't necessarily mean doubling the time spent; it means doubling the focus and the intensity so that you are more efficient and effective during the time spent.

Chris Heller, Encinitas, CA

In a shifted market there is little room for mistakes and that is a real challenge. The margin for error is very thin. Where there was once latitude, there isn't. You must be focused on the right tasks and you must execute them well. Efficiency and effectiveness are essential contributors to your bottom line.

One way to look at the necessary actions is by roles—yours and others. The challenge you might have is that you thought there were some roles you had delegated to others only to discover that you hadn't done so successfully. The net result is that you must personally start doing certain tasks again.

The critical actions that you identify must be carried out by you or personally overseen by you on a daily basis. Our research shows that the two actions real estate agents must take personal ownership of are lead generation and lead conversion. Nothing becomes more critical to success than finding motivated buyers and sellers and closing them to an appointment. Your active involvement in the lead conversion process gives you two invaluable gifts. First, you get an immediate and ongoing sense of the issues of the market—the buyer and seller objections that need to be overcome. Second, you will get an honest understanding of the conversion rates that are possible. No one on your team will be as talented or as invested in closing leads to appointments, and your direct participation allows you to set the standard and coach your team on how they too can meet it. It's what I call "management by wandering around." But it's not really wandering. I want to periodically and regularly insert myself into critical areas of the business. Sam Walton made a habit of visiting all his stores and working cash registers for hours. His interaction with customers gave him vital insight into what was and was not working.

This market is chaos, chaos is opportunity! It is much easier to slip by the competition when they have their heads down pouting!
Ben Kinney, Bellingham, WA

To put lead generation and lead conversion in less effective hands than yours could spell the difference between success and failure. Failure is never an option. As business analysts have often pointed out, "the seeds of failure are usually sown during times of success." The most humbling lesson of a shift is this—we succeed in good times not only because of what we do right, but also in spite of what we do wrong.

We make a goal board and look at it every day! Keep your goals posted in many places so you constantly see them. It helps you focus when you'd rather not.

Mary and Joe Charters
Gaithersburg, MD

The remaining eleven tactics involve making some of the most important choices you'll ever make and mastering some of the most important skills you'll ever master. What you did right in the past will be reevaluated and what you did wrong corrected. In each one, you will most likely have to ask, "Who should be doing this? Me or someone else?" The way to resolve this is by asking one more question: "Who will do this the best?" Don't fight the answer.

As you go through the list of necessary actions, don't be surprised if they're not special, unique, or new. Actually, they are the foundational components of any successful real estate career. Our research with the best agents in the industry for our book *The Millionaire Real Estate Agent* and our ongoing dialogues with them absolutely show that the top agents become top agents by mastering the fundamentals. Maybe the reason the basics are so often abandoned is the fact that they aren't special, unique, or new. When business gets tight, they reveal themselves as the timeless factors that determine the difference between success or failure. School is never out for the motivated. The basics are never outdated.

TACTIC #2
RE-MARGIN YOUR BUSINESS –
EXPENSE MANAGEMENT

It is not necessary to change. Survival is not mandatory.

W. EDWARDS DEMING

ANYONE WHO EXPECTS CHANGE to be comfortable hasn't been challenged enough. Change isn't easy and significant change is downright difficult. Yet long-term success requires it. My experience has taught me that the people most responsive to change are the ones most likely to survive and thrive. James Yorke, a University of Maryland mathematics and physics professor, put it perfectly when he said "the most successful people are those who are good at plan B." In other words, when change affects your plan, plan effective change.

To shift is to change. The market changes therefore you must change with it. With your thinking right and your role clear you must immediately identify the other effective business changes your current circumstances require. The first one is the only one that can get you back to profitability the fastest—cutting costs. The number one determinant of *thriving* is lead generation, but the number one determinant of *surviving* is expense management. When markets shift, the first change a business must make is "re-expense" itself. "Revenuing" your way out of a shift is iffy at best. Generating more income may be impossible in the short run and take too much time in the long run. This approach is always just too little too late. Now is the required speed when a shift occurs. Get your expenses lower—now!

I cannot overemphasize the importance of always working from a position of profitability. It is vital and must be protected at all times and at all costs. And therein lies the answer—time and costs. You must lower your costs now. To generate revenue you generate leads. To make a profit you manage expenses. Sam Walton explained his success this way: "We had to keep expenses to a minimum. That is where it started. Our money was made by controlling expenses." This is true for all businesses. The profit you seek will always be made in the way you manage your money. So when the market shifts, you must create a budget that matches your revenue. We call this re-margining your business.

Interestingly one might think that the goal of profit would provide the motivation necessary to do this, but research and personal experience have proven otherwise. Fear of financial loss is a more powerful motivator than the opportunity for financial gain. It just seems that the push we get from our fears is stronger than any pull towards the profits we desire. A swift kick in the behind turns out to be a pretty good motivator and that's okay.

Peter Drucker was famous for teaching this very straightforward point—you can't build a business by cutting back, but you can find your profit and save it. Every business must make a profit. To do this they must find a profit margin they can achieve and focus on getting there. The only true competitive weapon you have as a businessperson is a margin of profit. It is the foundation from which all of your competitiveness stems. If a market shift causes your income to drop but your expenses don't immediately drop in lockstep with it then your profit margin is gone. And along with it your competitiveness. If this lasts long enough you will go out of business because no profit and no competitiveness means no business.

This all seems like common sense. You cut to save and you spend to build. So what happens? Prosperity happens. In growing times we tend to become profitable with positive cash flow and loose with financial decision-making. We review the bottom line, see a profit, trust all's well and fail to scrutinize the detail. The fact is that for all of its positive indicators profit can also give a false reading. We allow an increase in our business profits to convince us that what we're doing

For every dollar we invest, we expect a multiple return.

Pam Kiker, Greenwood Village, CO

is working well. Really well. Thus we mistakenly justify our increased expenses as "the cost of doing business", say things like "it takes money to make money" and allow our rising revenue and present profit to cover up any mistakes or inefficiencies. Charlie Munger, Warren Buffett's partner, in *Warren Buffett Speaks* said "Name a business that has been ruined by downsizing. I can't name one. Name a company that has been ruined by bloat. I can name dozens." In up markets we tend to move fast and swell up. We're not as tight on our dollars or as tough on our results. We gain size and fail to see the bloat in it. We don't play "red light, green light" with our expenses very well and tend to just play green light, green light! Go! Go! Go!

In up markets we tend to acquire habits and patterns of doing things that don't stop us in good times, but grind us to a halt in bad. In other words, we do so much right that the market covers up the wrong. The first causes us to succeed and may be so powerful that it powers us right past the second. Good times seem to reward all that we do and profit seems to give permission to be permissive. Permission to avoid things you don't enjoy. Permission to do things you've always wanted to do. Permission to do things in the spur of the moment—all this leads to a lack of scrutiny, research, and accountability. Profit can act like a financial pillow and become a mental cushion or like a financial sofa inviting you to take a mental nap. But the truth is that there is never a good time to nod off and violate the fundamentals of finance. Always think financially awake and alert. That is what long-term successful business people do. They ask what should be done? What will it generate? What will it cost? Will it be profitable? They look and listen and they pay attention to the answers.

Business is never automatic or predictable. You can never predict with certainty the outcome of any action you take or financial decision you make. Each decision presents opportunity and risk. So think of spending money in your business as investing in your business. When you invest you expect to get your money back plus a return. And the same applies in your business. You're investing in your business every time you spend money. Therefore, sound business implores you to follow the basic philosophy "every dollar spent should return its original amount plus a reasonable profit." Think of this as "the cost plus" principle of converting your expenses into business investments.

Cut your expenses by 50 percent and you will see how business still goes on. It will shock you when you see how little you really need to spend.

Chris Cormack, Ashburn, VA

Everyone pursues growth, but few truly realize how profit happens. They prove this everyday by continuing to drive revenue while spending money where they shouldn't. Good markets hide this, tough markets expose it. If you don't pay attention to how profit is made and lost you'll most likely create and maintain a profit margin on the way up that will immediately disappear on the way down. Never to be found again.

Most agents tend to think they are as good as their last best year instead of the average over their careers. And they set up their expectations and expenses accordingly. They tend to think the trend of their last couple of good years

A boom market can cloud your financial vision and mask, among other things, poor expense control.

Pat Hiban, Ellicott City, MD

will continue and they underestimate the market's contribution to their success. Here is the dilemma—do you spend based on your average, your last year, your best year or your goals? The answer is none of the above.

No matter the market you always follow the philosophy of "lead with revenue." This means either always working from a position of profitability or, if just getting started, working from a position of having enough revenue already on the books so you know exactly when profitability will start. In a shifted market you drop your expenses until your inflow once again exceeds your outflow at an acceptable level and then you play red light, green light. You now grow your budget incrementally by holding each new expense accountable for contributing profit in line with your acceptable profit margin as you aim towards your goal. You're spending by "leading with revenue" and you're growing by the "cost-plus" business investment approach. It's the true win-win financial formula that works for any business at any time and in any market condition.

PROTECT YOUR MARGIN

When a shift hits initially everyone gets hit equally. The market doesn't discriminate so all boats float lower. What happens first is equal and without choice—what happens next is unequal and determined by choice. There is no expense that is untouchable. There is no cut too small. You must reduce expenses to match your income plus an acceptable profit margin. Be brutal. Cut! Cut! Cut! Cut once, cut twice and then keep cutting every week until you're there. Attack both variable and fixed expenses. Variable expenses might include hidden fees or add-on fees you've been unaware of, over-charges from lack of attention, unnecessary work that should be postponed or cancelled, waste that has gone unchecked and ineffective expenditures that have been returning zero results. From copies to couriers, from office supplies to subscriptions, from snail mail to express mail, the waste is there. Find it. Root it out. Get rid of it—now! Nothing should be untouchable and all expenses should feel the heat of your scrutiny.

This year I cut every marketing medium I used. When asked to continue, I offered half of what I paid before. I was surprised how many said yes!

David Fogg, Burbank, CA

This same approach applies to fixed expenses. Fixed expenses are always agreements that usually fall into the categories of car payment, rent, leases, advertising, phones, or salaries. Here you are best served by thinking of ways to turn fixed into variable. If you can get out of them then get out. If you can extend them to lower the monthly cost then extend them. If you can shift fixed costs to performance based then do it.

You're in the hunt for a positive net number and not getting there isn't an option. Deal straight with people. Tell them the truth and tell them what has to happen. You might be surprised at some of the results you and your team engineer and may wonder why you never did this before. As they say, necessity is the cause of most invention and a powerful motivator. Re-budgeting is your first issue and if you don't get it right it just may be your last one too. Cut expenses first—find your margin fast.

GET YOUR MONEY SMART AGAIN

Your money was once smart. It was invested each day based on past successful results so it was predictably productive each time it was spent. It was smart money. When the market shifts your money instantly becomes dumb. What worked no longer works so what it was spent on doesn't yield the same results. It is dumb money. It is often said that insanity is doing the same thing over and over and expecting different results. This couldn't be truer regarding money than when a market shifts. Warren Buffett teaches "the first step to financial recovery is to stop doing the wrong things. It's an old principle. You don't have to make it back the way you lost it." To get the results you want you'll have to pull back your expenses, find your margin of profit, figure out what works and then put your money behind it. First you get smart then your money gets smart. For every dollar spent expect multiple returns from it. Just keep this principle at the heart of your business spending and you can't go wrong. Until you get this don't spend another dollar.

This is how you build on success as opposed to piling failure on top of failure. Don't try to just spend your way out of a shift—make your way out through results. Define a benchmark dollar result you should expect from every dollar you spend and until you get that result don't spend any more. This is the most important business discipline you'll ever need. Learn it. Live it. Once it is ingrained into your business thinking you'll simply be adding success on top of success for the rest of your career. Your money will be smart. You'll be even smarter and financially better off.

Cutting expenses is so painful, but your pocketbook will thank you later.
Bob Guest, Austin, TX

When you get your money smart again and are working from a positive profit margin you are back in the game. The shift may have dropped you down but you're not out. You know what you're spending money on and what you're getting for it. You are putting your money where your priorities are. You're in control of your money instead of your money controlling you. Knowing what you spend, where it goes and what you get for it alerts you to opportunities you might otherwise miss. You'll know what you're doing, why you're doing it, and whether you can afford anything else. You're in the best possible decision-making position.

The key to re-margining and changing your budget is changing the way you think. If money matters then managing that money matters. To be an effective money manager you must be a "budget bully." Challenge everything and make nothing sacred. The goal is to guide your business and manage your money, as Owen D. Young, the former chairman of GE, said, by "taking advantage of the maximum number of opportunities and making the minimum number of errors." When you lead from a position of profit your world is full of possibilities.

TACTIC #3
DO MORE WITH LESS – LEVERAGE

When we are no longer able to change a situation,
we are challenged to change ourselves.

VIKTOR FRANKL

WHEN THE MARKET TURNS, it is time to roll up your sleeves and for everyone around you to do the same. It's time to work both smarter and harder. It's time to evaluate which resources and services must stay or go. It's time to consider effectiveness and efficiency as tools of necessity. It's time to see what bang you can get for the bucks you've got.

Cutting expenses and finding your margin doesn't necessarily mean slashing quality or delivering less. It does however, demand getting the job done with less money available to do it, and this will create a dynamic tension inside your business. Change and the speed of change always put pressure on you to do things better and yet more cost-effectively. Even worse, a swift shift can unexpectedly find you doing less and doing it less efficiently. It's in that moment you suddenly grasp the true challenge of a shift—to do more with less.

When the market shifts your organization must shift too. A market shift can be an opportunity to evaluate, upgrade, and top grade your business, an unsolicited gift of the shift. Instead of hiring just to get the work out, it may be time to reassess and top grade your people. Instead of just managing the flow it may be time to retool and upgrade your systems. Skip any fault-finding, finger-pointing, or blaming and go straight to a new vision for your business.

BACK TO BASICS

Don't let change throw you for a loop. Once you know what you must accomplish and you know what your margin can be, you must envision and promote a positive future. There is an old saying in sports "if you want to stay ahead then play like you're behind." The challenge you might have is that you've been ahead and played like it. Now you're behind so what do you do? You do what all great business people do—you focus tightly on the basics. You do that by asking yourself four straightforward questions. What are my business priorities? When do they need to get done? Who is the best person to do them? And, finally, how should they be done? We know the answer to the first question because it is the fundamental six priorities for your business.

THE SIX CORE COMPETENCIES OF A BUSINESS

1. Lead generate, capture, and convert to appointments
2. Present to buyers and sellers and get agreements
3. Show buyers and market sellers
4. Write and negotiate contracts
5. Coordinate the sale to closing
6. Manage the money

We know that to achieve your highest potential these six core competencies must be done consistently and done well. We also know the answer to the second question because these priorities show up for your business in this precise order and there is no skipping around. Your business success starts with generating leads and progresses from there. The real mission is to

More staff doesn't equate to more productivity. The phenomenal few can outperform, outproduce, and outpace the mediocre many.
Diane Kink, The Woodlands, TX

get all of these done in order at the highest level possible with the least amount of resources. The management of these resources is what the last two questions are about. If you know what needs to be done and when it must be done, then you're left with who and how—people and systems.

PEOPLE

People begins with you. So before you look at others take an honest look at yourself. Are you maximizing your own productivity? Are you doing what matters most? Are you doing what you get paid to do? As we said in *Tactic #1: Get Real, Get Right,* the role you play in your business is critical—now more than ever. Once you are clear about how your personal efforts are getting more of the important things done cost-effectively, the focus shifts to others in your business.

There are two types of people in your business. Those directly employed by you and those indirectly employed by you. Those directly employed by you are the ones to whom you write checks. Those indirectly employed are the vendors who support you. Both groups need to be effective because both are equally important to your success.

Let's first look at those you directly employ. Good times can obscure and even camouflage who isn't really working out or even actually working at all. Up markets can hide lesser talent because we predictably focus on our sales success in the moment and generally don't give the market enough credit for its role in our success. Face it, when it comes to people—up markets conceal and tough markets reveal.

The challenge in a shift is that in order to do more with less you must make sure that the less can do more. Think about it for a moment and you'll discover that you're facing the topic of talent. When you look at your organization through the filter of a shifting market you realize that no matter the circumstances you only ever have one critical issue with people: you either have the right ones or the wrong ones. It's always about quality and never about quantity. You can never have too many of the right ones, but you can certainly have too many of the wrong ones. And no matter the market too many rights never make up for even one wrong. In your business talent is someone who is a great match for the job you need them to do, who is motivated to do it, and can do it really well.

I'm asking everyone on the team to do more. We've even assigned each buyer agent additional tasks. We all have to do more without spending more.

Teri Brenkus, Las Vegas, NV

In *The Millionaire Real Estate Agent,* we identified these individuals as "cul-de-sac" talent. They have all the skills and motivation necessary to do the job you hire them for and they can perform at a very high level. However, these individuals may still be cul-de-sac talent in that they don't have the skills or motivation to grow beyond their current position.

"Capacity" talent, on the other hand, can do their job and much more. They will push you for a larger role and more responsibility. Capacity talent is your greatest asset in a shift. They want to do more and can do more. They require less of your time and will accomplish more in less time. They may cost more but will always make you more than they cost. Capacity talent, real talent, will see the shift as their opportunity to shine and they will stand out in your organization. Always keep in mind that you can't do more with less(er) talent, but, with real talent, you can always do more with less.

Leverage has given me a life worth living while I give my clients even better service. My kids appreciate it too!
Andy Hodes, Chattanooga, TN

Before you visit with your people do the math and make sure you know what your needs are. What needs to be accomplished and how much money do you have to pay for it? You're caught in between what you can afford and who you can't afford to lose. This is one of the most challenging leadership positions you will encounter. As you work through this, think assistance first and assistants second. Think part-timers, subcontractors, vendors, affiliates, or students. Review your needs and all your options for meeting them. Remember, you have a lot. You can combine positions, cut hours, or move to results-focused, bonus-based compensation. Any or all of these might need to be considered as you figure out how to keep talent with you, while keeping costs as low as possible.

When you're done thinking this through take stock and see where you are. For those already in your business, you need to find out who wants to work and can. Your approach will be as simple as following a seven step process.

SEVEN STEPS TO TALENT SHIFT

1. Sit down with your people and share your vision for your business. Tell them the truth about the situation, where the business is today and where you see it going.

2. Visit with each person to see if they're with you and are willing to do whatever it takes.

3. Realign job descriptions around the six core competencies that must get done. You might even consider moving from job descriptions to task descriptions. In this way, your key tasks can be mixed and matched, cross-trained and swapped without changing titles or compensation. Seek flexibility and avoid rigidity.

4. Set easy-to-measure goals, standards, and activities for each person. Be positive and clearly communicate what needs to happen. Then expect results or resignations— you'll accept either.

5. Establish a simple training schedule to make sure everyone knows what to do, how to do it, and what is expected of them. Training not only builds competence, but also confidence and positive expectations.

6. Meet weekly with each individual to evaluate their success and reach agreement on any corrective action. Don't make the mistake of believing that once changes are made, everyone is on board. You must inspect what you expect. Touch base regularly to check in and see how they're really doing.

7. Celebrate the small victories as well as the big ones. Celebrate the individual wins as well as the team's successes.

Keep it simple. Try to flatten your organization as much as possible. Less bureaucracy usually means more productivity. Create an environment of open communication and feedback. Remember that rule-making isn't nearly as productive as working from goals, action plans, and standards. Be aware that top-down imposed change can create frustration, fear, anxiety, unrest, and even resistance.

Talk to your people and share what you're going through and ask them what they're going through. Do your best to eliminate uncertainty and you will eliminate a lot of insecurity. Too much change too quickly can be difficult, so remember that people most likely will need new information to help understand and buy into it. And above all they'll need new and constant re-education. People will rarely make the leap in a shift on their own—they need to be led through change. If you do these things the right people will see the strength of your commitment and rally behind you.

For those who don't get it, they will have made it clear they can't play on your team. Nothing will help the wrong people at this point, but a new job somewhere else. One agent shared a telling story. She printed the letters D-E-C-K on four sheets of paper and placed them on the conference table in her office saying, "It's time for all hands on deck." But not everyone on her team put their hands on the table. Surprised and disappointed, she had to go back to her office and re-evaluate her team on the spot.

If you must fire people follow a process. Once you've made the decision to part company, move quickly but be respectful. You invited them into your business with positive anticipation for their future and you have to invite them out with the same attitude. There is no place for good guys and bad guys. The time is past for the blame game. It didn't work out, nobody is happy about it, and it is time to move on. The key is to frame out a win-win that works for everyone. Once the employee is gone there is no place for any further discussion about the circumstances. Just remember that "loose lips sink ships" and everyone associated with you will be paying attention. The respect you show those who are no longer with you builds respect with those who are.

TALENT SCOUTING IN FOUR STEPS

1. Check references
2. Get a behavioral profile
3. Conduct an in-depth interview
4. Test for knowledge and skills

When you need to hire new people always follow this simple four-step process. Check references and go deep; ideally you want to talk to people beyond the references your candidates provide and who are usually their unabashed advocates. Get a behavioral profile (ex: the DISC) to determine whether or not their natural behavior matches the job. Conduct an in-depth interview in order to determine their strengths and weaknesses. And, if possible, give them a specific test to prove their knowledge and skills.

The goal is to hire talent to your team. The hiring process is usually cheated on in good times and it's easy to understand why. When your business is growing, you need help fast and you tend to take the first person who comes along. You need help and you need it now. This is the mud approach to hiring—sling some people at a job and see who sticks. Circumstances have changed, you need talent now and the more talented team members you have, the fewer you'll need.

The same standard of having the right people applies to your vendors. Getting more and better support from your vendor team is critical. In fact, think "preferred partner" versus vendor. It'll make your thinking clearer. You need a phenomenal outside support team to work together with your inside support team to become one seamless, high-performance unit.

Make sure you have a loan officer who understands creative financing and is up to date on all available lending programs; a title officer who understands the closing process issues that arise during shifting times; inspectors who get the fickleness of buyers when operating in a perceived buyers' market; appraisers who know that transactions can hinge more than ever now on a tight, proper appraisal and are willing to listen to a valuation challenge and respect your market research.

Hold your preferred partners to the same high standards that you have for your team. Meet with them regularly. Set goals and review results with them. When you treat your outside support team with the same expectations of excellence you insist upon from your inside support team you will be amazed at the positive difference it makes for your business. With both your inside team and your outside team pulling together in the direction you've set for them you have the best chance of success.

SYSTEMS

You topgrade people and you upgrade systems. Now that you know what you need to do, when you need to do it, and who you have doing it, it's time to tackle your systems and how things are done. Good times usually plant seeds of system inefficiencies that during tough times sprout into choking weeds of ineffectiveness. We tend to add staff rather than improve systems and end up putting pressure on your budget instead of on your processes. The goal now is to quickly reevaluate how things are done to see what works and what doesn't. Again, we want to do more with less and that means we have to make our approaches to things simpler. To do this you must think efficient-effective and make maximum use of everything and everybody. The key is to ask what exactly needs to be accomplished to hit your minimum goals of sales and service quality without any extra effort or expense. Put another way, how can we execute a task with less effort and expense and still maintain high effectiveness? This is the efficiency question you face.

Usually with systems, the problem you face is the exact same one everyone faces. You are probably trying to do too many things and as a result not doing enough of the right things the right way. Trying to do too much will cost you time and money. Your procedures must be lean and mean. No more paperwork for paperwork's sake. No more filing for filing's sake. No more detail for detail's sake. Remember, complexity kills.

Everything must be extremely purposeful. Everything must be streamlined. The goal is to get right what you need to get right with as few steps and as few people doing it as possible. That means less red tape and fewer distractions. It means breaking things down to their basics to figure out what is the least you have to do right now so you can get the most done. Just boil things down to the basics that will get it done, get rid of all else and start from there. Get down to the basics, to what works at a truly simple level.

I am making the market obey me instead of me obeying the market! My business is important, but my life is precious.

Donna Grissom, Studio City, CA

In essence you're right-sizing your boat and jettisoning ballast. Simplify your business. Lay a more focused and efficient foundation. Find out what works and make the most of what you have.

GETTING LIGHT ON YOUR FEET

Change requires everyone to be on board. It's time for all hands on deck. To change really means to adapt. So just think of you and everyone working with you as being a part of an adaptive organization. An adaptive group always expects change whether forced on them or caused by them. And change causes more change. The point is for you and your people to not view what you do as static so that change appears to be this "big deal" that everyone fears, but see it as being adaptive and as a critical competitive advantage—an advantage you're always seeking. Change is good. It's good for the advantage it can give you.

To grow, let go. Let go of preconceptions of people and systems and what you think they should do. Start with what you have and build from there. Build core competencies around what really matters and associate with people who are on the same page as you. Now more than ever, your personal actions, your people, and your systems must be focused on the 20 percent that matters. There is no time or money in doing the 80 percent. Just let it go.

TACTIC #4
FIND THE MOTIVATED —
LEAD GENERATION

If your ship doesn't come in, swim out to it.
JONATHAN WINTERS

FEWER LEADS, FEWER SHOWINGS, and increased days-on-the-market— the minute these signs show up, take notice. Don't ignore them and don't wait to act. These are the early warning signals of what is most likely coming next—more inventory and fewer pendings. This is the sequence of a shift. Demand slows down and supply builds up. It starts with fewer leads and ends with even less closings. Buyers and sellers get thrown for a loop and they in turn throw the market for one. What felt like an unlimited supply of buyers and sellers suddenly feels very limited. Abundance quickly shifts to scarcity.

But just because the market has moved from more to less doesn't necessarily mean you have to. As leads become fewer, you must recognize the situation and make a more concerted effort to generate them. You can't sit back—you must be more rigorous and resolute in your lead generation than ever before and more so than anyone else. In fact now is the time to shift your lead generation activities into the highest gear possible.

The cause and challenge of a shift is simply one word—motivation. When a market has shifted what has really happened is that buyer and seller motivation has changed. Regardless of the economic causes or driving forces behind the shift, your market only shifts because the motive and rationale behind buying and selling has shifted. In other words, whenever and wherever economics shift so does motivation. And this becomes the number one challenge of a shift— finding the motivated. Where there was once a large quantity of quality leads, there isn't and the once clear pool feels more like a muddy puddle. The number of salable leads has decreased dramatically and the reason is motivation. It's almost as if all the buying and selling of the past sellers' market has borrowed against the buyers and sellers of this market and it's now time to pay up. Where the buyers and sellers had both personal reasons and positive market expectations as dual motivators they now just have their personal reasons.

Don't cling to buyers just because there's a scarcity of them.
Russell Shaw, Phoenix, AZ

Motives have narrowed significantly and fewer people pass the clear-cut motivation test of being able, ready, and willing. Fewer buyers can afford to, have the desire to, or are prepared to buy now at market prices. Fewer sellers can afford to, have the desire to, or are prepared to sell now at market prices. A market shift simply causes a smaller number of buyers and sellers to have the ability, readiness, or willingness to be involved in a real estate transaction at this moment. And this creates the difficulty you face. You can "motive-aid" someone to help them better understand why they should consider buying or selling in this market, but you can't motivate them. Their motives are their own. Their rationales or reasons are theirs and theirs alone. And since you can't actually motivate people, your only choice will be to find more of them. So this is why you must now ramp up your lead generation, because there are less of the motivated to find.

Frankly, this is when the true competitive nature of our business reveals itself and you realize it's time to stop trying to get your fair share of the market and do all you can to get your unfair share. The agents who are going to survive and thrive in any tough business market will be those who face reality and say "If it's to be, it's up to me and I need leads coming straight to me." The challenge is that when the market first shifts you are rarely sure what it will take to find enough motivated prospects to achieve your sales and income numbers. You have to be willing to do whatever it takes. You have to be motivated to find the motivated.

MOVE PAST YOUR MYTHS

Let's face facts. Lead generating to find potential customers just might not be your favorite business subject. If you're like most, it probably isn't why you got into real estate and isn't something that gets you excited to go to work everyday. The truth, however, is that you actually got into two businesses. You got into the helping people with their real estate needs business and you got into the lead generation business. They are inseparable. They are the yin and the yang of your professional world. The bottom line is that without motivated leads there are no people to help. To have sales you must have leads. One begets the other. Interestingly, the market shifting may have now exposed a real personal dilemma you must overcome—you love helping people but at the same time you haven't yet learned to love hunting for them.

Please realize that I'm actually describing myself. I must admit that I honestly didn't enjoy or fully embrace the lead generating part of our business at first. It wasn't until I realized that lead generating was something I had to do and master in order to get to do the things I really enjoyed doing that I actually buckled down and got serious about it. And then something magical happened. The more I did it, the better I got, and the better I got the more I liked it. It turns out that I had held a handful of myths in my head that were holding me back. Once they were dispelled I was over the hump and off and running.

From a distance, I thought lead generation was really difficult, but after I diligently applied myself to it for a reasonable length of time I came to see that it was actually quite easy and could even be fun. I was confusing effort with enjoyment. I also thought I was going to be too busy and wouldn't have the time to lead generate. However, as I focused on doing it every day I discovered it wasn't an issue of having time but an issue of making time and then protecting it. As I learned to manage my time better I discovered I had all the time I needed. Then intimidation set in. I believed I couldn't lead generate because I didn't know what to do or say and was afraid of making mistakes; however, as I consistently "got after it" I found that lead generation is nothing more than a set of tasks and skills that are well documented. I caught on that with practice and homework these actions are easily understood and learned. I saw that on top of being a "transaction knowledge and service business," our industry is a "script and dialogue skill-based business." I had to commit to getting onto the path of mastering these. I discovered that "time on the task over time" was the simple secret that helped me become very good.

Interestingly, what might have held me up the most was that I had naively bought into the popularly quoted myth that "it takes money to make money." As a result, I naturally assumed I couldn't successfully lead generate because I thought it would just cost too much from what little I had. However, once I experienced how buyers and sellers find and choose a real estate agent I then grasped two foundational truths. First, that lead generation doesn't have to cost money at all if I don't want it to and, second, that if and when I do spend money it doesn't have to be as risky as I had imagined.

And finally, I just plain fought it. I hadn't passed a sales behavioral profile test I'd been given in college, so I truly didn't feel at all like a natural lead generator. But as I looked around the industry, it dawned on me that very few people have the perfect sales profile and that no one is truly a natural lead generator. The gift of gab should never be mistaken for natural sales skill. It became obvious to me that everyone has to master the specific and meaningful scripts, dialogues, and skills of lead generation to be really successful.

Once I got these myths and erroneous thoughts out of my head, I was able to put my head down and get after it. In time, the results I had hoped for started to show up. When I was able to connect the dots between effort and results I had a huge aha. I now saw that

Lead generation has become critical! It's no longer waiting for people coming to us. We must be the initiators. If it's going to happen, we've got to make it happen.

Dan Harker, Dallas, TX

what I did on the front end with lead generation got me sales results on the back end. This connection opened my eyes to how effort and success were linked. I became motivated to put in the necessary effort and also began to enjoy it. I knew that when I generated leads, the desired results would follow.

I had to make peace with lead generation and so will you if you want to push through a market shift. When all is said and done one of two things is going to happen. You'll either get over your myths and get on with it or you'll eventually succumb to your myths and have to get out of it.

If your past sales success came (either in part or in total) from riding the wave of an increasing market, the odds are the easy business you enjoyed will have virtually disappeared. To get back on track there are three straightforward action steps you must take to get your sales business moving in a positive direction: 1) Stop doing what doesn't work; 2) Figure out what does work; and 3) Ramp it up!

STEP ONE: STOP DOING WHAT DOESN'T WORK

When you have fewer leads than you need you really do have a problem you can't ignore. Ayn Rand summed up this challenge extremely well when she wrote, "We can evade reality, but we cannot evade the consequences of evading reality." The consequences of evading the reality of your lead generation situation could be dire. The way to avoid this is to acknowledge your situation and do something about it. The first step is to stop doing what doesn't work. You start by realizing that time and money are really the two basic tools you have to generate leads, so you must absolutely stop spending any time or money on lead generation activities that aren't working. Seems obvious and sounds simple, right? But the trick isn't in getting it, it's in doing it.

Your goals haven't changed. You know what your annual income goal is and you know the number of sales you must close to hit it. What has changed is the number of appointments you are going on and the number of leads it takes to get those appointments. The question you're going to answer is "What am I doing or spending money on that is no longer effective since the market shifted?" You can only know this by associating your valid leads and your lead sources with your closed sales.

If you haven't already been tracking this get out paper and a pen and do the following exercise. Write down your top ten sources of leads. This could be individuals who send you referrals or it could be any methods you currently use. What you're trying to answer is "where do my leads come from?" Next, write beside each one the number of valid leads or closings that lead has brought you. Then prioritize them by numbering them from 1 – 10, with 1 being the most demonstrably effective and 10 being the least. Take the bottom five and stop allocating time or money to them and aim all your resources to the top five that are working. (Note: The total number isn't as important as the idea of only working the most effective ones.) Do this every month because effectiveness is an ongoing and never ending process of evaluation and adjustment to find the sweet spot—the "lead source zone" that's working for you.

IDENTIFYING YOUR LEAD SOURCE ZONE

FIGURE 10 In three simple steps you can quickly identify your lead sources,
prioritize them by what is and isn't working, and then narrow your focus on what is.

The one exception to this process is if any of the lower group on your list, while not always being immediately effective, still creates long-term lead generation opportunities. If you're doing one that meets this description, then you shouldn't necessarily give it up. But do try to get it to pull double duty. Your regular newsletter or e-letter might be a good example of this. The content should be geared for delivering short-term results as well as developing long-term relationships. In other words, pursue short-term and long-term goals at the same time. To have your best year plus a great career requires both. Lead generation effectiveness is the one true building block of all successful real estate careers and while its goal is always immediate business that is usually best accomplished through a dual focus on present and future business.

> *There are motivated buyers and sellers out there. The question is: Are we doing the right things to find them?*
>
> *Rick Brash, Calgary, AB, Canada*

So when it comes to evaluating results don't guess and don't get involved in overly optimistic thinking. If your leads have started to dry up then not everything you're doing is working. You need to spot what isn't and stop doing it. In other words, stop wasting precious time or spending scarce money. How much? All of it!

Having said that, you may find that it is impossible to hit your future goals without expanding your lead generation activities. So at some point, you may either want or need to invest some more money towards additional lead generating. When you do, start by only investing in what you know works and only initiate carefully planned efforts. As we said in *The Millionaire Real Estate Agent,* play "red light, green light." Red light means spending no more money until what you're doing proves its success. Only then would you green light additional dollar investments. Your new philosophy is to hold any and all dollars spent on lead generation accountable for generating motivated buyers and sellers that lead to closings.

When a market shifts, it requires you to take a step back and immediately stop doing what isn't working. By the way, you're not alone. What is happening to you is happening to everyone else in your market. The advice that works for you is the same advice that will work for them. The ones who succeed will be those who understand this the quickest and do something about it. That needs to be you.

STEP TWO: FIGURE OUT WHAT WORKS

Identifying what currently works and doesn't work is one thing. Knowing how to build an effective lead generation program is something else. While the exercise you just did roughly identified what is or is not currently working, most likely you will need to add more factors that will work. To do this you now need to understand why and how lead generation really works. This will enable you to move from having success to creating success, which becomes critical in a shift. Having sales happen is one thing. But now we need to make sales happen and that is something else entirely.

Most agents don't give adequate thought to building a successful lead generation program that works in any market. A shift makes it absolutely necessary. Anyone who doesn't move to mastering lead generation usually gets shifted right out of real estate. The proven formula you can use for truly understanding what will work in your market is the Two M's of Lead Generation: Message and Method.

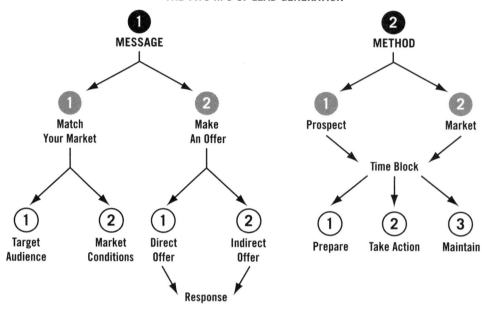

THE TWO M'S OF LEAD GENERATION

1 MESSAGE

1 Match Your Market
- **1 Target Audience**
- **2 Market Conditions**

2 Make An Offer
- **1 Direct Offer**
- **2 Indirect Offer**

Response

2 METHOD

1 Prospect

2 Market

Time Block
- **1 Prepare**
- **2 Take Action**
- **3 Maintain**

FIGURE 11

YOUR MESSAGE MATTERS

The first principle of lead generation messaging is that your message must match your market. This means that your lead generation message must match the motivation of the buyers and sellers in whatever market you're in. Always follow this standard—it's how you cause motivation to show up and reveal itself. When we say your message must match your market we're talking about two markets: The target market of buyers and sellers you communicate to and the market conditions of the market areas in which you operate. You convey a message to a targeted audience (your market) and you work in a targeted area (the market). It's about the issues and motivations of your targeted audience and the issues and conditions of the market area. You may have one or more targeted audiences and you can have one or more market areas. For some, their target audience and market area are one and the same because the targeted buyers and sellers they lead generate to encompass the entire general population of the market area they operate in. For others, the specific buyers and sellers they target are simply a subset of their overall area. Either approach can work. You just want to be clear on who you're addressing and on the current market conditions of that area.

Your message must match your market to be effective. This is a timeless business truth that transcends all markets and market conditions. In a constricting market this truth becomes critical since the message people respond to narrows greatly. When motivation is low there are fewer messages that work. The message you put out to attract prospective buyers and sellers is everything. *Why would they want to contact you in this market? What would they get if they did?* These two questions are at the heart of all effective messaging. The smartest lead generators know that people respond to messages that matter to them now. And this becomes the driving theme of all their lead generation activities. When the market shifts they immediately know that all their lead generation messages must now shift to match the new market.

Messaging is built on the proven idea that people will contact you if there is some direct benefit to them. The opportunity to get something they want or need drives their contact. Promoting your personal brand matters a lot because of the validity it creates for you, but in a shifted market personal branding alone without a lead generating message won't get you the motivated leads you need. The effective message makes the phone ring and it will do the heavy lifting of your lead generation. It will be the driving force behind why people contact you. They will connect with you when your message connects with their why—when it speaks to their personal motivations.

The second principle of lead generation messaging is your message must make an offer to get a response. When you create messages for buyers or sellers you must determine what kind of offers you will make based on what kind of responses you want. This theory is called "offer-response" messaging. Now, please know that this has been confusingly mislabeled by many as "direct-response" marketing for some strange reason I don't quite understand. The concept they are trying to describe is actually a foundational messaging principle that applies to both prospecting and marketing and includes two types of offers. When you lead generate you are simply making offers to people with the expectation of a response—thus the name "offer-response." Your two offer choices are to either make a direct offer to get an immediate response or to make an indirect offer to get an immediate response.

OFFER-RESPONSE MESSAGING

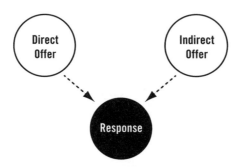

FIGURE 12 Your messages should make compelling direct and indirect offers that will evoke an immediate response from buyers and sellers.

A direct offer is exactly that—direct. It is an offer designed to get an immediate response from someone who wants to buy or sell with you now. An indirect offer is still an offer that seeks an immediate response, but not directly for using your services of helping them buy or sell. It is an offer to get something else from you now, thus it is called an indirect offer, which puts you into a relationship with them and opens the door to possibly doing business with you in the future. If you are offering a home for sale and they respond, that is a direct offer and an immediate response—they are immediately interested in buying. If, on the other hand, you offer a free report of some kind and they respond, that is an indirect offer and an immediate response—they are immediately interested in the report but haven't indicated an immediate interest in buying or selling. They are not seeking to hire you for what you directly do, but their response may give you the opportunity to build a relationship and serve them some time down the road.

Direct offers seek to generate immediate responses to buy or sell and indirect offers seek to generate immediate responses for something from you other than to buy or sell. One is a path to immediate business and one is a path to immediate services that might lead to future business. One takes a direct route to doing business and the other an indirect route—thus the labels direct and indirect. Regardless of which offer you make you always want people to respond *now*. To do this you must practice the simple concept of MOFIR—Make Offers For Immediate Response—at all times. You might have heard this explained in the past as "a call to action" for it is a tried-and-true messaging theory. Whether it is a direct or indirect offer you use in your message you should always call someone to action by putting forth an offer they will immediately respond to.

The bottom line is that to be an effective lead generator you need to make offers that motivated buyers or sellers will respond to right away.

Why would you ever make an indirect offer in a shifted market when making a direct offer would seem to be a straighter path to get you exactly what you want? The reason is that not everyone responds to direct offers. By casting out wider nets using both you're fishing for the two types of people out there and covering your bases at all times. And both work as well in a shifted market as they do under any other market conditions. The issue isn't about which is better because you really want to be doing both.

Lead generation is a 10 on a scale of 1 to 10. There is nothing more important for my business.

Gene Rivers, Tallahassee, FL

The priority is in making sure your offers always call for an immediate response. You're looking for opportunities to convert people to immediate business and you're also looking for opportunities to get into dialogue with people for future business. You can make any number of indirect offers ranging from specific information to free reports to something of economic value. Best-buy lists, free foreclosure home lists, property hotlines, custom property searches, reports you create such as the "five mistakes you can't afford to make when selling" and money-saving offers are all great examples of indirect offers. The key to making it effective is to appeal to people's motivation and do it differently than other agents so that it stands out.

Offering a free CMA, for example, is a fairly common indirect offer that sellers will regularly respond to under any market condition. Some would argue that it is a direct offer but they would be wrong. Remember that a direct offer is "buy a home through me" or "list with me." It is a direct offer when the only answer is that they do or don't do business with you. The free CMA doesn't pass this simple test because you're actually offering a free service and information that could lead to a listing at some point. That makes it an indirect offer. A simple free CMA, while tried and true, is probably being offered by nearly everyone in some manner, but since it is something people still want you'll just have to think outside the box when you make them the offer if you want to get your unfair share of responses. Focus on the market situation and the personal or logical motivations that would drive people to respond to an offer and then shape your indirect offer accordingly. By the way, follow the same approach with your direct offers too.

YOUR MESSAGE NEEDS A METHOD

Now that you're clear about the messages you will use you must pick your methods for getting them out. The two categories all lead generation methods fall into are prospecting and marketing. Prospecting is where you go get the leads and marketing is where you do things to cause the leads to come to you. Prospecting is you making contact with people and marketing is people making contact with you. Prospecting is seeking and marketing is attracting. Prospecting can be done by phone or in person while marketing is done through any published medium or broadcast media.

Although you'll consistently hear people say they do one or the other, research says you should do both. Doing both helps you avoid any risks of having "all your eggs in one basket" and this diversification actually increases your odds of long-term success. Also, both offer unique benefits. Prospecting gives you instant contact with the market and provides you the best timely feedback. It immediately lets you know what people are responding to and gives you the quickest proactive way to control results. Marketing gives you the opportunity to get to a wider audience faster and offers you the best chance for lead generation leverage. It can put your message in front of a lot of people efficiently and at the least cost per person possible. Your ongoing lead generation goal is always to get in the path of as many motivated buyers and sellers as you possibly can. To do that, you must do both.

Many people think of prospecting and marketing as mutually exclusive, but I encourage you to think bigger and see them as mutually supportive. Your prospecting can be supported or enhanced by your marketing and your marketing can be supported or enhanced by your prospecting. The only limits here are probably a lack of creativity. Continually seek ways to make both work at the same time. A simple example would be holding an open house (prospecting) and also passing out "best buy" lists (marketing). Or doing both prospecting (door knocking or calls) and marketing (direct mail) to get people to attend the open house.

As you look at the list in Figure 13 you realize that there are quite a variety of prospecting and marketing methods to choose from. Remember, the secret to successful lead generation is getting in the path of prospects with a message that matches their motivations for the market they're in. Once you understand the messages that work it is just a function of getting it in front of enough people who are motivated to buy or sell. Look at this list again, pick a few and get started. Which ones do you pick? The ones you think are most likely to work the fastest for you given your market.

PROSPECTING	MARKETING

PROSPECTING

1. TELEMARKETING
   - FSBOs (For Sale By Owners)
   - Expireds
   - Just Solds
   - Just Listeds
   - Past Clients
   - Allied Resources
   - Geographic Farm Area
   - Apartments
   - Corporations
   - Builders
   - Banks
   - Third-Party Companies
2. FACE-TO-FACE
   - Allied Resources (Meals)
   - Door-to-Door Canvasing
   - Open Houses
   - Client Parties
   - Networking Events
   - Social Functions and Community Events
   - Seminars
   - Booths at Events
   - Teaching and Speaking Opportunities

MARKETING

1. ADVERTISING
   - Newspapers
   - Personal Vehicles
   - Radio
   - Magazines
   - Bus Stop Benches
   - Billboards
   - Yellow Pages
   - Television
   - Grocery Carts
   - Moving Vans
2. PROMOTIONAL ITEMS (Magnets, Calendars . . .)
3. INTERNET WEB SITES
4. DIRECT MAIL
   - Postcard Campaigns
   - Just Sold/Just Listed Cards
   - Special Events Cards
   - Quarterly Market Updates
5. IVR and COMPUTER RETRIEVAL PROGRAMS
6. BROADCAST
   - Voice
   - E-mail
   - Fax
7. SIGNS/DIRECTIONAL SIGNS/BROCHURE BOXES
8. NAME BADGES/LOGO SHIRTS/CAR SIGNS
9. NEWS RELEASES/ADVICE COLUMNS
10. FARMING
    - Geographic
    - Demographic
    - Psychographic
11. SPONSORSHIP
    - Little League
    - Charities
    - Community Events

FIGURE 13 Whether it's prospecting or marketing or both, the methods are many!

You'll regularly hear some real estate agents saying one method works better than another. This may be true for them. However, I believe any method executed properly and consistently can be quite successful. And top agents rarely use just one method. So the question you should ask is not what methods you will do, but what methods you will do first. The answer should be simple and straightforward—the methods that will generate the most leads in the shortest amount of time, for the least amount of your effort and money invested.

Now, although there is no set formula for this, some target audiences are going to be better than others in a shifted market. You will want to prospect and market to those people you can directly identify as motivated, and to others who can identify them for you (because they know you and trust you). That first list would include: open houses, FSBOs, expired listings, foreclosures, builders with spec homes built, and relocation buyers or sellers, among others. The second list would be the people in your met database (your past clients, sphere of influence, friends, and acquaintances) who you believe will send you referrals. You're using messages and making offers trying to discover if they want or need to buy or sell in this market and trying to discover if they know of anyone who might want or need to buy or sell in this market. The thing to avoid is simply trolling for motivated people without any clue where they are. At some point, as you seek to increase your leads this will be acceptable, but not until you're already generating an adequate number of motivated leads that are closing. Quick leads first, more leads second, and lots of leads third.

Since prospecting can literally cost no money you should go straight to prospecting while you get comfortable with your marketing choices. Remember that prospecting is about converting your messages to effective verbal dialogues and scripts you must practice and learn. Marketing is about converting your messages effectively to the print medium or broadcast media you choose. Your effectiveness at either will be part knowledge and part experience. Get some basic training and then dive in. Don't wait to become an expert because you can't become one by studying—your greatest teacher and skill-builder is your personal experience.

The most successful real estate salespeople both prospect and market. Why? There are limits to your reach with prospecting that don't exist with marketing. Prospecting is something you must always show up to do. Marketing is something you unleash and then works without your having to be there. Prospecting is about seeking opportunities. It's the act of personally calling and contacting targeted people you haven't met or people you have met. Marketing is the opposite of prospecting. Instead of seeking opportunities, marketing is about attracting them. It's the work of placing your messages where you believe motivated buyers or sellers are most likely to see or hear them.

When leads become fewer, prospecting increases. The research for *The Millionaire Real Estate Agent* showed that top agents used the "marketing-based and prospecting-enhanced" approach, but experience teaches us that a shifted market requires that you move more towards prospecting. You could still be marketing-based, but you're probably doing more prospecting than you were. It is all about meeting your lead generation goals. Prospecting tends to uncover motivated leads faster and keeps you more in control. Because prospecting puts you in immediate contact with people you get immediate feedback—and that is what you want in a shifted market.

This isn't to say that marketing isn't effective. It is. What the research shows is that when markets shift for most top agents their lead generation will shift more in the direction of prospecting, but they don't quit marketing. For a few top agents, they will actually

My real estate business took off when I realized I had to ask for business and not be attached to the answer. I would have to get no's on my way to yes's, I just had to ask. The more I asked, the more I got.

Linda McKissack, Denton, TX

remain marketing-based and simply tweak where and how they do it, but this is a select group breathing "rare air." Even this group could benefit from adding or increasing some level of prospecting to their activities.

Time on the task over time will serve you well in mastering your approaches, but be careful that your behavioral style doesn't betray you. Most real estate agents fall into two broad behavioral types: those who like to take action first and those who like to study first. And although there are many behavioral assessments that call these various names, they all boil down to one simple concept—fear of making a mistake. Those who aren't afraid to make a mistake just jump right in and easily accept the idea that they'll learn as they go. Others shudder at this thought and think about all the mistakes they could make. They believe that only after they have thoroughly studied something and mastered it should they go out and take action. Honestly, I believe both are wrong.

Regardless of your behavioral style I think you should quickly study and learn the basics, then take action while you continue to study. Studying and practicing is one thing, doing it is another. Both are required to master anything at a high level. So the doer must also be the student and the student must also be the doer. The question remains: when do you take action and when do you study? Experience says that an ongoing cycle of study and practice, take action, study and practice, take action is the best approach. Don't be a slave to your preferred behavior style. You must gain some control over yourself no matter which natural style you are. You must do both to become your best.

Once we began using the phrase 'priced like bank-owned properties' our call traffic went up! The bank-owned language really works.
David Brownell, Las Vegas, NV

If you're an "action first" person, I want you to slow down long enough to study and practice 30 minutes each day before you take off.

A little research and role-playing will do so much for your effectiveness, you just won't believe it. So experience it. And remember that when you learn only from your experience, you're learning a lot less than you should.

If you're a "study first" person, I want you to realize that you can't know it all no matter how much you study. So get on a study program you're comfortable with and take action while you're on it. And remember, if experiential learning isn't on the program, you're arguably missing the most important part.

THE TRUE PROFESSIONAL

Consider this. Most difficulties in real estate transactions (from simple misunderstandings all the way to costly lawsuits) come from agents who think they know it all. They erroneously believe that the customer expects them to have all the answers and, as such, they think that being a professional is about always "knowing all the answers." This couldn't be further from the truth. In fact, it's unprofessional. A true professional knows what they know, knows what they don't know, and knows the difference between the two. So when they know, they tell and when they don't know, they go get advice. Professionals never fake or bluff their way ahead.

People want to work with someone who will get them the right answer no matter where it comes from. Notice the point?

They want the right answer not someone who knows the right answer. By now you certainly must realize that real estate transactions are never so time sensitive that there isn't time to stop and ask someone a question or do some research to verify something. Anyone who acts that way is just doing it because they want to or think they should, not because a transaction or customer requires it. People want to work with someone who says "I am a professional. That means I know what I know and I know what I don't know and I know the difference between the two. So, when I know, I'll just tell you and when I don't know, I'll go find the answer. This way you can always have confidence that I'm getting you the best answers possible." That is what a true professional does and that is what you should do. This definition of being a professional should set you free to move forward confident in your ability to offer professional service with the knowledge and experience you have.

No matter what your behavioral style, when you take action, really go after it. Don't just do a little and expect a lot. To get the best returns from any lead generation action you take you must go all out. An example of really working a lead generation method is the open house. Some just put a sign in the yard while others do much, much more.

TAKING OPEN HOUSES BEYOND THE BASICS

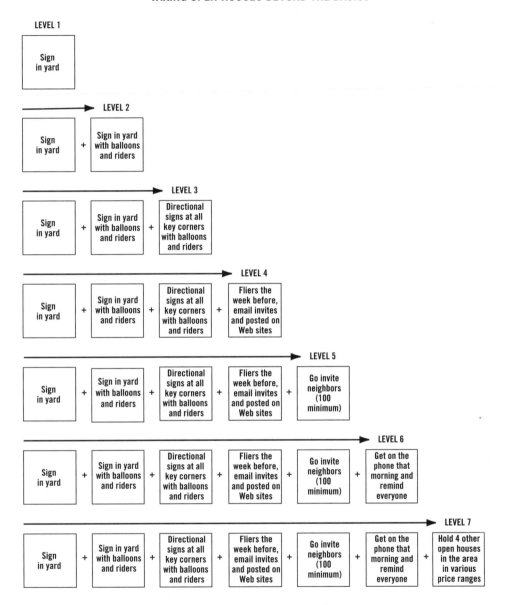

FIGURE 14 Some agents just stick a sign in the yard and call it lead generation.
Others go six steps beyond this and call it lead generation.
The big question is: What do you call lead generation?

Successfully generating leads in any market is about understanding how to create effective offer-response messages. Then it's about implementing effective lead generation methods to put your message in the path of your target audience (motivated buyers and sellers). And, finally, it's about weighing the responses and making necessary adjustments on an ongoing basis to improve your results.

In the end, you must decide how much you want to succeed and how much you're willing to do to make it happen. That may force you to acknowledge and work through your personal behavior style or challenges. Make no mistake about it, a shift requires you to do all you can with every lead generation method available. When there are fewer leads, you must give more effort. Don't get stuck in old ruts. Anything less than your best effort just won't cut it.

STEP THREE: RAMP IT UP

Now that you know what your messages need to be for your market and you know what lead generation methods you intend to use there is only one thing left to do—start lead generating. At the risk of being blatantly obvious, I feel compelled to point out that in order for you to truly be a successful lead generator, you must actually do lead generation. You must do it a lot. You can't do it one day here and one day there and you can't do it an hour here and an hour there. An inconsistent approach can get you leads, but it won't give you anywhere near the number of leads you'll need when the market shifts. You're going to need a lot of leads and that means you're going to have to do a lot of lead generating. You must do it every day. You must do it several hours every day. You must do it every work day for the rest of your career. You must ramp it up and keep it up. No negotiations. Got it?

To do this, you must subscribe to one simple belief: dealing with business never takes precedence over finding business. Never. You must adopt the position that until your lead generation is done every day, nothing else should get done. This may seem like a tough position for you to adopt, but adopt it you must. Otherwise you will constantly find other things that seem more important or allow other things to convince you they're more important.

When I was learning this concept, I put a sign over my desk that read "Until Your #1 Priority Is Done—Everything Else Is a Distraction!" This daily reminder helped me and it may help you. If you don't follow this, you haven't yet learned the true meaning of prioritizing.

The number one challenge you face won't be either of the first two issues we've covered, it will be this—consistently doing lead generation activities over time. It is the one true challenge all real estate agents face and the number one stumbling block that knocks most out of the game. Not getting lead generation done day in and day out may suffice in a hot market, but it will put you out of business in a cold one.

To ensure your lead generation is always your number one priority and that it gets done daily, you must acquire the discipline of "time blocking." Time blocking is setting aside daily blocks of time to execute your most important business priorities. Think of it as making appointments with yourself. Once done, you must protect that time against any and all distractions.

Before I explain how to time block, I want to confront one of the most disabling myths you can hold—the myth of being disciplined. One of the great dysfunctional goals people set for their lives is to become a "disciplined person." They say it all the time: "I just need to become disciplined" or "I really wish I were disciplined". There is no such thing as a disciplined person and even if there were why would you want to be one? The concept of a disciplined person is a myth. No one is disciplined in all things. No one. If someone looks like they are, they aren't. If someone tells you they are, they're not. Being a disciplined person simply isn't a possibility or a necessity. You can't be one, but the good news is that you don't need to be one.

My job is to follow my schedule. If I do that, everything works. If I don't, I should be fired. That's what happens out in the world.
Chris Heller, San Diego, CA

I believe that when you see someone who appears to be a disciplined person what you're really seeing is a person who has actually just acquired a few very key disciplines in a specific area. They have figured out what the handful of foundational disciplines are that they must do in order to be the best at what they're doing and that is all they've done. They've prioritized the disciplines they need and then have only gone after the most important ones.

When we did the original research for *The Millionaire Real Estate Agent,* we made an interesting discovery: The one thing all top producers have in common is that they consistently lead generate. On other issues top agents are very different, but on this one issue they all share a common bond. They are disciplined in doing their lead generation activities. They do many things differently but they all do one thing the same— they manage their time so that they get their lead generation activities done every day. The challenge of a shift is that you won't have any choice.

If you are inconsistent in doing your lead generation activities you will most likely need to be really concerned about surviving and you can absolutely forget about thriving.

If you struggle with the challenge of consistently lead generating don't fear for there is a simple solution for you. It is time tested and guaranteed to work. You must "time block" for it.

TIME BLOCKING — THREE THINGS FOR SUCCESS

MONDAY	TUESDAY	WEDNESDAY	THURSDAY	FRIDAY	SATURDAY	SUNDAY
Notes	1 8:30 to 11:30am Lead Generation	2 8:30 to 11:30am Lead Generation	3 8:30 to 11:30am Lead Generation	4 8:30 to 11:30am Lead Generation	5	6
7 8:00 to 9:00am Planning 9:00 to noon Lead Generation	8 8:30 to 11:30am Lead Generation	9 8:30 to 11:30am Lead Generation	10 8:30 to 11:30am Lead Generation	11 THREE-DAY FAMILY VACATION	12	13
14 8:00 to 9:00am Planning 9:00 to noon Lead Generation	15 8:30 to 11:30am Lead Generation	16 8:30 to 11:30am Lead Generation	17 8:30 to 11:30am Lead Generation	18 8:30 to 11:30am Lead Generation	19	20
21 8:00 to 9:00am Planning 9:00 to noon Lead Generation	22 8:30 to 11:30am Lead Generation	23 8:30 to 11:30am Lead Generation	24 8:30 to 11:30am Lead Generation	25 8:30 to 11:30am Lead Generation	26	27
28 8:00 to 9:00am Planning 9:00 to noon Lead Generation	29 8:30 to 11:30am Lead Generation	30 8:30 to 11:30am Lead Generation	31 8:30 to 11:30am Lead Generation	Notes		

FIGURE 15 A month-at-a-glance calendar combines the benefits of long-range vision with day-to-day and hourly planning.

Successful people annually time block three things. First they make a list of all the vacations and time off they want to take for the year and they time block them off on their calendar. This way they have guaranteed themselves, their family and their friends that personal time off comes first. Now they're simply working in-between their time off, instead of working all the time (and, as a result, taking too little time off, too late). Second they take out their calendar and time block a few hours every day devoted to nothing but lead generating. Third they time block an hour each week to plan their week. If they have others that work or report to them, then they actually block out a fourth slot each week to meet with these individuals and work with them on their goals, plans, actions and results. And that's it.

This is all the business time blocking you need to do. If you'll commit to this approach, you'll set the one discipline in motion you absolutely must have to be successful in a shifting market. Top agents know that this is the singular business-building block they must put in place. It will be the difference between staying in business or being forced out. It is that important. The formula for this time-blocking discipline is called the "3-3" and stands for three things done in three hours. Now, you can take more time but you don't need to do more than three things. Research says that you will need at least three hours a day of lead generation time and that you must do three things during it to be effective.

TIME BLOCKING: WHY I USE A PENCIL AND A MONTH-AT-A-GLANCE CALENDAR

I highly recommend that you use a month-at-a-glance calendar and use a pencil instead of a pen until you become an advanced time blocker. After all these years, I still use these simple tools because they still work well and there isn't a compelling alternative. I get a lot of pushback from agents who use handheld devices for this purpose, but there are real limitations to that approach. My philosophy is if you argue for your limitations you get to keep them. It's been my personal experience that when someone truly understands how time blocking works they discover that the most effective way to do it is by using a month-at-a-glance calendar. This type of calendar has one huge advantage that handheld devices can never overcome and it's in the name— month-at-a-glance.

Don't trade portability for vision. It is a poor exchange when your goal is to have real vision and to effectively manage your time. You need to know what opportunities you might miss when you say yes to something and you can only do this by seeing the entire month at one time. The pencil is so that you can practice the sacred rule of time blocking which is "If you erase you must replace!" Think of time blocking as a placeholder to ensure that you get something done regularly. Should you absolutely have to do something else during a time blocked period, and it will happen, then when you erase it you simply replace it at the earliest point you can fit it in. Abiding by this rule will ensure that what you intended to do gets done and that is the point of time blocking.

To absolutely ensure it gets done you must go to your calendar and block out the three-hour time slot each day. Time that you know you can keep each day without interruption. This is challenging but can be accomplished. You have to commit to doing it and then keep your commitment. The best time to do this is in the morning, when you are fresh and have the most energy. And since the world is just getting started, it will be the easiest time commitment to keep and the best time period to consistently catch people. Since you will invariably miss some people for a variety of reasons you will also have to commit some evening time as well. You'll need at least three hours in the morning everyday and an hour to an hour and a half in the evening two nights a week to accomplish your goals. The best times will be between 8:00 a.m. to 12 noon and between 7:00 p.m. to 9:00 in the evening.

WHAT DO YOU DO IN YOUR THREE HOURS?

Prepare ⟶ Take Action ⟶ Maintain

FIGURE 16 Three areas of focus for three hours a day, every day.

The three things you'll do during your lead generation time block each day are: prepare, take action and maintain. First, prepare. When prospecting create your messages and offers, assemble your call or door knocking list, rehearse scripts and role-play them, prepare handouts for any visits, do all the necessary preparatory work for your prospecting (like for an open house), and do any mail outs required to support your activities. If you're marketing, create your messages and offers, assemble a mailing list, plan any "touch" activities (such as 8 x 8, 12 Direct, or 33 Touch programs taught in *The Millionaire Real Estate Agent*), do any prep work on mailers or ads, work on your Web site, secure postage, take photos, and so forth. Give this preparation stage about thirty minutes (but no more than an hour) and then move on. If you give it much more than that, please realize you're simply preparing to lead generate but not actually doing it.

Now move on to taking action—the heart of your lead generation time block. You'll need a minimum of two hours for this so plan accordingly. If you're prospecting, make calls, go see people, host open houses, make follow-up calls and write notes. If you're marketing, do mail merge and mail, deliver mail and ad copy, write notes and respond to inquiries from all sources. Stick to this and don't skip out early. This is where your leads are generated. If you can allow more than two hours a day do it. You won't regret the time you put into taking action to generate leads—it is always time well invested.

ANATOMY OF THREE HOURS A DAY

1 Prepare ⟶ **2** Take Action ⟶ **3** Maintain

Prospecting Activities

- Assemble call list (current and past customers, sphere, FSBOs and expireds, cold calls)
- Rehearse scripts for calls (role-play)
- Prepare handouts for visits
- Prepare for open houses

- Mail out invitations to events
- Make calls
- See people (door knocking, networking, customer parties)
- Host open houses
- Make follow-up phone calls and visits

- Enter results into database
- Write follow-up notes
- Record your work
- Track results
- Schedule and calendar
- Fulfill promises

Marketing Activities

- Assemble mailing list
- Plan and maintain "touch" activities
- Prep, work on mailers, ads, messages (design, print, proof)
- Work on Web site
- Prep auto-responders
- Secure postage
- Take photos

- Mail merge and mail
- Deliver mail and ad copy
- Write note as a "warm" touch in your marketing plan (Thank You, Birthday, Thinking of You, etc.)

FIGURE 17 It's easy to allow preparation and maintenance to eat up the majority of your three hours. Don't! A minimum of one hour or more should be dedicated to taking action.

Finally, address any needed maintenance. This is the same for prospecting and marketing. Enter results into your database, write follow-up notes, record anything you need to record, track your results, do any scheduling and calendaring and fulfill any promises you made. While maintenance is important, preparation and taking action are more important.

Your goal is consistent lead generation and the way you do it is seeing your job as lead generation first and servicing second. The way to think about this is the way you think about going to the movies. When you go to the movies you turn off your cell phone, don't allow any distractions or disruptions and for a couple of hours you focus on the movie. Unless there is an absolute crisis you do not interrupt the movie. And it works for you. You do this all the time for personal pleasure so now I want you to do it for your business success. I want you to "go to the movies" every day, at least 5 days a week, for 3 hours in the morning and 1 to 1 ½ hours up to two evenings a week.

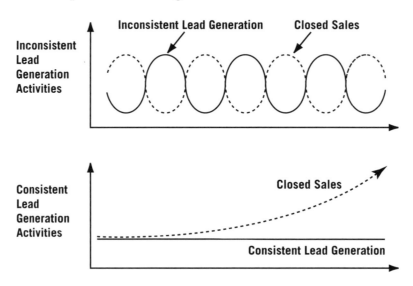

FIGURE 18 Consistent lead generation is the only way to get off the real estate roller coaster and enjoy steady growth over time.

Now in order to do this your environment must support this goal. That means your family, your friends, your office, and any team members must respect and support your time blocked periods. You're "at the movies" and not to be disturbed by anything or anyone until it's over—and it's a long movie!

GET IN THE PATH OF BUSINESS

Lead generation is a contact sport with simple rules. It means making contact with people through prospecting and marketing. Then, once you meet your new contacts you either do business with them immediately or you don't. Either way, once you've met them you put them in a database and stay in touch with them forever. Your number one job as a real estate agent is to find ways to get in the path of motivated buyers and sellers. Oddly, the tendency for most agents in a shifting market is to cocoon—to just wander around the office or stay at home and wait for things to change. Obviously this is a mistake. When the market changes, you don't slow down, you ramp it up. A shift requires you to do very specific things everyday if you want to succeed. You can't succeed sitting on the sidelines. Every day you must get in the game and make plays. It is crunch time for lead generation.

TACTIC #5
GET TO THE TABLE –
LEAD CONVERSION

Most people never run far enough on their
first wind to find they've got a second.

WILLIAM JAMES

THE MARKET IS LESS ACTIVE and motivated leads are less forthcoming. Your effort is there and yet results are sluggish. Shifts happen. When one does, you immediately consider any lead to be a good lead. In another time this might hold true, but not now. Not in a shift. As you ramp up your lead generating and experience the market you start to see the absolute nature of it—lots of leads but fewer good ones. Scarcity defines a shift. And instantly you get it. You recognize that for right now, good leads are great and great leads are golden, but leads that become timely appointments are what really matters.

If you do lead generation but don't get a name and number, what good is it? If you get a name and number, but can't get an appointment what good are they? Aha! As important as lead generating activities are if you can't get a name, number and ultimately an appointment, what have you really accomplished? Doing lead generating activity is one thing—getting an active lead from it is another. Without the ability to turn activities into leads and leads into appointments any lead generating activities you do are futile. In other words, conversion matters. It seriously matters and maybe more than you ever realized.

In a shifting market it matters the most because quite frankly, what you need more than anything else are appointments with motivated buyers and sellers. Right now. The essential truth is that your success in a shifting market will hinge entirely on your ability to convert leads.

You make this happen by doing two things well: generating leads and converting them to appointments. The ultimate success of your lead generating is directly dependent on your lead conversion ability. One can't work without the other. Yet many agents spend significant amounts of time and money on their lead production proficiency but then neglect their conversion competence. This is never an effective way to operate in any market but you absolutely can't do this when the market shifts.

I suddenly realized that I didn't have a lead generation problem; I had a lead conversion problem. We had lots of leads, but we weren't turning them into sales.

Bruce Hardie, Spokane, WA

The effort you give to converting leads must match the effort you give to generating them. Most entirely miss this. They look at their number of appointments and assume their lead generation isn't working. The bigger truth might be that their lead conversion isn't working.

While agents regularly talk about generating leads, they rarely give equal discussion time to converting them. Why? A lack of clarity. Most see them as one and the same, but they're not. They're two distinct efforts with your lead generation activity actually being the first. And when you say you've generated a real lead what you're really saying is that you have the name, contact information, and an appointment with a motivated person. That actually is the second effort of the process called conversion. Until you've done conversion, you don't really have a lead. You may have an inquiry, a Web hit, or a suspect, but you don't have a prospect. Don't fool yourself about this. You can't say you have a lead until you've talked with them and set an appointment.

I have a friend who is an avid fisherman. He loves to joke with others when they say they like to go fishing. He says, "You do? I like to go catching!" He makes a good point. We tend to speak of the activity we engage in rather than the outcome we seek. It's the difference between what we do and why we do it. Action versus purpose. When it comes to lead generation just realize that you're talking about two things—lead generating activities and lead converting to an appointment.

In a shifted market, you really have no choice but to acknowledge the importance of lead conversion to your success. Motivated leads can be scarce so each one becomes precious. That means you can't afford to waste even one. You not only must be able to convert leads to appointments, but also be able to convert as high a percentage as possible. Converting any and all you can becomes critical, so you must give it equal energy and attention. The challenge is that lead conversion is a process that gets interpreted as an event that just sort of occurs on its own. Thus it gets misunderstood and short-changed. For most it remains largely unexamined, often neglected, and seldom mastered.

If someone is able, ready, and willing to buy or sell right now, then conversion feels like an event that just happens. But that is not the case. Conversion is actually a collapsed process disguised as an event. Conversion can happen fast or slow, but it's always a process. The common perception is that prospects either just ask you to meet or you ask them. Straightforward and simple, right? Yes and no. On one hand, this is exactly what happens, but it rarely ever just happens. If you naively approach it as an event and only prepare for it this way, your conversion percent will be much lower than it could be or should be. Consistently getting every possible appointment from the leads you generate isn't complicated, but it does require preparation, practice, and purposeful action.

Our research regularly uncovered scenarios where an agent was allowing others, staff or sales agents on their team, to do all their lead converting. As the appointment-to-leads percentage trended lower and lower they started to hear the excuse that the "leads aren't as good as they used to be." To test this they took all the leads back and did the converting themselves. And guess what? The appointments always went up—significantly up. So, what did they learn? It wasn't about the leads, it was about their people. Their people were under performing at lead conversion. Even worse, because they didn't respect it they couldn't get better at it. In fact, many agents have discovered that outside of actually generating leads, personally handling converting leads to appointments is the most dollar productive thing they can do for their business. And this is right. It's that important.

Regardless of whether they want to do business immediately or in the future, the process of conversion is the same. The only difference is the time frame. Converting a lead begins with capturing (getting enough information to be able to make contact with the prospective seller or buyer), moves to connecting (engaging in meaningful contact where you get information, gain understanding and build a relationship) and ends with closing (by phone or in person) for an appointment (see Figure 19).

Without an appointment conversion hasn't happened. You've engaged in the lead generation activity without achieving your lead generation goal. And the only purpose in finding a lead is landing an appointment. It's all about getting to the table.

THE LEAD CONVERSION PROCESS

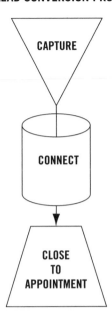

FIGURE 19 Getting appointments is the goal of your lead generation efforts. The capture, connect, and close process is a simple, reliable path to achieving consistent conversion.

THE TABLE

Shifts create urgency. The competition for leads becomes fierce and your only choice is to get your "unfair" share of them. This means you not only have to find leads before others, but also convert them to appointments before they get away to others. As quick as you can you have to get to the people who want to do business. Moods swing and circumstances change. In a shift the path from interest to appointment is fraught with distractions and interferences that can dissuade or discourage even the most motivated. The better you become at converting leads into appointments, the faster you will be able to move and the more opportunities you'll have.

National Association of REALTORS® (NAR®) research over the years has consistently communicated that the real competition in real estate is getting to the table—not at it. Their revealing statistics show that approximately two-thirds of all buyers and sellers only interview one agent and approximately half of the remainder only interview two. Getting to the table first or second is what matters. And this makes conversion more important than presentation. The competitive battle is almost single-handedly won simply by getting an appointment before someone else does. The number one challenge you face after you've encountered a lead opportunity is not making a winning presentation— it's winning the appointment.

Our industry is about getting appointments, buyer and seller agreements, and sales contracts. So if you don't get appointments you won't get any agreements and you won't get any contracts. To win at the table you must first get to the table. When you say you're "lead generating," be clear that you're actually "getting appointments"—you're getting to the table. If you aren't, then you're not actually lead generating.

CAPTURE, CONNECT, AND CLOSE

Lead conversion is simple but still requires more than just winging it. Unfortunately this is exactly what most agents do and what you should not do. It is as straightforward as asking for their information but not running them off in the process. It is as simple as finding common ground but not just finding things in common. It is as easy as just requesting a meeting but not as haphazard as just letting it come to pass. In other words, getting an appointment can just happen or it can consistently happen. Conversion success comes to those who intentionally and repeatedly do three things with every lead: capture, connect, and close.

Capturing should always focus on getting enough information from someone so that you can contact them. Your connecting must feel natural and allow you to assess their needs and establish a relationship. Your closing will seem effortless and likely lead to

Leads are priceless! Follow up with them until they buy, sell, or ask you to leave them alone.

> *Seychelle Van Poole-Engelhard*
> *Dallas, TX*

a decision to meet. You have a choice: repeatable and dependable or unpredictable and unreliable. You can come prepared or you can wing it—it's your call.

Many agents assume that a prospect will determine if they meet or not, but actually it will be you. Either your ability will cause a meeting to take place or your lack of ability will prevent it. This isn't a game of chance but a game of scripts and systems. Scripts ensure that you effectively say what needs to be said in the most powerful way with the least amount of effort. Because it is a script or dialogue you've practiced and internalized, you don't have to be a master of making things up as you go. You simply have to adapt what you know to any situation. Likewise, systems make sure that you are taking the right action at the right time with the least amount of effort. Painting by numbers doesn't require much thought or skill, but the outcome can be predictable and surprisingly successful. Systems and checklists can channel your customer responses in the same way.

Ultimately, the key to success in setting appointments boils down to two things: knowing what to say and then knowing what to do. You'll need to master your scripts and dialogues for the former, and implement simple systems and checklists for the latter. The question is which comes first? Some approaches will lead with scripts and follow with systems; others will lead with systems and then require scripts. All three steps in the conversion process will require both.

Top agents follow a proven path that allows them to consistently apply the right scripts and systems to each step in the process of capturing, connecting, and closing their leads. And the end result is what they're after—more appointments.

CAPTURING

You're in the sales business and that means you only get paid when someone buys or sells something. In the end, service and information are the two things you offer, market, and provide. At the same time, anything done for someone is done with the expectation that it leads to a sale or a listing sold. You must be clear on this point. Everything you might do for someone, while done with a true servant's heart, only gets rewarded financially when a sale occurs. To be successful in real estate sales you and everyone who works with you must have this mindset. In a shift where people believe tire-kicking, time-taking, and market-testing are their inalienable rights, it is an imperative.

Leads cost us money, so we really do need to hold each one accountable.
Jana Caudill, Crown Point, IN

The hard fact is that buyers and sellers approach you because they are interested in real estate, not your personal welfare. They assume you're doing just fine and that it isn't their concern. They will always engage you for information first, service second, and transacting business last. Clearly, in order to earn the right to transact business, you must always focus on and do your best with the first two. Prospects have their own needs in mind and that is how it should be. However, that means one very important thing to you—while providing what they need, you must also be vigilant in getting what you need.

The first goal when you encounter someone by prospecting or marketing is to capture their name and contact information. Any information you give out is done with the mindset of service with a purpose. It's not that we walk around worried about getting paid or calculating our commissions. That's nonsense and I've never met a great real estate agent who ever felt that way. Your customers' needs and your own aren't mutually exclusive. While serving others we also serve ourselves. In serving ourselves, we are in fact providing for and protecting the interests of those who are counting on us—our family, our close associates, and the causes we support.

When I first got in the real estate business I thought all that the world needed was an honest, servant-hearted, information-providing, will-do-whatever-it-takes-no-matter-how-long-it-takes, you-want-it-you-got-it real estate agent. That's who I became and it was the right thing to do. But that narrow way of thinking almost caused me to go broke. Along with my commitment to serve others I soon realized that I required something too. I actually needed to close transactions and in order to do that I had to first and foremost devote my time to those who would tell me who they were and how I could contact them. Ultimately, these were the only people I would talk to or provide information to and I called them "leads."

One of the most hotly debated topics I've ever encountered is the simple definition of a lead. It seems strange that some of the best and brightest in our field can't reach agreement on how to define the very fuel for our economic engine—leads! Responses range from simply someone we meet "who might someday do business with us" to someone "who needs to buy or sell in 90 days or less" and everything in-between. However, one thing is universally agreed upon—a lead is only a lead if you have captured a person's contact information. If you can't call them, email them, write them, or drop by their home or office and ultimately set an appointment, it's not a lead. It can't be.

I believe that capture is all about attitude. If you think you have a right to ask, you will. I often hear "I don't want to seem pushy or intimidating." My answer is always the same, "then don't be." This type of fear is inappropriate because asking is just asking and has no emotional energy attached to it. My experience is that pushy people are pushy and it has nothing to do with what they're doing. So, if you are you are and if you're not you're not. Asking someone for their name and number has nothing to do with that. You have every right to ask, at anytime you wish, the name and contact information of anyone and everyone you come in contact with.

It is not your job to give out as much free information as people want or do as much free work as they expect and then leave it to them to tell you when and if they want to be contacted. You shouldn't fear running someone off by asking for information. If they won't tell you or won't give it to you then that is what you need to know as early as possible. You're getting insight into whether or not they plan to work with you early in the game. You'll never hear the following in our industry: "that real estate agent was so slick they sold us a home we didn't even want." Nor will you ever hear: "that real estate agent was so pushy they talked us into selling our home." It just doesn't happen.

I've found that the best scripts are the most straightforward ones. In other words, just ask for what you want. Scripts like "Thanks for calling. I'm Gary Keller. May I ask your name?" and "Thanks and what is your phone number?" work really well when asked together. When asked separately a script like "If I were to need to get in touch with you what would that number be?" or "If I found exactly what you're looking for, how would I contact you?" or "If I found out that information you're wanting, how would I get it to you?" works well. Straightforward is usually the best approach and people just respond to it.

I have found that the agent who is the most consistent and persistent in their follow-up captures the lead and gets the business.
Debbie Tufts, Atlanta, GA

One of the reasons I never carry a business card is that I won't lie. When someone asks me for my card my reply (as I smile, pull out my pen, and poise to write) is "Thanks for asking. I'm sorry I don't have one with me, but what is your name and address and I'll get one to you." This is very straightforward and works every time. Remember, you're in the capture business.

This same attitude and approach works well when you are capturing through marketing. Whether it's at an open house (written on the guest log: "The owner has asked us to let them know who has dropped by and how we might get your feedback. Thanks for signing in!"), using an interactive voice response system ("Call 1-800-the-home for more details on this home!") which automatically catches their phone number or Internet registration forms ("For a virtual tour, click here" or "For the lowest financing options click here"—which then asks for their contact information before letting them continue), always remember that you must have a capturing system in place. If you don't, then you're just giving out information for free with little chance of getting compensated for it. Capturing a prospective buyer or seller's contact information allows you to be in business while helping others with theirs. It also lets you be proactive and own the next steps, connecting and closing.

Leads are leads. It does not matter how you acquire the lead, what matters is how you deal with the lead and turn it into business.
Dave VanDermyden, Roseville, CA

CONNECTING

Once you've captured a name and number it's time to connect. It's time to quickly lay a foundation for a working relationship. The fundamental theme of connecting is curiosity—to know who someone is, to understand their wants and needs, and to become aware of their worries and concerns. At this point, you are investigating not selling. You are a consultant who genuinely wants to understand their situation and offer help if needed. Your goal is to generate trust and build confidence, first yours and then theirs. It is your chance to show them what it feels like to work with you. Their experience of talking with you at this point will have more to do with them hiring you than almost any other thing you can do, say or send to them.

During the connect step things will feel like they're slowing down for just a moment. And that is good. The fundamental philosophy of connecting is "people don't care how much you know until they know how much you care." In other words, this isn't where you "tell and sell" your way to success, but where you "ask and listen" your way into their head and heart. You've gotten what you needed, a name and number, so now you move to connecting.

When you connect with someone you demonstrate that you care. The two tools you'll use are your mouth and ears, but not equally. You have two ears and one mouth for a reason and this is when you use them accordingly. You will ask and then listen and listen. Then you'll ask again and then listen and listen again. (Be sure to take notes. It guarantees you will remember what they said and if you happen to be with them, they'll see you care.) And just when you think that you should talk, ask and listen some more. You don't talk your way into a trust relationship with someone, you ask and listen your way. While they're talking they are also making a decision—whether or not to go to the next step with you.

Connecting is more than making small talk. Connecting is not "Oh, you play golf? I play golf. Golf, golf, golf, golf, golf ..." or "Oh, you like dogs? I like dogs. Dogs, dogs, dogs, dogs, dogs ..." It is an intuitive and natural approach that seeks the answer to six basic questions that allows them to open up and reveal themselves to you. It follows a timeless formula you are surely familiar with: who, what, why, when, where and how.

THE SIX CONNECTION QUESTIONS

1. Who are they?
2. What do they want or need to do?
3. Where do they want or need to do it?
4. Why do they want or need to do it?
5. When do they want or need to do it?
6. How do they plan to do it?

Make a note: you're not specifically looking for what they "need" right now. Wants and needs are very different. For now, you're going to ask what they want or need interchangeably as you feel like it. Later on, when you meet with them, you'll absolutely distinguish between what they want and need.

While you want your questioning to sound conversational, please understand that while you are connecting, you're also qualifying. The questions are the same but the style is different. In effect, while you're qualifying, they're connecting. So your six connecting questions might sound like this:

1. *"Back up and, if you would, please tell me a little about yourself?"*
You're looking for as much personal information about them and their situation as they are willing to share: marital status, kids, pets, jobs, etc. These are the details that you'll later put in your database to reconnect with them in the future.

2. *"Thanks for sharing that. Now, if you would, please tell me what you want to do?"* or *"So you folks called about Bandera Drive, are you looking for a new home?"* or *"So you folks called to get the pricing information on Bandera Drive, are you thinking of selling your home and looking for price comparisons?"* You're beginning to assess their wants, needs, and current plans.

3. *"Thanks for sharing that. Now, if you would, can you share with me where you're thinking of moving?"* or *"Where is your current home located?"* or *"Do you have a home now that you might need to sell?"* Now, you're trying to get an understanding of their current situation.

4. *"Thanks for sharing that. Now, if you would, can you share with me why you're doing this?"* or *"Why you're needing to move?"* or *"What this move will mean to you?"* You're trying to determine their motivation.

5. *"Thanks for sharing that. Now, if you would, can you please share with me when you'd like to do this?"* You're getting a feel for their timetable.

6. *"Thanks for sharing that. Now, if you would, can you please share with me what you've already done to plan for this?"* or *"How do you plan to do this?"* You're accessing what they have already done, their expectations and perhaps their experience.

You may have noticed that these scripts feel repetitive. And they are. The interesting thing about scripts is that they are observed one way and experienced another. When you read them or role-play them, they can feel stilted and overly repetitive. That's how it can feel to you. But when received, they can feel warm, sincere, and natural.

Clearly, since we don't know what their answers will be, this sample script feels a little contrived, but don't just write it off. To them it will feel courteous, organized, and professional and that is why it works. Actually, they're the questions you need the answers to in order to connect. Note the intentional repetition of the phrases "thanks for sharing," "if you would," and "can you please share." These are key phrases you must memorize and constantly use. Another question I frequently ask is "would you be offended if I ask?" This works well because it actually sounds to them like you've asked if they'd literally be offended, which they won't be, but when they answer "no" they're actually saying "yes," giving you permission to proceed. This is what I call a "negative-positive" and it's one of the most powerful ways you can put a question to someone.

This is how you connect—straightforward, without fear, full of questions, and with lots of listening. Once connected, you and they are ready for closure.

CLOSING

Closing is where the rubber meets the road. It is where a prospect becomes a lead and your lead generating activities require you to go—getting an appointment. It's called "closing" someone and although it's old sales language, you'd better dust it off and revisit it. An appointment is the real outcome you seek and it requires real scripts to get you there. The positive thing about the concept of closing is that it leads to decisions and outcomes. The word "close" means "end in mind" and that you're bringing something to conclusion. And that is exactly what you're doing. You're concluding this discussion and seeing if there is a new one that can take place.

So it's time for closure. You've gotten a name and contact information and you have successfully connected with your prospect. There is only one thing left to do—meet. Setting up the meeting is your responsibility. Some agents think the meeting happens naturally without doing anything. Other agents act as if that's all they care about. Both fall short. The right approach to close for a meeting is the only approach—just ask. Ask to meet, ask when to meet, ask where to meet, ask if you should, could, want, or must meet. Yes, yes, yes, yes, yes, yes, and yes. Just ask.

Nothing is going to happen if you don't ask. If it does, it's pure luck and that's no way to run a business. Truthfully, if you've gotten their name and number and you've genuinely connected with them, then asking to meet is a natural thing to do. In fact, they expect it and want it. People want to buy, but hate to be sold. People want to make the right decision and they fear being talked into the wrong one. People want help, but are hesitant to ask for it. So you have to help them out—you have to ask for them. They want and need you to be in charge in a caring way.

I still remember my very first listing appointment with a FSBO, Gene Vollie Smith. A wonderful man, Gene owned a house a few doors down from where he lived

> *You can't serve them if you don't meet with them.*
>
> *Jeff Hooper, Ottawa, ON, Canada*

and was selling it himself. I called on Gene and during the connect stage he out of nowhere just asked me, "Gary, what would you charge me to handle this for me?" I was flabbergasted. So, I told him, took the listing, sold it in one week, closed it in about a month and have never ever had anyone just ask me that way again! For the rest of my career, I've had to do the asking. And unless Gene is still out there buying and selling—so will you. To consistently close for an appointment you just have to know how to ask and how to respond.

Asking

You'll ask people for an appointment either by phone, in-person, or in writing. Always remember that asking in writing will have the lowest conversion rate due to your lack of ability to respond to any issues they may have. But, any and all of these methods can be effective.

TEN CLASSIC CLOSES THAT WORK

1. The Hard Close
2. The Soft Close
3. The Direct Close
4. The Indirect Close
5. The Trial Close
6. The Assumptive Close
7. The Negative-Positive Close
8. The Take Back Close
9. The Tie Down Close
10. The Alternative Choice Close

Many agents ask, "Why am I always being told to close, close, close, close...close early and close often?" There is a time-tested reason. While people talk in absolutes, they seldom think in absolutes. Most of the time a "no" isn't an absolute no and a "yes" isn't an absolute yes. There is a continuum (see Figure 20). People use the words without being committed to them and you don't really know where they are on that continuum. Every "no" can become a "yes" and every "yes" can become a "no." Closing is the process you use to find out where they are and to what they are committed. As a salesperson, you aren't attached to their decision—your goal is just to help them to make one.

THE DECISION CONTINUUM

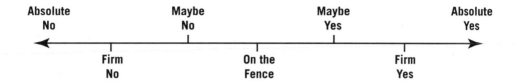

Absolute No	Maybe No	Maybe Yes	Absolute Yes
Firm No	On the Fence	Firm Yes	

FIGURE 20 Between the absolutes there are degrees of yes and no.

In this context, the yes or no we seek is about getting an appointment. While this concept is bigger than just asking for an appointment, it directly applies to it. So, in closing, let's take a closer look at the different ways you can be a closer.

1. The Hard Close: "Let's meet!"

2. The Soft Close: "I've really enjoyed visiting with you. Would you like to get together to discuss this further?"

3. The Direct Close: "Can we meet today?"

4. The Indirect Close: "Would it be okay if I got you some information to look over and then we can meet to discuss?"

5. The Trial Close: "Have we gone over enough today that meeting would be our next step?"

6. The Assumptive Close: "It sounds like we should meet. I am available most times this week so what works best for you?"

7. The Negative-Positive Close: "Would you be offended if I asked if we could meet to go over this?"

8. The Take Back Close: "I've really enjoyed visiting with you. To be honest, I'm not sure if I can be of help or not, but I'd be honored if we could meet to find out."

9. The Tie Down Close: "Wouldn't it make sense for us to meet in the next day or so?"

10. The Alternative Choice Close: "What works better for you? Meeting today, sometime this afternoon, or tomorrow morning?"

As you can see, there are many ways to ask someone for an appointment. And they will all work—if you'll just learn them and then use them.

Responding

When you ask someone to meet, they will either just say yes or give you a reason why they can't. This is the moment to remember that selling isn't verbal warfare, so don't get flustered, feel threatened, or get indignant. Learn how to respond and let the conversation take its natural course. In the end if they can meet and have a good enough reason to meet they will meet. And if they don't then they won't. And that's okay. You really don't care what their answer ultimately is because you're not into getting people to do anything they don't want to do. You're just going to ask and respond until they agree that meeting with you makes sense or it doesn't. Either way you both win.

When you ask someone to meet you're starting a dialogue you can anticipate and practice. Here are some of the possible responses you will hear if you ask enough people to meet with you: no thanks, not now, not yet, we'll need to think about it, we have an agent, we know an agent, we're not sure what we want to do, we're just looking, we're just investigating our options right now, we're not in a hurry, we don't need to do anything, we'll get back to you on that, and on and on and on. Your job is to go through each of these, write down their response, and then you write down your response options. Then grab another agent and the two of you role-play using your answers.

If you do this an hour a day for one week, I promise you that you'll begin to feel comfortable with asking people to meet. If you then practice this the first 30 minutes of your lead generation time block each workday, guess what—you'll become so good at it that you can't wait to ask people to meet just so you can discuss it with them.

I'll always be grateful for Tim Leggett. Tim was my role-playing partner for a few weeks when I was first learning how to ask for appointments. We'd go into a conference room every morning and start by one of us simply saying, "Can we meet?" The other would then respond (and the answer was never "yes") and we'd be off and running. Within a few weeks of this I was so comfortable with people's possible responses that we ended this partnership and I threw myself into lead generating all the way. The same will happen to you.

CULTIVATION

Even though the lead conversion process of capturing, connecting, and closing is the path you seek, there will always be a small percentage of leads that can't be converted directly to an appointment. No matter how skilled you are and how hard you try, an immediate meeting with them just isn't in the cards. There will be a few people who are just not ready or willing to meet with you but who are still worth pursuing. This is when your cultivation system becomes your indirect path to an appointment. It can be as simple as touching base regularly or as systematic as entering them in your database and implementing a touch program. While you will always seek to meet with prospective sellers or buyers immediately, if you can't but still believe they are motivated, you should stay in close contact until you can get an appointment. This is the purpose of cultivation.

CULTIVATING LEADS FOR FUTURE CONVERSION

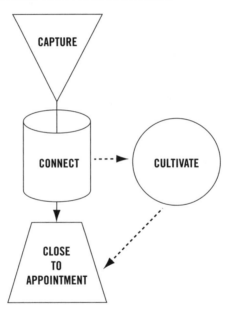

FIGURE 21 When the straight path of capture-connect-close just isn't possible, think cultivation. You stay in close contact until an appointment becomes an option.

Most agents struggle with cultivation. If they connect but can't immediately close for an appointment, they usually let the lead slip. They simply don't get back to the people. Oddly enough it surprises them and disappoints them when they hear that those people listed their house or bought a home with another agent. Many times they never even hear about it. The business just slides away to someone else. They seem to have no clue as to why their lead generation efforts aren't building a pipeline of business. They don't have a pipeline, because they don't cultivate the leads that can't immediately be closed for an appointment.

The process of cementing a relationship (8 x 8 programs) and saturating (33 Touch programs) is well-covered in *The Millionaire Real Estate Agent*. Cultivation is a specific and purposeful application of these principles. Here you are looking to convert a potential lead you already have. You know they want to buy or sell but you aren't sure when. They may not know either. A simple cultivation approach allows you to stay in touch and be there when they decide. You can't know or predict when they will come to a decision, but if you're reconnecting with them in a systematic way you'll have a great chance of being there when they do. That's when you'll be able to close for an appointment.

....

GARY AND THE BOX

When I first got started in the business, I developed a simple method for tracking all my active leads. I had a 3 x 5 index card box divided into two sections: A – Z and January – December. Every time I generated an active lead, I created two 3 x 5 index cards. One had their contact information, including everything I knew about them—that card went in my permanent record, my A through Z file. This is the group I used for my regular touch program. The other card was my "active leads" card that had just their contact information and all the information about their buying or selling needs—that card went in my January – December file ac-cording to when I next needed to contact them. Whatever month I was working in, I'd simply grab that stack of cards and contact them accordingly. Sometimes the cards would go back in the stack for a near-term follow-up and sometimes they'd be re-filed in a future month. It all depended on my sense of their current motivation. This system is simple and effective.

Clearly technology can do the same thing as index cards, and once you start consistently generating a lot of leads, a contact management computer program will be required. But even then it isn't wise to leave the active cultivation job to your technology. You must personally make the contacts. You need to reconnect to see where they are, provide information, and continue to build the relationship.

Lead cultivation, contacting leads that wouldn't originally set an appointment with you, is a vital part of your time-blocked lead generation time. Some of that time will be connecting and closing new leads you've just captured and some of it will be cultivating those leads you've captured and connected with before. For this second group you will need to constantly review and assess where your pros-pects are in the process, answer their current questions, and continue to close for an appointment.

There is really no additional script for this; just continue to use your connecting and closing scripts. You simply want to keep moving the re-lationship along—be friendly and caring, offer more information or ser-vices they can respond to, and emphasize the benefits of getting together face-to-face. While some leads may require long-term cultivation, don't ever assume waiting to meet is in their best interest. The sooner they meet with you and actively begin the process of selling or buying their house the more likely they are to get the best deal the market can deliver and the sooner a transaction will be completed.

THE SELLER TABLE THAT MATTERS

As you navigate from capturing a name and number to closing for an appointment, remember one key issue you must deal with: which seller table constitutes an appointment. Not all tables have the same value. By table, I mean either the conversation you have at the kitchen table or on the phone. Depending on the market you may consider getting them on the phone as the only appointment setting you'll need. Other markets may require getting to the kitchen table.

In a sellers' market the battle is for getting seller listings—homes sell fast, inventory stays low, and homeowners think anyone can sell their house. In this kind of market you must get to the kitchen table to give you a chance to assess motivation and have a shot at taking the listing. Typically you will not do much prequalification over the phone and you will try to get to the kitchen table as fast as possible. In a buyers' market not all listings may be worth taking.

In a shifted market unmotivated or unrealistic sellers can cost you time and money. The decision as to whether you will take an overpriced listing is really yours to make. In our experience, top agents' philosophies differ greatly on this and either side has shown they can be very success-ful. You will want to do more phone prequalification and assessment of motivation before you go on any appointment. You will likely be more selective in who you give priority to in your follow-up. You want to get to the table that matters; the one that is motivated to sell, realistic in their expectations and respectful of the value you are bringing.

BE A LEAD CONVERTER

Lead conversion is one of the most skill-based aspects of your real estate sale business. And after lead generation, lead conversion is the most business-critical activity you must master. It is one of the last things you delegate and arguably the highest dollar-productive use of your time. Getting appointments to make presentations is, in fact, a moment of truth. Get an appointment and it's all downhill from there. Fail to get an appointment and there is no hill to climb. It is where the "possible business" that comes from your lead generating activities can turn into "probably business" and, ultimately, into "profitable business." If you commit to mastering the skills of lead conversion, you will lift yourself above your competition. You will be even more than a lead generator, you will be a lead converter. You won't just be "fishing" you'll be "catching."

TACTIC #6
CATCH PEOPLE IN YOUR WEB –
INTERNET LEAD CONVERSION

You can't expect to meet the challenges of today with
yesterday's tools and expect to be in business tomorrow.

UNKNOWN

A SHIFT FORCES YOU TO RETHINK almost everything you do. The scarcity of business and the competition for it tugs at your pocketbook and tests your willpower. One crucial area you may have to reassess is your Internet strategy, which sits at the crossroads of expense management and lead generation. The shift has forced you to re-margin your business, cutting spending on everything that isn't leading to real financial results. As a result, the expenses of your Internet strategy are now under serious scrutiny. The shift has also forced you to refocus your lead generation on methods that deliver motivated leads ready to buy or sell today and even demand that your long-term activities yield as much near-term business as possible. Consequently, the results from your Internet strategy are now under serious scrutiny, as well. And here's the hitch: generating a quality lead from the Internet is difficult in good times—in a shift, it can be downright daunting.

If your Web site isn't consistently generating appointments with motivated buyers and sellers then it isn't earning its keep. Contrary to a lot of tech talk success on the Internet isn't measured in clicks, unique visitors, page views, or even registrations. It's measured just one way: in appointments to do business.

Unfortunately, many agents have long operated under the misconception that a Web site is more about professional branding or validity than about lead generation. They build a site without much forethought or strategy simply because they believe their buyers and sellers expect them to have one. They're working under the mistaken myth of if I build it, they will come. As a result they spend precious time, effort, and money to build what is essentially an online business card or, at best, a virtual brochure. They provide information for information sake. That's why so many come to understand that while the Internet can be a great source of leads, it can also be a great source of financial loss and frustration. And usually they experience the financial loss and frustration long before the leads.

> *You can lead generate all day, but if you don't have a system in place to convert those leads, you're wasting your time and money.*
>
> *Kurt Buehler, Flower Mound, TX*

The hard truth is that buyers don't really care if you have a Web site. They just want to look at all the homes for sale and research neighborhoods to live in, and they'll use any site that allows them to do this. Sellers don't really care if you have a Web site. They just want to know the value of their home and the sites where it will be marketed for sale. Like buyers they will use any site that allows them to do this. If your site doesn't meet these clear-cut expectations in a manner that causes buyers and sellers to want to use your site and, ultimately, you, then the Web isn't working for you.

The most straightforward way I can put it is this: a Web site is a tool for you to offer consumers what they want in exchange for what you want. It's a vehicle that enables you to offer them real estate information in exchange for their contact information—a win-win information swap that must be the foundation of your entire Internet strategy. Your Web site may accomplish more, but you won't accept anything less. When you view it in this light and hold it accountable to this approach, your Web site can become one of the most powerful lead generating and appointment converting tools in your arsenal.

Because there is so much confusion about the Internet's role in our industry any advanced discussion on how your Web site strategy might adapt to a market shift is premature until we've reviewed the fundamentals of an effective Internet lead generation plan.

THE INTERNET LEAD GENERATION MODEL

Our extensive research, interviews, and mastermind sessions with some of the most successful Internet agents in our industry led us to a surprisingly simple three-step approach to Internet lead generation. The model encompasses three areas of focus—creating and maintaining an Internet presence, lead generating for traffic, and converting those leads to appointments (see Figure 22). The big aha is that contrary to what some may think "Internet consumers" don't really exist.

History reveals that when any niche becomes the majority they are no longer a niche. This is exactly what has happened with the Internet regarding real estate. Mountains of research report that essentially all our customers today are Internet customers, which makes them, well, our customers. Why is this significant? It gets us out of the myths of "Internet customers" and "Internet specialists," limiting beliefs that imply unique buyers and sellers who require extraordinary effort and highly specialized expertise. That's simply no longer true. For all intents and purposes, everyone is now using the Internet and we're all Internet agents. The Internet is no longer about the extraordinary, it's about the ordinary; and it is as much a part of our daily work as mobile phones and cars.

THE INTERNET LEAD GENERATION MODEL

FIGURE 22 In the beginning, build a great site with lead generation in mind. Then market it online and offline. Those efforts result in leads to be converted to appointments. Based on your results, you may or may not need to modify the site for better results.

1. CREATE AND MAINTAIN AN INTERNET PRESENCE

A successful Web site doesn't have to do a lot, but it must do a few things really well. Thankfully this doesn't have to cost a lot of money, require technical expertise on your part, or even occupy much of your time. The widespread adoption of the Internet in real estate has both made things affordable and created a cottage industry of service providers to help you. Many of the features that were once the domain of costly custom Web sites are now common on affordable template sites. As such, the vast majority of agents should begin with template Web sites and only graduate to custom sites when their lead generation results demand it.

So, what are the few important things your site must do well? Or, in other words, what are the elements of a great real estate sales Web site? To begin with, your site needs to have a professional, up-to-date look that lends credibility to your image and brand. Don't confuse this with cutting-edge, award-winning design. Unless you've purposefully chosen this as a point of differentiation between you and your competitors (and you know for a fact it's money well-invested), your Web site design need only meet your customers' basic expectations. And that doesn't require a consultant. After all, you're an Internet-empowered consumer yourself—you search on Google and Yahoo!, buy books on Amazon, watch videos on YouTube, fill your attic on eBay and later empty it with the help of Craigslist. You recognize sites that just make you scratch your head, close the browser, and move on. You also recognize an uncluttered, easy-to-navigate professional site when you see one. Make sure your site is one of those.

While most technology professionals capably design template or custom sites to meet these basic consumer design expectations meeting your lead generation expectations is not as easy. Consumers surf real estate Web sites a little like they browse car lots on Sunday afternoons. The reason you see so many folks peering through car windows on Sundays is that the car lot is closed and the potential car buyers can take a leisurely look at the vehicles without getting "sold." It's a no-hassle opportunity to kick tires and check out the merchandise. However, this desire to remain anonymous is in direct conflict with the goals of the dealership.

You and your Web site have the same dilemma. Remember, your site's primary purpose is to capture leads that become appointments. So you'll have to look beyond design and aesthetics to verify that any Web site you purchase or create has effective points of contact. You must aggressively think offer-response and lead capture at every turn on your site.

Are potential buyers and sellers given reasons and easy-to-find ways to phone or email you? These points of contact should be well-placed and easily found on the page. They also have to be labeled in plain language, avoiding real estate jargon, so that your potential customers understand what you're offering. For example, a common mistake is to offer people a "Free CMA." Instead, try something simple and widely understood like "My Home's Value." If they are ready or willing to make contact with you,

My team monitors the IDX search patterns of leads we're cultivating, so the moment we notice an increase in search activity we know that this is the time to seize the moment and convert that lead to an appointment before someone else does.

Ben Kinney, Bellingham, WA

then it should be simple and easy to do so. Make them work and they will contact someone else.

You will also want a compelling, memorable Web site address or domain name. In fact, you'll probably have more than one. Of course you'll have your main Internet address like YourName.com or YourBrand.com, but you'll also have buyer, seller, or niche addresses like YourAreaHomes.com or YourNiche.com. These unique and simple sites will be named for the special area they feature. The goal of such sites is to pull people to you by giving them numerous ways to find you while they're looking for what they want. In some cases, you may use some of these secondary domain names in your marketing and simply have them pointed or redirected to your primary Web site. In other cases, they might be stand-alone sites that serve the niche target of your marketing efforts. As a result, depending on the scope of your Internet lead generation focus, you may own a handful or hundreds.

Finally, research tells us that your buyers and sellers clearly expect a few critical elements. Buyers want the ability to search all the homes in an area (Internet Data Exchange searches or IDX), get instant notifications on properties that meet their criteria (buyer instant notifications or BINs), and save search criteria for future visits (search savers). Besides those tools, they are also looking for information on communities, neighborhoods, schools, and the home-buying process. Likewise, sellers want to know how much their home is worth (a home valuation or CMA request form). As for content, sellers want market statistics and information on the home selling process. You must meet or exceed buyer and seller expectations in these areas or they'll go elsewhere.

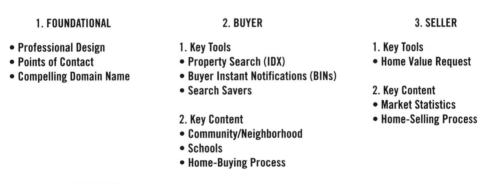

THE ELEMENTS OF A GREAT AGENT WEB SITE

1. FOUNDATIONAL
- Professional Design
- Points of Contact
- Compelling Domain Name

2. BUYER
1. Key Tools
- Property Search (IDX)
- Buyer Instant Notifications (BINs)
- Search Savers

2. Key Content
- Community/Neighborhood
- Schools
- Home-Buying Process

3. SELLER
1. Key Tools
- Home Value Request

2. Key Content
- Market Statistics
- Home-Selling Process

FIGURE 23 Many agents who don't have specific features on their Web site (such as instant notification) simply offer them on their site as personal services which they then can fulfill with their MLS tools.

This checklist is just that—a checklist. These tools are common enough that it shouldn't be a struggle to incorporate any into your Web site. The real challenge is to make sure that when a buyer or seller visits your site, these features are appropriately spotlighted and not lost in a left-hand navigation bar that runs twenty-two items long. The first thing a buyer or seller must see is exactly what they came for. Everything else is a distraction.

When your Web site meets these achievable yet nonnegotiable standards you will know that you can lead generate to it with confidence. This is very important. Having exactly what people want is more than half the battle. As technology evolves, tools change and vendors come and go, don't lose sight of what buyers and sellers are primarily seeking. It won't change. So when you offer what they want, your site will be "sticky" as techies say, because when visitors who find your site find what they want, they tend to hang around. This core understanding of their wants and needs must be the driving force in how you build, update, and maintain your Web site. When the buyers and sellers who find you on the Web get what they want and have every opportunity to give you what you want—their contact information—you have a chance to get what you need: an appointment.

2. LEAD GENERATE FOR TRAFFIC

No matter how great your Web site, if no one ever visits it then it is, in effect, useless. People must find your site or you might as well not have one. A great site with no traffic is nothing; a great site with great traffic is everything. To be successful with your site you must have a strong lead generation plan that pulls, pushes, and leads people to it. The most effective lead generation plan will use both offline and online marketing to accomplish this.

The Internet age has collapsed many traditional competitive borders. Territories that were once highly local are now practically global. Local booksellers compete with Amazon. Area car dealerships wage war with CarMax. But do local real estate agents really have to go toe-to-toe with national Internet real estate companies? Research emphatically tells us *no*. Real estate is a uniquely local industry and your best competitive advantage still stems from your local market knowledge and position.

The challenge in competing with these companies is that they are throwing big money at online marketing. Their number one target is search engine placement for all the generic key word searches but they've also gobbled up great general domain names like homes.com and REALTOR.com. In this game of search engine placement if your business doesn't appear in the top three or four results, you are invisible to consumers using only search engines to find Web sites. It takes dollars invested in search engine optimization or pay-per-click to get results. So here's the truth: Very few, if any, can cost-effectively compete nationally (or even regionally) against these big, well-funded Internet players in their big-name search engine game. That's where their focus is and where they heavily invest to create a competitive advantage. But, don't despair. There is an even bigger truth: That's all these big national companies can do, and they can't cost-effectively compete against individuals with targeted and offline marketing. The research is compelling on this—that's where you should invest to create your online competitive advantage.

For every Web site you own, you have the ability to obtain local, specific domain names that matter in your market and point back to your site. You can counter realestate.com with yoursubdivision.com.

From neighborhoods to individual street names to local activities or amenities, you can niche your way to spectacular success and keep your competition local in scale. And this same tactical advantage exists in search engine placement and pay-per-click. National and regional players neither have the knowledge nor the resources to counter your ability to tap into the mindset and awareness of your local customers. Our research suggests that the more precise someone makes their Web search (e.g., "south Tampa golf course homes" versus "golf resort properties") the higher their motivation. A precise search is indicative of someone who has a clearer sense of their wants and needs and is further along in the process. Savvy local real estate agents have the advantage. Targeted Internet lead generation strategies allow you to be a big fish in a strategically defined pond and capture anyone attracted to it.

Another essential to winning the Internet lead generation game is to think beyond high-tech marketing. In fact, I'm going to suggest you think low-tech, especially in the beginning. High-tech lead generation methods such as search engine optimization, pay-per-click, and listing aggregators can be highly effective when aimed at a locally defined target market. But they can be wonderfully complemented and actually surpassed by incorporating your Web site (or Web sites) into all your existing low-tech lead generation materials. Your Web address should appear on your yard signs, letterhead, business cards, brochures, fliers, direct mail, all advertising... in short, on anything and everything you use to market your business. Most of the high-tech agents we surveyed confessed that as much as 50 percent of their traffic came from offline marketing. It's a bit counterintuitive but the best way to succeed online is to market your Web site offline.

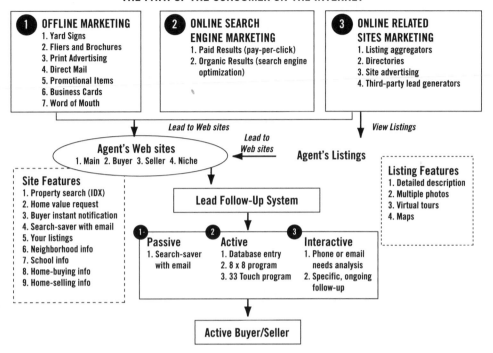

THE PATH OF THE CONSUMER ON THE INTERNET

1 OFFLINE MARKETING
1. Yard Signs
2. Fliers and Brochures
3. Print Advertising
4. Direct Mail
5. Promotional Items
6. Business Cards
7. Word of Mouth

2 ONLINE SEARCH ENGINE MARKETING
1. Paid Results (pay-per-click)
2. Organic Results (search engine optimization)

3 ONLINE RELATED SITES MARKETING
1. Listing aggregators
2. Directories
3. Site advertising
4. Third-party lead generators

Lead to Web sites

View Listings

Agent's Web sites
1. Main 2. Buyer 3. Seller 4. Niche

Lead to Web sites

Agent's Listings

Site Features
1. Property search (IDX)
2. Home value request
3. Buyer instant notification
4. Search-saver with email
5. Your listings
6. Neighborhood info
7. School info
8. Home-buying info
9. Home-selling info

Listing Features
1. Detailed description
2. Multiple photos
3. Virtual tours
4. Maps

Lead Follow-Up System

1 Passive
1. Search-saver with email

2 Active
1. Database entry
2. 8 x 8 program
3. 33 Touch program

3 Interactive
1. Phone or email needs analysis
2. Specific, ongoing follow-up

Active Buyer/Seller

FIGURE 24 For every way to attract customers online, there is an equally effective method offline. When the two work together and you have a solid lead follow-up and conversion plan, your Web site can be at the center of successful lead generation.

So, the path that buyers and sellers follow to find you on the Internet can originate online, but as often as not, can begin offline as well (see Figure 24). The key is to make sure your online and your offline marketing complement each other. Possibly one way to do that is to make your Web site an integral component of your lead generation and conversion plan. Some of the most successful agents we work with aggressively route the public to their site. All their offline marketing includes their main Web site address. They also have targeted search engine marketing that directs online traffic to their site. And, leveraging their listings, they post their properties on multiple sites and with listing aggregators, all of which direct visitors to contact the agent or to visit the agent's site. And once visitors arrive, lead capture and conversion is waiting. Central to this approach is a well thought-out method to capture inquiries so you can close for an appointment. Without a strong conversion plan in place sending everyone to your Web site is like sending them to outer space. It's a great trip for them but you'll never see them again.

Finally, if you own multiple targeted domain names or Web sites (for specific groups of buyers, sellers, or niche audiences), you'll want to fit them into your larger strategy as economically as possible. Domain names can simply be redirected to your main site and you can then measure the traffic generated by these campaigns with simple Web metrics. (What we mean by Web metrics are any of the tools that measure traffic to your Web site and give you visibility into what someone does while they are on your site. For instance, Google offers a popular free tool called Google Analytics to do this for you.) If you choose to maintain stand-alone sites you'll want to keep

Most of the time an Internet lead is just a name and email address. Your goal with every contact is to gather one more piece of information until you know enough to get the appointment.

Antonio Atacan, Philadelphia, PA

some things in mind. First, multiple sites can be a little like multiple store fronts. Each site will require its own regular upkeep and maintenance, so make sure your business is equipped to handle this. You, someone on your team, or a contractor will have to monitor and regularly update the sites. Second, as much as possible, you should leverage the tools you created for your primary site. For instance, if you have an IDX search feature, it can be "framed out" or designed into multiple sites. Ideally, you won't have to build duplicate tools for each site but rather have the same set of tools hooked up to all of them. The Internet allows for amazing economies of scale so make sure you take full advantage of them.

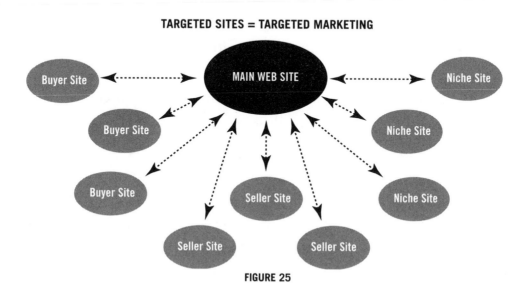

TARGETED SITES = TARGETED MARKETING

FIGURE 25

3. CAPTURE, CONNECT, CULTIVATE, AND CLOSE LEADS

On the one hand, the lead conversion strategy for the Internet isn't all that different from what we discussed in *Tactic #5 Get to the Table*. The process is the same—capture, connect, close, and when you can't close, cultivate. There are a couple of critical differences. The first is in the capture step. If a prospect makes a sign call or an ad call to your office you can verbally capture, connect, and close. If they call your IVR (interactive voice response or 1-800 number) it immediately captures their phone number through caller ID or they leave a message, again allowing you to call them back, connect, and close. The Internet doesn't present you with such a direct and controllable path to an appointment.

With the Internet, you must be intentional about capturing enough useful information to be able to get back to prospects. If that doesn't happen, you don't really have a lead—your Web site may generate a lot of traffic but it won't generate any transactions. You may gain some bragging rights among the techies, but you don't earn any points with true business people. Make sure your site has a way for the consumer to register but also a good reason to do it.

Personalize your email responses and show your personality! I mean, really, who wants to work with a boring agent? We make our Web sites come alive with great content and reasons to register with us. An amazing percent of our business now comes from the Internet.

Ida Terbet, Raleigh, NC

Can they easily register for you to supply them with compelling services and information? These could be the same exact offer-response hooks you use in your other lead generation methods (from special reports like "common mistakes to avoid" to personal services like prequalifying or a property price valuation). Just be sure they are clearly visible on every page. And finally, since most visitors will be on your site to look at properties, you must decide how far you will let them go before you ask them to register. It's a delicate balance with which you'll need to experiment. The important thing to remember is that the offers will have to be very persuasive to get the immediate response you seek.

The other vital distinction is in regard to lead cultivation. You're either going to capture a name and a number or a name and an email address. If someone gives you a name and a number online you simply call them back and handle it just like any other captured inquiry. But if all you get online is an email address, you're put in a passive-type position where you must cultivate the relationship to see if they'll ever give you their name and phone number. Research shows that buyers and sellers captured on the Internet often begin their online search as much as 18 months before they intend to buy or sell. Remember the car lot on Sunday analogy? Well it's true. The Internet allows buyers and sellers to arrive early in the process and start looking around. The cultivation process we described in *Tactic #5 Get to the Table* is much more active with live inquiries but tends to be more passive with online inquiries.

Online cultivation is akin to having an "Internet farm," in the same way you'd have a geographic farm. It's actually closer to a marketing plan than a conversion plan with a couple of key exceptions: you must still respond quickly to have a chance to cultivate them and technology makes it economical to have many contacts.

Let's first address response time. Speed wins this contest almost every time. Buyers and sellers who decide it's time to stop being anonymous and start the active process expect reasonably timed responses to their Internet queries. Once they have registered or emailed you, fast response is critical. Internet usage has everyone accustomed to fast response times, so you should think in terms of responding in less than 24 minutes rather than hours.

> *When an Internet lead comes in, my chances of conversion are highest if I can call them while they are still on my site.*
> *Sue Adler, Short Hills, NJ*

An auto-response email that is warm and service-oriented is a great first step and an excellent way to ensure you give this quick response. But an immediate phone call or personal email is even better. If you can't do it personally, then your staff can do this. There are also call-center services that can do it for you, 24-7-365. Anyone who does this for you must make the quick response in your name and get enough information so that you can contact them yourself when you become available.

Now please understand that some younger people or those who are tech-oriented actually prefer and enjoy being followed up via email and text messaging. For them, this can be the right way to begin a relationship which can then lead to a phone call or an appointment to meet. So it's not necessarily wrong to respond by email if that's all you have because that is probably how they'd like you to respond. The mantra "respond like they respond" isn't a bad one to follow at all. And this is where a contact management system can become critical if you hope to track and cultivate dozens or even hundreds of online prospects in your Internet farm over time. A good system will be able to record when you contacted them, what was said, what services were agreed upon and when the next contact needs to take place.

The key is to target your site to a specific niche audience like your farm—but don't get so localized that you limit your traffic.
    Cary Sylvester, Austin, TX

Most Web site packages for template or custom sites can easily incorporate saved searches or buyer instant notification systems. These tools are excellent for managing the large numbers of online prospects you might have in your contact management system. The most successful agents follow up quickly whenever users register for these services with a personal offer to help them refine their search criteria. This is a great chance to connect and possibly close the prospect for an appointment. The Internet brings you many people who have set timelines and expectations that are usually longer and slower than necessary. They actually could, would and perhaps should buy or sell right now but they've let the market shift lull them into slow motion. Be sure to give them every opportunity to move faster and encourage them to get a "real-life perspective" about what's going on in the market right now. For those who can't be converted you have the opportunity to gauge

If you can help them to begin looking, they will begin to get excited, see the advantages of buying now, and actually be closing on their next home long before they thought they would.
Bruce Hardie, Spokane, WA

their motivation and offer other services (like a prequalification consultation with a mortgage vendor or a free estimate of their home's value) that can move them along in the process. And remember it's not just what you offer but how you offer it that can make the difference. So don't just focus on the offers you make. Experiment with how and when you make them until you find what will work.

You might also consider investigating tools that offer you a glimpse into buyer and seller activity. They can measure when and how often people revisit their saved searches or view properties online. Periods of increased activity thus become your queue to reach out, reconnect, and offer your assistance—and get an appointment. So if you are going to engage in serious Internet-based lead generation and conversion during a shift, be sure to thoroughly research the technical tools for contact management and lead cultivation that could help you succeed.

In our research with top agents on their Web strategies, we made a concerted effort to establish a baseline measure for success in lead capture and closing. Much like our lead generation modeling in *The Millionaire Real*

Estate Agent, we believe that if you can put numbers behind your expectations then you'll have a quantifiable goal to reach for and, eventually, surpass.

POINTS OF CONVERSION	SELLER RATES	BUYER RATES
Visitors by Type	15%	85%
Visitors by Registrations	20%	3.25%
Registrations to Appointment	5%	5%

FIGURE 26 Average Internet conversion rates based on surveys with top agents.

As you can see the majority of visitors are buyers. Interestingly, because sellers tend to be more motivated in their quest to determine the value of their homes, sellers are much more likely to register. The net result for you: for every 700 visitors you drive to your site you should be able to capture approximately twenty seller and twenty buyer registrations that should yield an average of one buyer appointment and one seller appointment. Bear in mind these are averages that don't reflect your efforts in your market. Some agents far surpass these benchmarks and others fall far short. Tweaking your site and its offers through trial and error should get the numbers up and make the difference.

That sums up the foundation for your Internet lead generation. You'll need to create and maintain a Web site that is designed to capture and close leads to appointments. You'll employ offer-response marketing both online and offline to targeted audiences designed to drive traffic to the site and, once there, get them to register or contact you directly.

And finally you'll have systems for capturing, connecting, cultivating, and closing those leads to appointments to do business with you. With this clear understanding in mind, let's look at how you'll implement this strategy in a shifting market.

INTERNET LEADS IN A SHIFTING MARKET

Shifts force you to reevaluate everything you do, especially an area like the Internet that carries fixed ongoing costs. You might even be asking yourself if the Internet is really where you should be spending precious time, money, and effort. It is if it can deliver and that will depend on the quality of the offers you make around and on your Web site.

Earlier, I shared research on the average conversion rates for an effective real estate Web site. Those numbers showed agents got one buyer appointment and one seller appointment for every 700 visitors. I also mentioned that some agents surpassed those benchmarks. Our research actually revealed a select group of agents who were doubling these conversion rates on the buyer side (with 7 percent of buyers registering and 10 percent being closed to appointments). That translates to an average of four buyer appointments instead of just one. What these agents did differently was master the what and where of Internet offer-response.

An attendee at an Internet Lead Conversion Summit we sponsored summed up the difference between good Internet offer-response marketing and great Internet offer-response marketing as the difference between offering "thin bait" and "fat bait." He explained that your Web site must have "thin bait" that attracts people to your site and keeps them there for a while. But then, he warned, you must offer something more, the fat bait, for them to want to register. Thin bait lures while fat bait hooks. You'll need both to catch the most leads and succeed at your highest level.

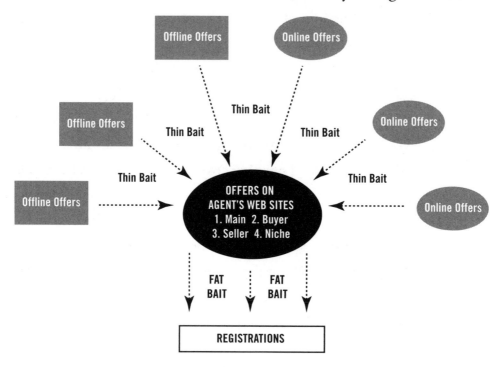

FIGURE 27 "Thin bait" gets people to your site—it's what they expect. "Fat bait" consists of the special or unexpected offers that get them to register.

Thin bait is everything people expect to find at your site. All the properties for sale in the market, community and neighborhood information, home value resources and market statistics are what they are looking for. These are the things you'll cleverly market to pull buyers and sellers to your Web site. The key is to make sure that your bait stands out from the crowd.

Fat bait can be more detailed information on the listings, virtual tours, detailed neighborhood information, community calendars, property tax and mortgage calculators, and other additional "valuable" information. The list is endless so be creative. Take a look at the other offline offers you're making in a shifted market ("Best Buy" lists, foreclosure tours, short sale information, pricing studies, etc.) and consider incorporating them online. In addition to that, you can offer timely services such as mortgage refinancing or home staging consultations for homeowners or first-time homebuyers, investment and financing seminars for buyers. Beyond these you can also offer free reports (examples include "The Five Secrets to Getting Your Home Sold Now" or "The Three Mistakes Buyers Make in a Buyers' Market") that match the market conditions of the moment. The more interesting and attractive you make your offers the more leads they will generate. It is well worth your time to give this your best thinking and testing. Don't be satisfied with just doing average marketing for average results—create unique, valuable offers that will earn you outstanding results. Just as you advise your sellers, stand out from the crowd and be more compelling than your competition.

Besides bait, the other issue you'll have to master is when and where to capture buyer registrations. There are four widely issued strategies (see Figure 28) ranging from up-front registration to open searches with registration attached to ongoing use. Not having a registration is not an option. Front-end registration tends to get more registrations but yields fewer appointments on average. While a few may go to other sites (where no registration is required), proponents of this strategy insist these are few in number and less motivated in general. On the other end, open searches with registration required to save a search or get email drip notifications does get fewer registrations but these tend to be more easily converted to appointments. While this method allows for a lot of anonymous searches, proponents argue that those individuals who do register tend to be farther along in the process and more committed to working with you. In the end, both strategies are absolutely valid; however, the wisdom of the shift says you must experiment until you find methods that yield you the most appointments.

FOUR LEAD CAPTURE STRATEGIES

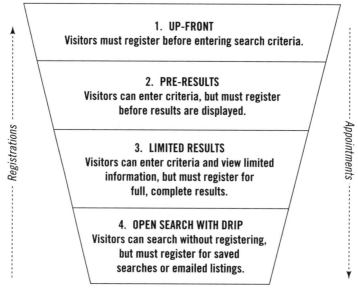

Higher Percentage of Registrations, Lower Percentage of Appointments

1. UP-FRONT
Visitors must register before entering search criteria.

2. PRE-RESULTS
Visitors can enter criteria, but must register before results are displayed.

3. LIMITED RESULTS
Visitors can enter criteria and view limited information, but must register for full, complete results.

4. OPEN SEARCH WITH DRIP
Visitors can search without registering, but must register for saved searches or emailed listings.

Registrations

Appointments

Lower Percentage of Registrations, Higher Percentage of Appointments

FIGURE 28 A shift will force you to make a decision on when and where you capture buyer registrations to improve results.

Our research showed you might actually get more registrations with "up-front." It's a bit counter-intuitive and I struggled with it until I thought about it. More people are given the opportunity to register "up front" while fewer people are serious enough to want to save their searches or get email notifications. So the "up-front" strategy captures more registrations while the "open search" captures a smaller but more motivated group, thus the higher appointments. It makes sense when you look at it that way.

Rather than automatically adopting the fourth strategy there are valid concerns you should think about before you decide. In particular, if you are well-equipped to follow up with and cultivate large numbers of leads, the up-front strategy may be better for you. Agents skilled in cultivation that have effective teams or technology to support their lead conversion programs should have the best ability to

Simply put, the goal of your Web site is to offer consumers what they want—real estate information—in exchange for what you want—their contact information.
Bryon Ellington, Austin, TX

take advantage of this strategy. But beware, large numbers of unqualified leads can quickly swamp the unprepared. And then confusion over who is and is not a lead can result in lost time, lower conversion rates, and less actual business. If you have any doubts about your ability to cultivate large numbers of captured inquires over time choose the fourth option and focus your resources on fewer but higher quality leads. Experiment and see which strategy works best for you.

No matter which way you go however, I want you to be like impatient Eric. A while back my son John, my coauthor Jay and my friend Don Hobbs and I went fly fishing in Montana with two guides. Funny thing is we not only caught a lot of fish, but we also were taught an incredible lesson in lead generating. Before we began, Don told me that whoever went with Eric would catch the most fish no matter their skill, experience or time on the water. And guess what? He was right. Each day Eric's boat landed the most trout. Why? Because Eric was impatient. If a lure or hole wasn't delivering results, he gave it little time before he made a change. He would row to another hole or tie on a new fly. The other guide's approach was the opposite. His favorite line was "leave your fly there...I like it" and he would fish a particular spot or fly for extended periods of time. Don't get me wrong, this guide was plenty good but Eric was simply legendary. At the end of our trip our biggest catch besides some great fish was the lesson we learned about lures and locations. If something isn't working, move on or expect to come home empty-handed.

If your marketing isn't sending enough people to your site or your offers aren't getting registration responses—do something different immediately. Be like Eric and don't wait too long before you make a change. Be impatient.

I want you to step back and think of your Web site as one big open house. You're there to sell the house and you're there to get leads. Most visitors aren't going to buy that house, but they are going to buy a house. They are researching. Take the opportunity to capture their contact information so you can assess their needs and get into relationship. While the vast majority is just looking, follow up quickly and systematically so you can close all the motivated leads to appointments to do business. Just as some say open houses aren't very effective for lead generation, many believe the Internet is equally unproductive and best left to a handful of specialists. The truth is these leads generate opportunities and are only as good as your capture, con-

I don't believe in forced registration for IDX because it's so readily available for free. However, for my own listings, I have buyers register to see the floorplans and virtual tours because this is something of value that they can't get anywhere else.

Sue Adler, Short Hills, NJ

nect, cultivate, and close system. Focus on having a great site that is cleverly marketed and makes timely, compelling offer-response marketing messages. Then make sure you deploy a quick response follow-up program to reap Internet rewards.

No matter the market, you must have some presence on the Internet. That's no longer a question or an option. Using the power of the Internet to communicate with clients, share information about your services, and validate your standing as a professional real estate agent is critical to your business. Technology and the Internet are no longer a choice. The question is do you move from simply communicating to effectively lead generating? In a shift we don't think you have a choice. You must make your technology earn its keep.

TACTIC #7
PRICE AHEAD OF THE MARKET—
SELLER PRICING STRATEGIES

The ability to learn faster than your competitors
may be the only sustainable competitive advantage.

ARIE DE GEUS

THE MOMENT THE MEDIA DECLARES a "real estate shift," it's as if the market just got doused in a cold shower. The result is fearful buyers, pickier buyers, and eventually fewer buyers. The remaining few claim that if they can't get a good buy then they'll just say good-bye for now. The market has cooled off. Cautious consumers appear willing to let good deals die and great opportunities pass them by in hopes of getting a steal. They start missing the forest for the trees. Wary of paying too much, buyers go too far and begin to offer too little, and only properties that appear to be serious bargains get serious attention. Sellers who are slow to recognize this shift will quickly become overpriced and consequently be overlooked.

This isn't rocket science. When the market shifts, first buyers and then sellers become overly guarded and set in motion another intriguing game of *The Price Is Right*. In this version, instead of guessing there is no top, buyers now predict there is no bottom. When previously they were aggressively pushing prices forward, now they're equally aggressive in trying to pull them back. The truth is the market remains full of people who genuinely want to buy and sell. The question is—at what price? The answer sorts both sellers and buyers into a range of categories from "not interested" to "still motivated." This sorting now defines and shapes the marketplace. The desire to do business hasn't gone away, but the heat has gone out of the market. The motivated few are the ones you are looking for and the ones you can help.

A shift exposes and magnifies the classic real estate price conflict that has always existed: the asking price a seller wants versus the price a buyer is willing to pay. To illustrate this conflict and how the market determines who has the upper hand, I'll share a story:

At the bar exam three different would-be attorneys forget their pens. One asks a test proctor if he has an extra pen. He does, but only one. The first attorney says, "I'll give you a dollar for the pen." The second attorney chimes in, "I'll give you two dollars!" Then the third says, "Hey, I'll give you three!"...By the next time the bar exam is given, all the attorneys know not to forget a pen and all the test proctors have heard they should bring extras. This time only one attorney forgets and when he asks a proctor for a pen, the proctor answers, "Sure. I'll sell it to you for three dollars." Then another proctor jumps in and says, "I'll sell you one for two dollars." But before the attorney can pull out his billfold, a third proctor offers, "I'll sell you mine for just a dollar."

We're in a race against time. The best price you'll get is the one you get now. If you wait, it will be lower.

Jackie Ellis, Boynton Beach, FL

In a sellers' market the power of pricing favors the seller and buyers will compete for a limited supply. A shift means this power is now in favor of the buyer and that sellers will compete to attract the limited supply of buyers. Our goal in representing a seller in a shift is to use pricing to empower them as much as possible. And that's not easy.

THE WINDOW OF OPPORTUNITY

If someone is to buy their house, sellers must be aware of and buy into the concept of a "window of opportunity." This phenomenon means that when a home first comes on the market it attracts attention from those agents who are currently working with motivated buyers or those agents who are motivated by the price to go find one. If any agent or their buyer believes that a house is poorly priced, it loses its opportunity and doesn't draw their attention. Basically, it gets written off from the beginning. Once this happens it isn't easy to get those agents or buyers back, even with a series of price reductions or home improvements. First impressions are the original pictures framed in the mind and heart—they are usually lasting ones. When memories and opinions get set, they are typically tough to change.

In a buyers' market, sellers are often going through the five stages of grief: 1. Denial, 2. Anger, 3. Bargaining, 4. Depression, then 5. Acceptance. My job is to counsel them through it.

Martin Bouma, Ann Arbor, MI

The first time someone sees a property is called the "window of opportunity" because it's the single best chance to create the impression that will sell the house. It is the best marketing message a seller can send: We're priced right and serious to sell. If a property isn't appropriately priced for the market from the outset, a seller will likely miss this important first. Your job is to get them to grasp why pricing it right must happen right now. They only get one chance to make a good first impression. Making the wrong impression will cost a seller time and money.

THE PRICE REDUCTION EFFECT

FIGURE 29 Sellers with a price reduction need 2 to 3 times longer to sell, potentially delaying their move and increasing their carrying costs[3].

Pricing houses for a successful sale is never as simple as some might think. Continually changing market conditions and circumstances make pricing a skill as well as a science. The research, analysis, and judgment that go into competitive pricing aren't readily evident in most agents' listing presentations. And truthfully, some real estate agents don't actually approach it with the thoroughness it deserves. A market shift absolutely underscores the importance of pricing and exposes cavalier agents who don't give it researched attention and serious thought. The most successful agents become masters of pricing and masterful in getting their sellers to trust the findings and act on them.

Buyers are always looking for value. Regardless of the market, they want the best property available at the lowest price. A shift doesn't change

[3]Based on 2008 research on single-family home pricing in 36 Atlanta First Multiple Listing Service (FMLS) areas.

this, it actually accentuates it. This happens because of what a shift does change—the direction and speed at which a buyer thinks prices are going. As an agent you know this, so you not only advise your sellers on what their home will likely sell for, but also the general pricing of the market. You are making an observation and a forecast. The observation is the science and the forecast is the skill. Observation of current pricing is a science that requires a thorough, rational, fact-based analysis. Forecasting is an acquired skill, an inexact ability to predict market direction and speed. The information to do this is there and available, but someone must put in the time and effort to uncover it, interpret it, learn from it, and use it.

THE ART OF PRICING PERSUASION

A seller not only needs you to master the science and skill of pricing, but also the art of persuasion. In a shift, most sellers are actually "tryers" who never become solds. The market becomes oversaturated with unsuccessful wannabes who didn't get the formula of direction and speed correct. If they are to become true sellers then they're going to need competent professional guidance to price their houses to sell in the desired time frame. For sellers in a

I always tell my sellers to price ahead of the market. Whether it's going up or going down, the key is to price your house ahead of it.
Gary Gentry, Austin, TX

shift, the need for an agent who has mastered the science, the skill, and the art of pricing becomes critical.

The essence of the pricing science is identifying the right comparable properties. The right comps make the analysis more accurate and a seller's acceptance more likely. So what makes a property comparable? There are four main factors: location, size, amenities, and condition. Then you must factor in when it sold or went pending. You may also use properties currently on the market to get a sense of the current competition.

Whether you use recent pendings and solds or active listings and expireds, you are attempting to assess the price range in which a home will sell. In the final analysis, all else being equal—and that's what you've done in selecting comps—the price impacts marketability and ultimately salability. That's what all motivated sellers must understand and their agent must persuade them about.

In addition to their home's immediate value, sellers are also challenged to come to terms with another reality of the marketplace—the direction and speed at which the market is moving. This is determined by studying the area economy, grasping the motivations of available buyers, and reconciling this with listed, pending, and sold data from the market. Patterns will emerge and require interpretation. Sometimes they're obvious and sometimes they're not. Either way, sellers need to know. They need to understand the full extent of the market trends and the implications for pricing.

THE MARKET IS LIKE A SEESAW

FIGURE 30 Market cycles are like a seesaw. It's the balance between the number of buyers on one side and the number of sellers on the other. More sellers drive prices down; more buyers drive prices up.

The direction in which a market is going and the speed at which it's moving determine pricing strategies. Properties that are appropriately priced for the market will always make the best impression. They'll be the first shown, the most talked about, the first to receive offers, and the most likely to sell. But if the price doesn't match the direction of the market then buyers will merely move on and never even give it a second thought. Since they won't even look at it, they'll never get to experience the property's real appeal. The best way to truly serve a seller in a shift is to persuade them to outthink the other sellers they must compete against. When the buyers pull back successful sellers must be persuaded to step out in front. They must "price ahead of the market."

DON'T CHASE THE MARKET—LET THE MARKET CHASE YOU!

Statistically speaking, sellers will find themselves facing one of three real estate markets: a buyers' market, a sellers' market, or a balanced market. And as they're confronted with each market they'll discover they have three pricing strategies from which to choose—price at the market, behind the market, or ahead of the market.

In practice, only the "buyer and seller markets" are considered when choosing a pricing strategy. The reason a "balanced market" is taken off the table is because that transitional period between a "buyers' and a sellers' market" is short-lived. Transitional markets are usually fleeting. As such, markets usually move in one direction or the other with little to no pause in between. It's why you hear people say "we're in a buyers' market" or "we're in a sellers' market" but virtually never hear them say "we're in a balanced market." This is important to grasp because it is this thinking that drives pricing strategy decisions.

Not chasing the market means pricing your listings ahead of it. When a house isn't priced ahead of the market it's essentially behind the opportunity curve—the opportunity to get the best price possible. This may seem paradoxical but it is actually the foundational principle of successful pricing in a shift. Successful pricing means getting the maximum price for a house in that market, but the strategies can differ based upon the direction of the market. Sellers must first decide if they really need to or want to sell. This is their decision to make. Once they decide to sell, our job as agents is to show them how to make that happen. Once they see how the market really works they can then decide what they want to do.

As soon as a market price has been established the question every seller must then answer is, "what should my asking price be?" This is a strategic question not a value question. What a house is worth is the answer to a value question, but what a house will sell for is the answer to a sales price question. They are clearly different questions.

I help sellers see that they have to be smarter than other sellers—they have to be wicked competitors on pricing to essentially put the other listings in their area "out of business."
Donna Grissom, Studio City, CA

When a seller is ready to sell there is only one thing they want to know: "what is the best price their house will sell for right now?" When sellers go to price their property, two things matter: where the market is now and the direction it's going. And that is why they must be strategic if they want to get the best price in the right time.

When a seller wants to sell, and a property valuation has determined a price range for what the home might sell for at that time, a pricing strategy must now be chosen. Before a seller chooses a strategy they must make a very important decision: do they want to sell for the maximum price now or do they want to maximize the price possible? When asked this question literally every seller immediately answers "both," which means they have misunderstood the question. Getting the maximum price now

There is a gap between what a seller thinks and the realistic price they can get. That gap is where your skills must work.
Dave Norberg, San Diego, CA

or getting the maximum price possible presents two different choices in a sellers' market. In a buyers' market they are in fact the same. In other words, in a buyers' market maximum price and minimum time are the same strategy.

Successful pricing means getting the maximum price now for a house. But getting a maximum price now doesn't necessarily mean getting the maximum price possible. When home values are on the rise, sellers can clearly price their home to sell at its maximum price now. This is choosing "at the market" pricing. If they want to sell quicker, then they can choose "behind the market" pricing by offering a price below the market. This would mean they're strategically making less money in return for a faster sale—a tradeoff only they can justify.

The seller also has the opportunity to anticipate where the market is going and if time isn't an issue, see if they can maximize their financial opportunity. If they have the time, this could mean holding off from selling for a while longer until the market prices rise enough to pay their price. While there is risk in this strategy in that it is truly trying to time the market, it can work. They could also consider marketing it now at that "future" price, but unless it is an amazing property it will simply fail the "window of opportunity" test and become "shopped." In other words, the seller would run the risk of simply being another overpriced listing on the market. A rising market can actually forgive a small over-pricing on a highly desirable property, but never a big one.

FIGURE 31 In a market with rising home values, if a seller wants a price that's ahead of the market, the market may go up enough to make that price attractive for buyers. Time can cure some mistakes and make people look smart.

When home prices are falling sellers are in a real bind. Pricing "behind the market" when prices are rising means sellers could be leaving money on the table for a quicker sale. But pricing behind the market when prices are falling means sellers just won't ever sell. In a declining market, selling now and maximizing the price turn out to require the exact same strategy. Buyers always want a great buy, but when they're shopping for a house in a clear buyers' market they are in essence looking for an even greater buy. They're looking for a bargain. If everything is priced the same then what goes through their mind is "where is the bottom?" Buyers know they're in a shift, but if everything is priced alike they get confused because it appears to them that sellers still want too much. This is a real dilemma so they tend to become "fence-sitters." Value is a comparative concept so when everything is priced the same, buyers become uncertain about where the value is. In a rising market they have faith that values are at their lowest and they don't fear current prices. But in a falling market they have no faith in current prices and fear paying too much. As a result, they're looking for the lowest priced home as an indication of the best value.

Sellers also have a dilemma because in a falling market it usually means all sellers are going to have to take a price cut. The market price is getting ready to fall across the board. This is when anyone who wants to sell in a shift must become very strategic. Sellers have to realize they must stand out now and get sold or they'll be chasing the market all the way to the bottom. If they price at the market they'll in essence always be overpriced for what the market will pay at that moment. Their only real choice, if they want to maximize their price and sell now, is to price "ahead of the market." This means dropping their price below it. How far below it now becomes the critical question.

All sellers naturally fear underselling their house, and rightfully so. However, in a shifting market the greater risk is in overpricing. This happens by pricing it "at the market" and this is where it gets a little confusing and tough for a seller to swallow. Unless they're underpricing it they will end up underselling it. Time is not on their side. Buyers in a shift are shopping for a good deal. This means they're hunting for the lowest priced home. This means less than any of the other homes. Sellers in a shift must outthink the other sellers, the tryers, by getting ahead of them. If a home isn't priced ahead of the market, it may well be priced out of the market. Once sellers fall behind, they can end up chasing the market all the way down and losing the margin they would have gained by pricing it right in the first place.

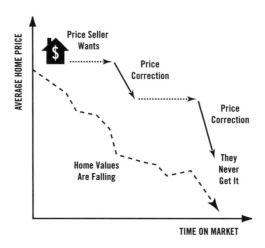

FIGURE 32 If sellers fall behind a market with falling home values, they can end up chasing the market down, because home values are always falling faster than their price reductions.

"We're in a race against time," is what you tell every seller, "The best price you'll get is the one you get now. If you wait, it will just be lower." Pricing at the market is really overpricing in a shift and simply too high a risk to take. Whether the market is on the way up or on the way down, sellers should always price to the market they're headed to.

The way to guide a seller to understanding the market is to show them graphs (see Figures 33 and 34) and then talk them through each of the numbered points. This creates a logical analysis of the thinking behind your pricing recommendations. It is a way for you to help them discover the facts and overcome their fears or misunderstandings. It is your way to empower them and give them the competitive advantage they want.

Graphs are available as free downloads at www.MillionaireSystems.com/shift.

THE COST OF OVERPRICING IN A *STABLE* MARKET

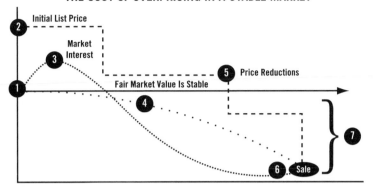

(1) Fair Market Value is driven by what buyers will pay for perceived worth.

(2) Seller hopes a higher initial price will draw a higher offer.

(3) Market interest is highest for new listings and wanes after two to four weeks.

(4) As listings become "stale," market psychology reduces the Salable Price.

(5) Price reductions are necessary to attract buyer attention.

(6) The actual List Price corresponds with the current Salable Price.

(7) As counterintuitive as it seems, properties initially priced above Fair Market Value tend to sell for less than they could have if their original prices had looked more attractive to buyers.

FIGURE 33

THE COST OF OVERPRICING IN A *SHIFTED* MARKET

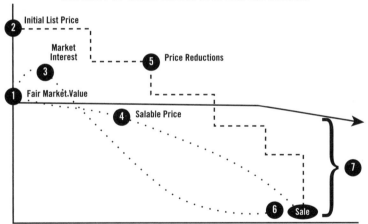

(1) Fair Market Value declines during a Market Shift.

(2) Seller hopes a higher initial price will draw a higher offer.

(3) Market interest is fragile (with high inventory) and wanes quickly.

(4) Salable Price is impacted by declining market values, "staleness," and competition.

(5) Small price reductions only "chase down the market."

(6) Properties sell when buyers see very attractive prices.

(7) The *Cost of Overpricing* is amplified after a shift!

FIGURE 34

THE CHALLENGE

Research supports the fact that sellers and buyers are typically out of sync with the realities of the market. In a sellers' market, sellers tend to dwell in the future and buyers in the past. Sellers want to push prices up and buyers want to hold the line. In a buyers' market, buyers want to place themselves in the future and sellers want to dwell in the past. Buyers want to push prices down and sellers want to hold the line. The net result is a chasm between a buyer's and seller's perception of what a home is currently worth.

Effective consultations about pricing can bridge that gap but it's not easy. The challenge is that in a buyers' market buyers usually make offers in anticipation of the market dropping. This means that it's up to the real estate agent to pull the seller forward not just to where the market is today, but to where it is likely to be in a few weeks or even months. Given this reality, in a shift, sellers need a knowledgeable agent more than ever. Specifically, they need professional—and brutally honest—pricing advice.

It's best to turn unrealistic sellers down during the listing appointment, rather than disappoint them later.

Matt Fetick, West Chester, PA

In the end, it's a "pay me now or pay me later" proposition for both you and the seller. If you can't get them to face the realities up front, you may find yourself back with them in a few weeks explaining why the home hasn't shown, much less sold, and talking price reductions. For the seller, they risk chasing the market and netting far less than if they'd priced it strategically from day one.

The most frustrating situation is when a seller lists their house behind the market, attracts an interested buyer who makes a below list price offer and the seller rejects it. You might have to remind the seller that they should treat every offer as if it will be the only offer they will ever get. This doesn't mean they should accept a low-ball offer, but it does mean they will have to do a reality check on how intent they are in selling. When they reject an offer, it's like they are "buying back" the home at that price with the expectation they can resell it and get what they want. No one would ever buy a home this way, but sellers re-buy their own home every day and usually lose big in the process.

In a real buyers' market, I really encourage a seller to take the first offer. You never know if you'll ever get another one.

Michaelann Byerly, New Tampa, FL

Dave Jenks illustrated this point by sharing a personal experience. In 1995 the market had shifted and sales were tough to come by when he put his home up for sale. He had it listed at $195,000, quickly got an offer for $180,000, and just flat-out rejected it. As knowledgeable as he was, he still fell into the "seller-buys-the-home-back trap." A year later, after twelve months of carrying costs, he says he had to accept an offer of $170,000 to get it sold and get out from underneath it. He says he knows exactly what it's like to chase the market and he didn't feel very smart or very happy with the outcome.

THE TALE OF TWO MARKETS

In a recent interview with a top agent in Massachusetts, I asked how things were going in his local area. "Our market is really a tale of two markets," he said. "Eighty percent of the homes are overpriced and twenty percent are well-priced. The well-priced properties are getting multiple offers. The overpriced properties are getting none."

I immediately realized that in every market, in every time, there are two markets—one where properties are priced to sell and another where properties are priced to sit. A seller is either in the market or out of it. And unlike a sellers' market where time on the market can pull overpriced homes back into the market, after a downshift, every day just pushes overpriced homes farther and farther out of the market. Based on this critical understanding, we recommend that a dialogue with a seller might go like this:

AGENT: Mr. and Mrs. Seller, just because a house is on the market doesn't mean it's in the market. In every market, there are actually two markets. There are properties that are priced well enough and in good enough condition to attract interested buyers. Those homes attract offers and sell. Then there are homes that are overpriced or are in less than ideal condition that don't attract buyers and just sit on the market. So, if you look at this graph [Figure 35], you can see that some houses are in the market and some are out of the market. Does that make sense?

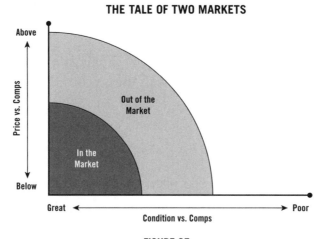

FIGURE 35

Seller: Sure. I've seen the same thing on eBay. People who auction good stuff with a fair reserve price attract a lot of bidding. Others try to pawn something off with an unrealistic reserve and they don't get any bids at all.

Agent: Great, that's the point. Buyers have a sense of what's a fair value and what's not and they just won't show up if you're not in the ballpark.

    Now, when we were in a sellers' market, we saw a lot of multiple offers and it wasn't so much whether a home would sell, it was a question of how long it would take and how much it would sell for. As you can see [Figure 36], almost all the homes were "in the market."

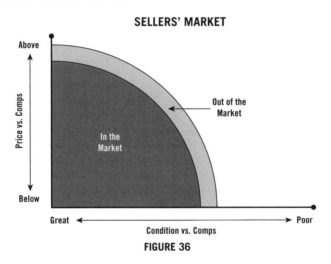

FIGURE 36

Seller: I understand but what does that mean to me today?

Agent: Well in a buyers' market like we're in today [Figure 37], many homes aren't really in the market at all. There is a lot of inventory but there aren't as many buyers. The buyers who are looking expect a great value—a good home at a good price. And with all the competition for their attention, they have a lot of choices. They start to be really picky.

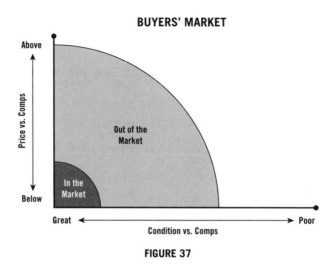

FIGURE 37

Seller: I guess that's why it's called a buyers' market, right?

Agent: Yes. That's why it's very important for us to get your home in the best condition possible and then to price it correctly and competitively. Buyers are looking for value pricing and if we don't meet those expectations, we'll look over-priced and be overlooked.

As you can see [Figure 38], the market of homes that are actually selling is small and competitive and if we don't get "in the market," we risk ending up "out of the market" with no showings and no offers, or, worse, in "no man's land" where we get enough interest to think we might be "in the market" but no offers. We need to price ahead of the market. Let's make the market instead of chasing it. As your agent I can't change the market conditions, but it is my job to show you how to get your house sold in the existing market conditions.

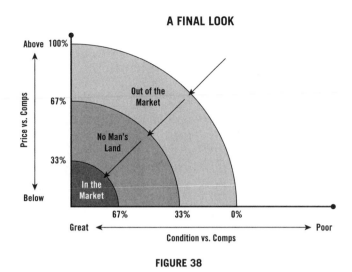

A FINAL LOOK

FIGURE 38

SELLER: I'm pretty sure I get it. It just makes me wish we'd decided to sell earlier.

AGENT: The truth is that this actually may be a good time to sell and even a solid financial opportunity for your family. Yes, we may not be able to price the home as high as we could have last year, but if you don't sell now you'll be selling for even less next year.

SELLER: So how do we do that?

AGENT: I've prepared some research on the prices of the other homes available in this area and neighborhoods like it, as well as some numbers that reflect what is and isn't selling. Or to put it another way, what is and isn't "in the market." I previewed a lot of those homes and we can decide together how best to price your house to sell....

The "Tale of Two Markets" is a simple, proven way to engage your sellers in the realities of effective pricing and staging (discussed in *Tactic*

#8: Stand Out from the Competition). Remember, it's not about you—it's about the market. The current state of the market is the determining factor for pricing. You don't make the market, you simply show them how to get their home sold in the market. You are actually bringing them the solution and showing them how to help their own cause. These charts and dialogues should give you the confidence to advise your sellers and the conviction to be strong in your approach. Truthfully, this is what they expect you to do as their fiduciary agent. To do less is to serve less than honorably in your role as a real estate professional.

We do an absorption rate CMA rather than comp sales. We take six months of active, pending, and sold units within a one-mile radius to find out how many months of inventory (exists) for that area. We want our sellers to be at the best price, terms, and conditions for that one-mile radius.

Bradley Chais, Tampa, FL

TO TAKE OR NOT TO TAKE AN OVERPRICED LISTING?

Even the best researched and most impassioned presentations can sometimes fall on deaf ears. If the seller insists on listing their home at too high a price, what is a real estate agent to do? In our experience, agents usually fall into two distinct schools of thought—never take an overpriced listing or always take the listing no matter the price.

Many insist that you should never take an overpriced listing. From their point of view overpriced properties can be a liability in terms of time, money, and reputation. Listing a home takes hours, involves real marketing expenses and, if it doesn't sell, it's your reputation that is eroding in the front yard. Agents who adopt this philosophy aim at ramping up their lead generation so they have so many listing opportunities that saying no to a listing doesn't feel like saying no to income. Still this approach isn't for everyone.

Others see listings as a marketing opportunity that shouldn't be ignored. Research for *The Millionaire Real Estate Agent* absolutely supports this. Many top agents reported that they could reasonably expect to net two buyers from a well-marketed home. That's a real opportunity if done right. So many take the path of list all you can and market the best you can. They view this approach as a market share and buyer opportunity equal to a potential listing selling.

So each approach has its supporters. We have interviewed too many successful agents on either side of the argument to tell you which approach you should follow. Experience will show which strategy is best for you.

The market is what it is. Our goal is to beat the competition to the closing table before prices drop further.

Larry Bartow, Brandon, FL

A home has the most value the day it hits the market.

Mike Mendoza, Phoenix, AZ

We do believe that regardless of which approach you choose, you fundamentally always want a motivated seller. If they're not truly motivated, time has shown that neither approach will work very well for you.

SEVEN MAXIMS FOR PRICING IN A SHIFTED MARKET

1. Be a student of your market—know your numbers.
2. Focus your main comps on actives—pendings and solds may already be out of date.
3. Be a student of property—preview them so you understand what is selling and why.
4. Keep your presentation as current as possible—let your ongoing research do the talking.
5. Prequalify for motivation—sellers who most need to sell, sell most often.
6. Price ahead of the market—to avoid chasing it.
7. Always secure price reductions in advance—to avoid falling behind the market.

THE PRICE IS RIGHT

Bob Barker's *The Price Is Right* was an enduring phenomenon highlighted by his trademark call, "Come on down!" While that catch phrase might take on ominous meaning for home prices in a shifting market there is something we can learn from the longest-running game show ever—everyone loves to be a pricing expert, but very few are. The wisdom here is to be purposeful in your conversations with sellers, providing them with the necessary data and engaging them in the process of pricing their house to sell. Just like on the game show only the ones who get the price right will ever win.

TACTIC #8
STAND OUT FROM THE COMPETITION – SELLER STAGING STRATEGIES

*Opportunity is missed by most people because
it is dressed in overalls and looks like work.*

THOMAS A. EDISON

"WHAT YOU SEE IS WHAT YOU GET!" is one of the common expressions in our society. It is also the first half of one of the great truths in real estate. The other half is "and will pay for." Real estate buyers understand this and take it literally. They believe that what they see is all they get and this determines all they'll pay. The challenge sellers constantly face is that very few people have the imagination to visualize beyond what they see. Most buyers are unable to envision how a property will look when it is in its best condition—even if they could, they rarely see themselves doing it. So someone must do it for them. Smart sellers realize this and work hard to show their home in its best light. When the market shifts and fewer homes are selling savvy sellers recognize that their home must outshine the competition. They know that to make the house go it must show. They know that in a shift it's showtime!

Whenever we say price is the number one issue in getting a home sold, what we're really saying is that its price must match its condition. Price and condition are irrevocably intertwined. Priced right means priced right for what you get and overpriced means overpriced for what you get. It's that simple. Staging a home means showing off what you get in that home in the best possible way so the seller gets the best possible price. Staging a home is about dressing it up for success and highlighting its assets.

TO STAGE OR NOT TO STAGE

A seller should never ask if they should stage. This is simply the wrong type of thinking and the wrong question. The question they should ask is how should I stage? Staging is an essential part of the marketing process. It can entice buyers to take a look and perhaps get hooked on a home. This process of preparing a house to put it on the market – from simple clean-up and clean-out to extensive repairs and improvements – always directly impacts how quickly a home will sell and for what price. In a shift it may determine if it even sells at all. Staging is that important. In fact, a review of more than 2,800 properties in eight cities found that "staged homes, on average, sold in half the time that non-staged homes did. The sellers with staged homes ended up with 6.3 percent more than their asking price, on average."[4] In other words, staging helps get sellers what they want most—to sell their homes in the least amount of time for the most amount of money.

> *I tell my sellers that once they decide to sell their house, they no longer live in it—clean it up, fix it up and start packing. It needs to show like a new model home.*
>
> *Gary Gentry, Austin, TX*

The significance of staging really stands out when you consider our earlier pricing discussion and the way we select CMA comps. In finding the right price we attempt to make all the other variables equal: location,

[4]From an October 2006 *USA Today* article which cites a Coldwell Banker Residential Brokerage report.

size, amenities, and condition. The first can't be changed and the second is difficult to change. The last two can be and should be changed anytime a serious seller wants to sell. And that is what we call staging—adding cost-effective amenities and improving the condition of the home (via cleaning, painting, floor treatments, repairs, etc.). When a seller does this one of two things happens: 1) the house becomes more valuable than the other comparable properties in that price range, or 2) the house gets moved into a higher price range category where it becomes the lowest priced. In either case, the house now has a better "face" value than its competition and that is what a seller wants.

We're selling a lifestyle. Their new home must be the vision of how they want to live – not how they are living now!

Susan Murphy, Hermosa Beach, CA

BEAUTY IS IN THE EYE OF THE BUYER

Oddly enough, while almost any seller grasps the necessity and sees the logic of staging a house in a buyers' market, far fewer see the necessity of staging their home. After all, they've spent years and thousands of dollars fixing it, improving it, and filling it with all their favorite stuff. They have their own personal tastes and decorate their homes accordingly. And frankly that's how it should be. It's their home and they should have it as they please. However, the moment a house goes on the market, a seller's personal taste must go out the window. It's now time to have it as a buyer pleases. Their house must now appeal to the largest possible segment of likely buyers. In a shift, with fewer buyers to go around this becomes imperative.

TIP: A PICTURE IS WORTH A THOUSAND WORDS

One of the most effective methods to convince a seller to get on the staging bandwagon is also one of the simplest. Go out and take pictures of a cluttered closet and an uncluttered closet, a cluttered kitchen and an uncluttered one, and so on until you have the main areas of a house fairly represented. If you have before and after photos of a house that was staged, that's even better.

When it comes time to sit down with a seller pull out the photos and have the following conversation: "Mr. and Mrs. Seller, let me show you some examples of what I mean by staging....Now, let me ask you a question. All things being equal, which rooms and ultimately which home will catch the buyer's attention?" Invariably, sellers choose the pictures of the staged home to which you reply, "It's interesting. You have, in every case, selected the rooms of the home that was properly staged. I assume this means that you can see the wisdom in staging yours as well..." This is an approach people respond well to. I encourage you to think of this as a consulting session where you present the best possible information to help a seller make the best possible decision.

A buyers' market is definitely a stagers' market. Buyers are looking for a great deal, so the home they choose must look like a great deal. Buyers are looking for great value, so the home they'll choose must look like a great value. The home must look like it is worth what the seller is asking. A seller won't get a second chance to make a first impression. Sellers are in competition with more homes than they care to count and they want to come out on top. You'll have to tour these competitive listings and make note of the look, standard features, and amenities in their price range. What these houses have in common becomes the minimum buyers will expect from your seller and, if the seller truly wants to sell, they'll have to meet almost every expectation and exceed many.

Remember that in any market unless the price absolutely and completely reflects it, buyers want great-looking homes in move-in condition. This is the appeal of new homes and can't be ignored by a resale seller. It's always tough news for a seller to hear, and in a shift this can be downright painful. Cash or the equity to borrow against is usually in short supply and yet repair allowances rarely fly in a shifted market. It's hard to ask a seller to spend money on repairs and cosmetics and then ask them to take a beating on the price. But if they're going to sell they will have to execute the necessary dress up. This is about getting the house sold at the maximum price the market will bear. If the seller can't do this then they probably shouldn't sell. In the

I have shifted from rarely staging to doing it every time. Since the Internet has replaced the first showing, staging the home for the pictures is the most important marketing thing I do.

Shannon Aronson, Short Hills, NJ

end the cost of staging your home may not increase the price you get, but it may just get the house sold.

FROM CURB APPEAL TO CLOSING THE DEAL

Staging always follows the "3P – 2F Formula": plantings, paint, pictures, fixtures, and furnishings. If you follow this simple strategy and checklist you're on the right path to successful staging.

So where to begin? Good staging works a little like a great novel—it grabs you on page one and doesn't let you go until the last page. Page one for a bestseller is the view from a drive-by. So, the battle begins with curb appeal—if the house isn't appealing enough on the outside to coax them out of the car, it doesn't matter how beautiful it is on the inside. Paint and plants are the cornerstones of curb appeal and will do the trick every time. Plus the cost can be minimal so no owner should have permission to ignore them. And because this same curbside view is almost always framed at the top of every Internet listing page or promotional flier, it can make a big difference in terms of first impressions. Curb appeal can also be a magnet, attracting potential buyers to your home.

We tell our sellers they have thirty seconds to make the buyer fall in love, so their home must be staged like a model home.

Barbara Van Poole, Dallas, TX

Staging starts at the street. Look at everything from simple lawn maintenance and landscaping to trimming back trees and shrubs to create better views of the house on the outside (and possibly more light on the inside). Does the house need power washing or a fresh coat of paint? Does the roofing need to be repaired? It's amazing how much the outside of a home reflects the TLC the owner gave the interior. Sometimes you can tell a book by its cover. And whether or not it's fair that's exactly what buyers do. Poor outside appearance is, for most, the sign of poor maintenance and hidden problems. If the external appearance sends a negative message then a potential buyer will look more closely at the inside of the house, expecting to find (or possibly inventing some) problems that will prevent the house from selling.

THE "BUYER EXPERIENCE" DETERMINES STAGING PRIORITIES

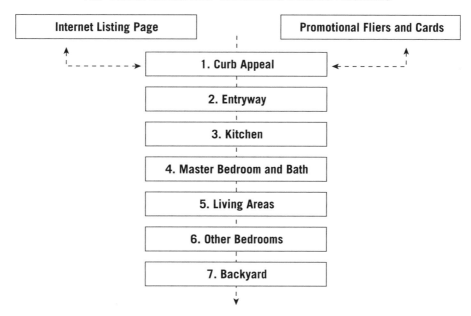

FIGURE 39 The view from the street is critical. It figures prominently into
your marketing where buyers make the decision to go see a property.
Once they're outside, it determines whether they'll get out of the car to see the inside.

From there, the drama generally unfolds along the lines of the buyer experience. They spend time at the front door, while their agent opens the lockbox, so lay out the proverbial welcome mat! Again, the "3P – 2F Formula" applies so think about it as you walk through the house to stage it. Plantings, paint, pictures, fixtures, and furnishings will be what a potential buyer sees as well as the house.

THE 3P-2F FORMULA

1. Plantings   1. Fixtures
2. Paint   2. Furnishings
3. Pictures

FIGURE 40 Prioritize these five whenever you're looking for quick cosmetic improvements in a listing for sale.

The entrance area or foyer says a lot about the house; it's the first impression of the inside so make it count. Next in priority are the areas of the house that are most important to the buyer: the kitchen, the master bedroom, and then the other bedrooms. Staging the house through these areas follows timeless wisdom. First and foremost is to make it inviting. The best stagers not only make the house look great, but also create a vision of what living in the home would be like for the buyer. From candles and place settings on the dinning room table to a good book and reading glasses on a nightstand, the goal is to show and sell the experience. Anything that would tend to dispel that vision must go. Personal items like family or wedding pictures can absolutely break the spell and are often the first things packed up. If it isn't necessary or doesn't add to the charm of the home it needs to be removed and stored for the seller's next home.

Next, clean it up and minimize the clutter. That's why job one is boxing up as much as possible. Rearrange and remove furniture to create an impression of spaciousness and a natural flow through the house. I've seen agents back up a moving truck to haul away excess furnishings. For sellers who have truly decided to sell, adopting this attitude signals a beneficial shift in attitude. The seller can psychologically "move on," packing their things, turning over ownership of the house to the future buyer and, in the process, making it much more attractive and salable. I've heard it described as hotel living and that's an accurate description. The best hotels invite guests to feel at home. The house you have listed should say the same thing to any prospective buyer.

Just remember, you don't have to be the one that does all the staging recommendations. If you can then great, but you have other options. While many agents are students of the staging game and enjoy the physical work of staging a home, many others choose to delegate it to their staff or a professional. There is no right or wrong. Since there is a cost to hiring a staging professional, most of the agents we interviewed recommended providing one or two hours of consultation as a part of their listing package (most often paid by the agent at closing should the home sell). Sellers always have the option of retaining the stager for a more extensive consultation or to coordinate the work on their own. The advantage to having a third-party staging professional is that you don't have to deliver the bad news about any obvious clutter, precious knick-knacks or favorite furniture. Either way you go you must become their partner and adviser in finding ways to accomplish the recommendations. You're their consultant and it's the market that is telling them what must be done.

I'm finding that we're getting big laundry lists from people wanting everything done to the house and if you don't do just about all of it they'll walk.

Sharon Hamilton, Santa Rosa, CA

MY FAIR LISTING

Staging accentuates the true value of a home – its notable amenities and features – and when done effectively, can actually create value. The smartest and most experienced sellers know this and welcome the opportunity to enhance the value of the home and odds of selling the home. After pricing, it's the most effective way to get a seller's house shown and sold in a shifted market. Pricing and staging are the issues of the day in a shift. Think of them as a price war

There are two priorities for your house to sell: price and pristine. If either is missing, your house will sit on the market unsold.

David Eiglarsh, Fort Lauderdale, FL

and a beauty pageant all rolled up into one. If your seller can master both issues, they'll win the battle and be crowned with a contract. You win their respect, their business, and their referrals. The truth that any seller must know is that in the end, pricing gets you in the game—staging gets you the offer.

TACTIC #9
CREATE URGENCY–
OVERCOMING BUYER RELUCTANCE

If someone is going down the wrong road, he doesn't need motivation to speed him up. He needs education to turn him around.

JIM ROHN

A BUYERS' MARKET SHOULD BE JUST THAT—a buyers' market. It's not a fence-sitting, waiting, loitering, delaying, dawdling, postponing, vacillating, hesitating, wavering, faltering, pausing, foot-shuffling market. It's a buyers' market. By its very name it means buyers should be doing one thing and one thing only—buying. So where are the buyers and why aren't they buying?

The great irony of a buyers' market is that even though the opportunity to buy is high, buyer urgency tends to hit an all-time low. The media becomes the excited purveyor of negative news and uninformed advice, and buyers buy it all. Actually, it feels like the only thing they're buying. Their reluctance is ironic since not so long ago buyers were incredibly excited about buying—and it was a sellers' market. Prices were escalating and it was perhaps one of the most difficult times to buy value and yet people were buying like there was no tomorrow. Buyers were afraid of losing out by not buying even though the advantage was all to the seller. Now a shift has occurred and it's a true buyers' market and what happens? Fear is still in the driver's seat but the tables are turned—the fear of paying too much seems to stop most in their tracks and immobilizes them.

When they should have been afraid of paying too much they weren't and now that they shouldn't be afraid of paying too much they are. It's one of the great paradoxical moments of any market and the herd instinct at its most pure. Reluctance in the face of great opportunity becomes an agonizingly defining characteristic of a shift.

THE MYTH THAT FUELS RELUCTANCE

In a shift buyers can easily lose sight of the primary reasons driving their home purchase – a different neighborhood, a better school district, proximity to work or recreation, a different floor plan, more space – and become hyperfocused on price and price alone. With so many homes for sale, too many potential buyers buy into the biggest myth of a shift— they think that they can time the market. Believing in this myth results in a false sense that the buyer has all the time in the world. This fixation on finding "the greatest deal ever" clouds their thinking and causes many to miss out on the great deals that are possible.

Buyers can't wait for headlines to say, "Buy Now." Headlines will only let you know when the best time to buy has passed.
Shaun Rawls, Atlanta, GA

There are two types of buyers in regards to timing. There are those who believe they can time the market and there are those who believe timing will find them. The ones who believe in timing believe that they can come in and out of the market and always time it to make the best possible buying and selling decisions. The ones who think the opposite believe that if you just always stay in the market then timing will simply find you. History supports the latter—it says that if you're always in the market actively paying attention, although you may never sell at the highest peak or buy at the absolute bottom, you can buy right and always do well over time. Logic says that you can't predictably time the market to be able to buy at the absolute bottom and sell at the absolute top.

Timers are waiters—those who wait for prices to come down. If the market has dropped then prices are down. Waiters will wonder if they are as low as they'll go. The problem is that no one can know this until prices are already headed back up. So, then the real question a waiter should be asking is "if prices have already significantly dropped is it safe to buy now?" You believe it is and can explain why.

A simple technique to prove to a potential buyer, or even a seller, that they can't perfectly time the market is to do this easy demonstration: Take out a blank sheet of paper and pen. Now, starting at the top of the paper, draw a line going down and at the same time ask the buyer to stop you when they know the market has bottomed out.

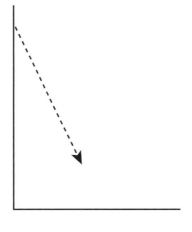

FIGURE 41

Guess what? As long as your line keeps going straight down they won't be able to. Then as you get to the bottom of the page curve the line so that it bottoms out and starts back up.

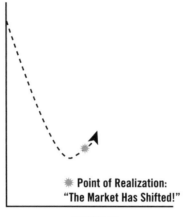

✳ Point of Realization: "The Market Has Shifted!"

FIGURE 42

Watch. The moment you start back up they'll say "there!" but of course they missed the bottom. They did and they will every time you do this presentation. Now, keep drawing your line up while asking them to tell you when the market has peaked.

✳ Point of Realization: "The Market Has Shifted!"

FIGURE 43

Again, they won't be able to tell you until you've rounded the top and started back down. Then they'll say "there!" and once again they'll be behind the peak.

Points of Realization:
"The Market Has Shifted!"

FIGURE 44

This should be a moment of truth for them. Hopefully, they now realize that the only way they'll ever know the market has bottomed is after it has started back up and the only way they'll know the market has peaked is after it has started back down.

A buyer cannot perfectly time a market—no one can. They can look at indicators that will point out the direction in which a market is going and they can absolutely mark how far it has fallen or risen, but after that the only way to know a market has bottomed or topped out is after it has. In other words perfect timing is luck. The smartest people know

Creating a Best Buy List has re-energized my team. We are finding the best deals, sharing them with the team, and letting our buyers know. It's an exciting process and now we've got some sales.

David Brownell, Las Vegas, NV

this and the smartest money never goes looking for it. They play in the safe zone.

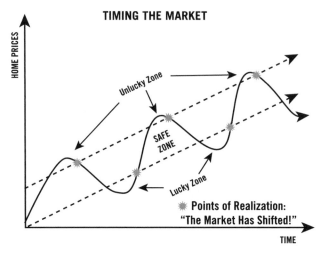

FIGURE 45 No one can perfectly time the market—but anyone can "play it safe" in the safe zone.

You know the market has bottomed out when it starts back up and you know the market has peaked when it starts back down. The safe zone is where smart people plan to buy and sell. Anyone who buys at the top of a market is just unlucky and anyone who buys at the bottom of a market is just lucky.

People who buy in a buyers' market are the smart ones. They're buying in the safe zone and living in the area of certainty. They're not unrealistic and they're not greedy. They know they can't predict the end of a bust, but they can see when a market has fallen considerably. They can't see the end or the speed at which it will climb afterward so they focus on what they can count on.

People who attempt to predict the bottom in a buyers' market are essentially undecided while wondering, "Have we hit bottom yet?" The real buyers in a buyers' market aren't trying to predict the floor but are just trying to buy smart. They aren't looking for a killing because they know that's a matter of luck not planning. They know they could just as easily miss it as hit it. They're looking for a sound decision with a predictable result and therefore ask the question: "Has the market dropped enough now to make a sensible purchase?" More often than not, when they're asking this question they are already in the safe zone and the answer is yes. These are the real buyers in a buyers' market.

UNDERSTANDING URGENCY

Understanding buyer urgency – its root cause and how to respond to a lack of it – is imperative in a shift. When buyers are more reluctant than ever to make offers and more than willing to walk away from signed contracts, you must be prepared. You must help buyers rediscover a sense of urgency.

Only buyers who are "able, ready, and willing" to buy a home ever actually buy one. Able, ready, and "waiting" may or may not. As a result, when you first meet a potential buyer the three fundamental things you want to understand are their ability, readiness, and willingness to buy now. The answers determine if they really qualify as a buyer in a shift.

The first thing you want to know is a buyer's ability to buy—their financial capacity to purchase a home in a certain price range. Second, you want to know their readiness to buy—the personal reasons that are motivating them to purchase a home. Third, you want to know their willingness to buy—their sense of urgency of when they want or need to buy a home. While all three must exist for someone to be a buyer, in a shift someone's willingness to buy is what gets your attention. You're very interested in their timeline because in a shift you can only afford to work with buyers whose time frame is now. Knowing a buyer's level of urgency is just another way of knowing their timing and just how "willing" they are to buy right now.

BUYER URGENCY

1. **ABLE**
   - Available Cash
   - Creditworthiness

2. **READY**
   - Personal Reasons

3. **WILLING**
   - Market Expectations

FIGURE 46 A buyer's ability, readiness, and willingness to buy are all directly impacted by a shift. However, of all these factors, readiness (the practical motivations and personal reasons for moving) tend to be the most "shift-proof."

Ability always comes first and is tied to factual answers to some basic questions: Do they qualify for an appropriate loan or pay cash? Do they have money for the down payment and closing costs or can they get it? These are show-stoppers for you and why a buyer's ability to buy is one of the first things you assess. Consequently, if a buyer isn't already prequalified to buy, your first job is to put them in the capable hands of a loan officer.

In a shift the availability and cost of money can also play a crucial role in a buyer's ability to buy. Tightened lending standards or higher interest rates can absolutely act like a blast of arctic air on the real estate market. At the beginning of my career, interest rates soared so high that buyers had to ask sellers to buy down interest rates by paying as many as sixteen discount points! Can you imagine? Even ready and willing buyers were often rebuffed by sellers in that market. Due to the cost of money creative financing became the only way to give buyers the ability to buy. Though not the same, after the subprime, free-lending ways of the early- to mid-2000s, mortgage lenders created another "ability" crisis for buyers. In response to the previous loose lending practices suddenly lenders tightened their lending standards. They quit offering many popular programs, asked for stricter appraisals, required higher credit scores, and even demanded more money down. In both shifts many buyers were less able to buy and some could no longer even qualify.

To counter such challenges you must find workable financing solutions and counterattack or put to rest any false ideas buyers might have about their ability to buy a home. Knowledge and a great loan officer are the keys. By teaming up with a loan officer immediately you'll not only serve the best interests of the buyer, but also increase the number of people you can help. As soon as you meet someone help them understand whether they qualify. And if they do qualify then help them find out if they can buy what they want and need.

This may be actually the best time to sell and buy. Buyers have more choices and the prices are great.

Jim McKissack, Denton, TX

Readiness is about wants and needs. It's a buyer's personal reasons for buying a home. These are the things you discover in the course of qualifying someone and doing your buyer consultation. You are determining what they want and must have in a home. Readiness always underpins a buyer's motivation. In fact, it is their motivation. It is the "why" that leads them to buy.

A buyer's personal reasons for moving, buying up, or owning instead of renting are possibly the most powerful determinants of their readiness to buy. Think of it as a spectrum. On one end you have "maybe someday" and on the other you have "right now, today!" Personal reasons tend to be the most "shift-proof." Real buyers have real wants and needs. Their wants drive them and their needs compel them.

When I was in the fourth grade my parents sold our first home and bought a larger one that was closer to our schools. Three months later we had to move again because dad took a new job that required we live in the school district where he would be working. Personal wants are powerful in their own right, but needs are the most powerful. They have to happen and thus create absolute buyers. No matter the exact reason, personal needs create buyers no matter the market.

Make your buyer prequalification and consultation time count. If you don't have a firm grasp of their personal reasons for moving you've missed out on one of the most powerful sources for reducing reluctance and reinforcing urgency. Once you understand someone's motives you can help them overcome any doubts or reluctance by reminding them of what they are going to gain by buying now.

If you show buyers what they want, they'll be motivated to buy.

Steve Cohen, Boston, MA

Willingness is simply about action. It's about a buyer mentally and emotionally making a choice about when they'll buy. A buyer can be able and ready, but if they're not willing then they're just waiting. The truth is that a shift in the market can absolutely impact a buyer's willingness, making them more wary and less eager to buy. It's the fear of making a mistake overruling the faith they can make a good decision, and it can cause even the most able and ready to become less willing to buy at that moment. The challenge is that once someone has the belief that they should wait it can be very hard for them to move off of this position. Only willing buyers buy.

In a true sellers' market buyers usually fear missing out on accelerating home values. Once a market starts to shift however, they then fear overpaying. This is troublesome since the fear of overpaying can not only make buyers reluctant to make offers but can also lead to buyer's remorse. Buyer reluctance leads to fewer contracts and buyer remorse leads to more cancellations. Some days it can truly feel like you're running up a descending escalator, exerting a lot of energy and effort with little progress to show for it—one step forward, two steps back. Willingness not only has to be there at the start of the buying process, but it has to be checked on regularly to make sure it remains intact. Just as an unwilling buyer can become willing, a willing buyer can become unwilling. This means you must be on your toes from start to finish or you could be in for a surprise.

To get willing buyers to the closing table and into their new home you will have to check in regularly with them until they move in. Don't back off and don't assume anything. Don't take your willing buyer for granted. Touch base regularly and often. Head off any issues you see coming. Willing buyers buy into the process every step of the way. Everyone else has to be continually reenergized and recommitted to get to the closing table. Willingness in a shift is a precious thing. Nurture it, support it, and appreciate it.

Buyers can easily become paralyzed in a shift. Too much information, too many choices, and too many opinions can cause confusion and fear. Able and ready buyers become confused about what to do and afraid to make a mistake. Instead of stepping up and being willing to buy, they back off and try to wait the market out. You must help people find confidence and clarity if they are to become willing buyers.

All of this—buyer ability, readiness, and willingness—add up to one key decision for you: are they worth investing your time, money, and effort when all those resources are already stretched? In a shift, you'll want to think of this as a simple yes or no question; either they are able, ready and willing or they aren't. There are no shades of gray. Buyers who are willing have a sense of urgency. Buyers who aren't willing are reluctant. You want to avoid the reluctant and you want to work with the urgent. If you can't help a buyer overcome their reluctance today it may be better to drop them into your cultivation program and check back with them another day. Your focus must be on the motivated. While it's true you can't motivate a buyer, you can "motive-aid" them. There are proven ways you can educate buyers on the market, support their tapping into their personal reasons for moving, and help them overcome their fears in order to rally them to become buyers now.

{
THREE WAYS TO ENERGIZE BUYER URGENCY
1. Become the Local Economist of Choice
2. Help Them Tap Into Their Why
3. Address Buyer Reluctance
}

1) BE THE LOCAL ECONOMIST OF CHOICE

I once heard someone laughingly say, "Some of my best thinking was done by other people." I don't know about the "best" part of this, but unfortunately, when it comes to buying real estate in a shift I do believe that most buyers are letting others do too much of their thinking for them. These other people might include family, friends, and the media. On one hand, there's nothing wrong with this. A lot of good information can come from these sources. On the other hand, if these are the only real estate information sources people are using then they're not getting the entire story.

So what's missing? Expert advice. While we read and ask people for information and advice on a variety of subjects, when we need specific information and opinions to make serious decisions we seek a professional. From health issues to diagnosing our car's engine woes, we invariably put the most weight on the information and opinion of a trained professional who specializes in a specific area. Right? Absolutely. So why not real estate as well? Because everyone, including the media, thinks they're an expert!

Buyers need professional advice in a shift more than ever. The challenge is that most don't realize it. They've read the newspapers and magazines, listened to the news, talked to some friends and family members, and formed an opinion. So far so good. The problem is that more than likely, they've not gotten the entire story about the market or how to approach it. They believe they are fully informed, but they're not. The media rarely tells the whole story and most people have limited experience. As a result, buyers are either half-informed or misinformed. And either is dangerous because they lead to decisions that are poorly formed. So what can you do? Become the professional voice they listen to. Become their economist of choice.

Buyers bring their ability and readiness to buy to the market. So what are they getting from others? Some knowledge and some instruction, but mostly economic and market perspective. It's usually these opinions by others that steal away a buyer's willingness and this is where you can provide a valuable service. By providing useful information and a balanced perspective you can create more willing buyers. Most people allow their level of willingness to be greatly impacted by the perception others have about the market. Your goal is to round out their economic understanding and market knowledge so they have the complete picture.

> *If you want to be the best buyer's agent, know every home for sale in your marketplace.*
> Brad Korn, Kansas City, MO

Willingness lives in a buyer's market expectations. Notice, I didn't write market realities. Expectations are what drive willingness. They can be fact based, but tend to be more emotion based. A buyer's sense of the market can become a tailwind that drives them forward or a headwind that stops them cold. Some people look like buyers because they are able and ready to buy, but then you find out that instead of willing to buy they're waiting. Their perception of the market, wherever they got it from, is that they should wait.

If you are to reach your sales goals in a shift, you must develop a strategy for returning your buyers to reason and confidence. You must help them understand that this is a good time to buy—not because it benefits you, but because it benefits them. You start by influencing their rational thinking with numbers and facts. If you don't do this, you'll never get a chance to address any emotional resistance they may have built up.

Find every way possible to overcome the media-driven real estate malaise. Be the one with the facts. Challenge yourself to become the "local real estate economist of choice" for any potential buyer you meet. Educate them that real estate is a cyclical business. All of this has happened before and it will happen again. What goes up must come down. More important, what goes down has always come back up. Home values will most certainly continue their long-standing trend of appreciation over time. At the very least inflation will see to that. And equity buildup through mortgage debt paydown still remains a proven path to financial wealth.[5] You will have to constantly educate and remind buyers of these economic certainties.

The extreme mobility of buyers today has led to some unrealistic expectations that surface in a shift. It is a case of people wanting to bend market reality to reflect their mobile lifestyle. Somehow, people have been led to believe that they can buy and sell every three to five years and make a killing on both ends. This economic idea is quite unrealistic. Any successful real estate investor will tell you that real wealth comes from the combination of any appreciation plus debt pay down. And for home buyers this can be further enhanced by any available tax advantages for homeownership. While it is often possible to buy good value (or "make your money going in"), not every home sale results in a windfall. When my parents sold their first home they lost money. They did it anyway. Why? They wanted another home.

As an expert you can teach buyers about realistic economic expectations. They can't sell high and buy low at the same time. If they sell

---

[5] If you're unsure how this conversation goes, let *The Millionaire Real Estate Investor* be your guide. Unlike many other books on investing in real estate, it stresses the stable, realistic, and proven path to wealth.

and then buy during a sellers' market, they will get more when they sell and then pay more when they buy. When they sell and then buy in a buyers' market, they will get less from their sale, but be able to make it up with greater savings when they buy. In the end, home ownership is best viewed as a long-term investment just like the stock market or any other sound investment. Short-term buying will always put anyone at the mercy of the market. The biggest gains are made from holding over longer periods of time, not constantly buying and selling in the short term. Buyers should know that buying the family home and playing the market are two entirely different things.

As an agent and local real estate economist you must communicate the economic and market facts to buyers every chance you get. In your newsletter, on your Web site or blog, in your marketing pieces and advertising, continuously communicate local market statistics, financial information, and economic facts. Give a historical perspective as well as a current one. Offset a national perspective with a local one. Show buyers the local market information—your area's job growth, population growth, household income increases, and the factual decline in area home values. Share current interest rates and financing options. In a buyers' market, the presentation of these facts generally adds up to a powerful argument to buy now. In fact, you will regularly point out how this translates into a buying opportunity that, once gone, most likely won't come back until the next cycle. And then it will be at higher prices. It's your job to help buyers understand this.

The key here is to not appear to be self-serving or simply offering up your own opinions. Cite independent sources and quote experts. Often the same articles that create a gloomy outlook for sellers report real market statistics that can prove it is an opportune time for buyers. If the local real estate section interprets a decline in local prices as creating risk, you can use those same stats to make your case that it is a great time to buy value or trade up.

Market expectations are a powerful source of motivation for buyers and you want to be the one setting these expectations. It is unlikely that anyone giving your buyers advice – whether from a national columnist, a coworker, and even family – knows as much as you know about the local market. You are the research-based expert; you are the trusted adviser.

Finally, share the success stories of people who recently made the decision to buy and are very happy that they followed through with their purchase. I can't overstate the importance of collecting and sharing these authentic personal stories. By sharing them, it will give a buyer reassurance both that it's okay to buy and that others are

I believe every agent on my team must wake up with the goal of finding and motivating buyers. We need to convince them of the incredible opportunities this market offers.
Russell Rhodes, Dallas, TX

in fact doing it. The market isn't dead or dormant and they need to see that. Also, realize that it's only natural for buyers to be a little skeptical when you are telling them "it's a good time to buy." Show them they're not alone by backing up your sound advice with credible success stories.

When the market shifts you must become more than just a real estate salesperson to a buyer. You must actually become their local market authority, the real estate expert they know and trust so that anything they hear about real estate, they will filter through your advice. Be their local economist of choice.

2) TAP INTO THEIR WHY

At the end of the day, nothing trumps a buyer's personal motivations and reasons for moving. Compelling personal motives guide people through their lives and sit at the heart of their biggest decisions. Buying a home is no different. There are some pretty big and important reasons attached to buying a home. The list can be as long and varied as you can imagine. People move because....now you finish the sentence. What did you choose? A new job, a new baby, a new marriage, retirement, being closer to family or certain places, a divorce, a death, a bright vision of a new life elsewhere? Tapping into someone's list of reasons is getting them in touch with their heart as well as their head. Invariably, a factual reason for buying has an emotional string attached to it. Tapping into someone's why is helping them find that string and pulling it so that the heart sits equally with the head. Whatever the reason, I've learned that these internal motivations are among the most powerful of all. So, especially in a shift, you must tap into their reasons for moving.

The best way to get to understand a client's motivation is to ask personal questions. *Why are you thinking about buying? Really, tell me more. Now, what will that do for you? What will that mean for your family?* When you have their answer, you must keep it on the tip of your tongue and at the top of their mind. It is the central topic that defines all of your conversations.

In our book, *Your First Home,* I tell the story of Steve and Denise. Their story happened in a true buyers' market. They were getting married so we met to discuss them buying their very first home. As we visited

I drew a line down the middle of a sheet of paper and wrote "wants" on one side and "needs" on the other. I then had them share with me all their wants and needs for their first home. High interest rates had made it a buyers' market, but since their price range was low for the area where they wanted to live I was having trouble finding even one house to show them. As luck would have it the day we were to look at houses the perfect home for them, right in their chosen area, came on the market. We were the very first buyers to go through it and as we got back to the front door I almost had a heart attack when I heard Denise say to Steve "and just think, this is the first one we've seen." I asked them to sit on the couch right there in the home. Then I pulled out their wants and needs sheet we had done together, handed it to them and said "this home has everything you want and everything you need, right?" They quickly went through it and agreed. Then I said "if you leave here without buying this home, it will be gone. The very next buyer who walks in will buy this house and it will be gone forever. Can you live with that?" They bought it on the spot and never regretted it.

Talking about personal wants and needs is not manipulation. It's simply reminding people what they want to buy and why. I actually consider it my fiduciary duty. I've learned that in life it's much better to be able to say "I'm glad I did" rather than "I wish I had." I believe it. In fact, I know it's a lesson to live by and it has guided me well in advising my customers. And I've had countless notes, letters, calls and conversations (sometimes many years later) with buyers who thanked me for reminding them why they were looking—for helping them overcome their doubts. Cold feet can lead to regrets. Reluctance can translate into remorse. Believe me, those aren't the memories you'll cherish as a professional. On the other hand, you will cherish the emotional thank-you's from clients who are so happy that you helped them overcome their fears and get into a home they love. In the end, your buyers must make the decision. Your job is to help them make the best decision for their family and their circumstances. And, often, that will require you to tap into their motivations and keep them tapped into it from the first time you meet all the way through closing.

3) OVERCOME BUYER RELUCTANCE

When people have a good reason to buy—they do just that. Except in a shift. When the market changes it can throw people off balance. They were going along with their life and then the market tosses a wrench into the engine driving their decisions. All of a sudden they're not sure of themselves and are hesitant to move forward. They want and may even need to buy, but yet they hold back. It's frustrating for you and it's frustrating for them. They need someone to intervene and help them overcome their reluctance. They need someone to show them that it's okay and give them permission to buy now.

In the end, you are being the highest level of fiduciary when you don't let should-be buyers cave-in to their sense that it is better to wait. The reality that people must face is that their expectations may be faulty. Reluctant buyers clearly think that prices will go lower. That will certainly be true for overpriced houses in any market and might even be true for all of the houses in this market. But if prices have already significantly dropped then the best homes may not go much lower. So unless they're a psychic or a gambler, it's time to buy.

Since no one can predict the market and prices have already dropped considerably, waiting any longer no longer really makes any sense. Test this with any buyer. Ask them the question: "Do you think that prices have dropped?" They'll answer, "Yes." Next ask, "Do you think they'll ever go back up?" Again, they'll say, "Yes, eventually." Then ask, "So, aren't you then saying that it's actually okay to be out buying again?" They're caught and may or may not answer. That's okay. Go ahead and ask them one last question: "Given how you feel, if we found the home today that met all your needs and your most important wants, is there any reason why you wouldn't make an offer to purchase that home today?" Pause and add one last thing: "Sellers are in the same situation you're in. They also know prices will come back up some day, but they don't know when. Genuine sellers want to or need to sell now, but they have fears too. They don't know if prices will go lower either so if they can sell today they will. That means they are ready to deal because they're afraid today might be the best price they get. This makes most very willing to consider all reasonable offers."

The problem with a buyer waiting for the market to get better is that by the time they realize it has, it will be too late and they will be competing for their dream home with multiple offers.

Ron Young, Bluebell, PA

Once the market settles or shows any sign of improvement, opportunities start slipping away. The very moment sellers no longer have to make concessions they won't. And, since there is almost always group-think at play with all of the waiting buyers, the pent-up demand will show back up and buyers may be faced with mounting competition for the best homes available.

This is a great time to use the "Tale of Two Markets" graphs we shared on pages 149 to 154 in *Tactic #7: Price Ahead of the Market.* Homes that are priced well and in good condition are always the first to sell. Aren't these the very homes your buyers would want to purchase? Of course they are, but to do that they will have to get off the sidelines, stop being spectators, and get out into the market.

This is the time to put your sales skills to work. A buyers' market is a skill-based market and you are best served to practice your scripts, find a coach, engage in regular role-play with a partner, and get familiar with the proven best practices for helping your buyers make good decisions. Let's take a look at four classic strategies for helping buyers overcome their reluctance. Just as your consultation is designed to identify and assess a buyer's ability and readiness to buy, careful consultation can also help initiate a buyer's willingness to buy.

FOUR STRATEGIES TO OVERCOME BUYER RELUCTANCE

1.   Why Wait?—The Hazards of Timing the Market
2.   Trade Up—The Opportunity of a Down Market
3.   Less Is More—Narrowing the Field
4.   Find a Best Buy—Get While the Gettin's Good

WHY WAIT?—THE HAZARDS OF TIMING THE MARKET

Buyers who choose to wait "until prices come down more" are also gambling that interest rates will hold steady or drop. What is not widely understood is the impact interest rates can have on the real monthly costs of homeownership. Even a 10 percent drop in home prices is immediately nullified by a mere 1 percentage point increase in interest rates on a 30-year mortgage loan. By the way, this relationship between interest rates and home pricing remains essentially the same at any price point.

BUY NOW OR WAIT?	**SCENARIO 1:** Home prices decrease by 5% Interest rates increase by 0.5%	**SCENARIO 2:** Home prices decrease by 10% Interest rates increase by 1.0%
Home Price $200,000	**Home Price: -5%** $190,000	**Home Price: -10%** $180,000
Interest Rate 6.0%	**Interest Rate: + 0.5%** 6.5%	**Interest Rate: + 1.0%** 7.0%
Payment $1,199	**Payment** $1,201	**Payment** $1,198

FIGURE 47 Even a slight increase in mortgage interest rates can offset a significant drop in home prices. There is little to gain in this scenario and much to lose if home prices rebound or rates jump.

You want your buyers to avoid trying to time the market. Not only does it almost never work, but it certainly can't be done from the sidelines. They have to be in the market to take advantage of the market.

TRADE UP—THE OPPORTUNITY OF A DOWN MARKET

Many of your buyers will also be selling a home—they're actually feeling the buyers' market from both sides. It's only natural they focus on the impact of the current market on the sale of their house, the fact that they will likely get a lower sales price than in the recent past, rather than

Figure 47 is available as a free download at www.MillionaireSystems.com/shift.

the opportunity that selling will give them to buy. If they are planning on trading up, you will need to highlight how saving on the larger home purchase will offset any loss on the sale their current house.

A BUYERS' MARKET IS A TRADING-UP MARKET!

If home prices dropped by 5%, here's what it could look like if you decided to trade up:

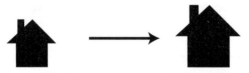

Home Price = $200,000
Sell at $190,000 = *$10,000 Loss*

Home Price = $400,000
Buy at $380,000 = *$20,000 Savings*

The smaller loss at sale will be compensated by greater savings at purchase, resulting in a significant net gain.

FIGURE 48 Falling home prices are a great opportunity for a savvy homeowner looking to move up. Even though your home sale price may be lower, the smaller loss at sale can be compensated by greater savings at purchase.

This kind of trade-up is often the exact same strategy employed by successful real estate investors. When you buy a larger and better home, you are saving more on the purchase than you may have lost on the sale of your previous home, and the new home is often better positioned for appreciation when the market rebounds. If we take the homes in Figure 48, and the market were to rebound in subsequent years and appreciate by 10 percent, the larger home would go up in value by $38,000 while the smaller home only grew by $19,000. My wife Mary and I systematically traded up our homes, each time focusing on buying a greater value than we were leaving behind. Each move, over time, helped us improve our net worth and accelerate the growth rate of our financial bottom line. It's a proven strategy and one of the best opportunities of a shift. In fact, on average over 60 percent of the average individual's net worth is in their home. Make sure your move-up buyers understand this.

Figure 48 is available as a free download at www.MillionaireSystems.com/shift.

LESS IS MORE—NARROWING THE FIELD

One of the challenges for buyers in a shift is simply that there are too many choices. When home inventories rise from a few thousand to ten thousand or more, buyers may show some superficial interest but have an extremely difficult time getting serious. It can begin to feel like they're looking for a needle in a haystack or searching for a diamond in the rough. Research backs the notion that "too much of a good thing" is both mentally exhausting and ultimately unproductive.

Barry Schwartz, psychologist and author of *The Paradox of Choice: Why More Is Less,* states "there's a point where all of this choice starts to be not only unproductive, but counterproductive—a source of pain, regret, worry about missed opportunities and unrealistically high expectations." One study by researchers at Columbia University and Stanford University empirically proved the downside of excessive choice. They chose jams and jellies for their study, and most of us know why. It's not uncommon to find half an aisle devoted to every flavor under the sun and plenty of artificial ones too. This team showed that buyers tend to show more interest in a larger assortment but had a much harder time deciding on one to actually purchase. In fact, buyers were ten times more likely to buy if they chose among six than among twenty-four flavors. The best retailers have taken this kind of research to the bank.

Apple famously mocked up an entire store inside a warehouse and brought in focus group after focus group until they had created the ideal space to highlight their computer and digital lifestyle wares. After just a few years in the retail business, their stores sold an average of almost $4,500 per square foot—far outpacing traditional retail powerhouses like Best Buy, Tiffany & Co., and Neiman Marcus. Why? If you've ever experienced their stores, you understand that this is a company that mastered the art of presentation and narrowing the field to a few choices.

So what does this mean for you? Your job is to help your buyers narrow the field. This is hands-on, personal consultation time. If their search criteria are yielding dozens, even hundreds of potential homes, science tells us they are likely to be overwhelmed, shut down or, worse, make a poor "first good choice" kind of decision. You must either pre-sort their choices or sit with them and patiently help them sort the stack. The goal is a handful of great choices.

LESS IS MORE — NARROW THE FIELD!

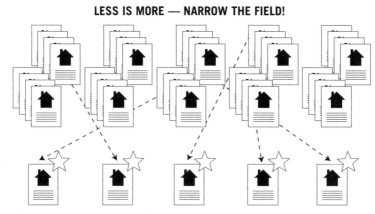

When you help buyers reduce the choices, you'll find they are able to choose.

FIGURE 49 Winnowing the selection down from many good selections to a few great ones is hard work—and your buyers need your help. Careful and personal consultation will help them identify the best options for them and they will thank you for it.

Take the discards and physically tear them up. Drop them in the trash can. Make the point that those homes are no longer under consideration. The few that remain are the best options and these are the homes you will tour with your buyers. Each one potentially represents a great match and now they must choose from a few. Less is more! Do the same kind of sorting and filtering as you look at homes. Have them compare the current home being viewed with the others they have looked at and remove those that are not in the running. There should never be more than five or so homes that are under consideration at any one time. The best agents understand the benefit of this step-by-step selection process. They know it helps the customer decide, it speeds up the home search and it makes their work with buyers more efficient. They make this their standard practice and, in a shift, so must you.

FIND A BEST BUY—GET WHILE THE GETTIN'S GOOD

One aspect of the "less is more" theme that can help you overcome buyer reluctance is a "Best Buy List." This is a list you have compiled of the current best buys in the market. It will be based on your consistent tracking of new listings, price reductions, and pre-foreclosure or foreclosed properties. It will be one of the most useful outcomes of your daily previewing of homes.

Agents have typically used market knowledge to advise sellers on pricing. When they are working on getting a listing they research comparables to help the seller understand what the house will likely sell for. What is interesting is that agents rarely do this for buyers. So, this becomes a great opportunity to continually pull buyers into the home buying process plus it might actually help you stand out from the competition. A Best Buy List actually becomes your unique intellectual property and a powerful magnet for people to work with you.

"For access to my Best Buy List, updated daily, register now (or call now)" is a provocative and attention-getting statement. It is a powerful offer-response you can use in both your marketing and prospecting. It just might be the most effective indirect offer you make. It is a reason for them to want to work with you. It is a reason for them to get off their reluctance and respond.

Another great benefit of a Best Buy List is that it can create additional buyer urgency. "Hi Tom, a home just hit my Best Buy List that could be exactly what you and Sarah are looking for. I'm not sure if it is even still available, but if it is could we set a time as soon as possible to go see it?"

Here's the point: you can't create urgency if there isn't a good reason for it and you certainly can't fake it. Buyers can see through false optimism and manipulative selling techniques almost every time. And, when they see it, they lose faith in you and the market. You must find real, honest, and compelling ways to help them feel optimistic about the market and comfortable with you as their expert guide.

OPPORTUNITY TIME

Markets always favor one sector or another. An up market favors a seller and a down market favors a buyer. They're characterized by the opportunities that define them. A sellers' market is a good time to sell and a risky time to buy. In a buyers' market only serious sellers sell, so all buyers are in a favorable position. The type of market indicates who has the advantage.

Reluctance is about unwillingness. Some will come right out and tell you they're waiting. Others won't, but you'll feel the unwillingness anyway. It'll show up as lingering, lagging, and delays. People reluctant to buy or sell will allow time to pass and so miss opportunities. Their actions will speak louder than any words possibly could. Either way they're missing out on the next big sale and it's your job to see that they don't.

At the end of the day, building buyer urgency is about expert knowledge of the market, careful consultation on their personal wants and needs, skill at communicating the opportunities of the market, and assertiveness in challenging their thinking. You are the dedicated professional they hired to help them make good decisions and take the right actions. Earn the right to be that person and have the courage to act on what you know to be true. More people will thank you, more people will refer you to others, and you will execute more sales. Creating urgency is a learned skill. And, once learned, it will create new opportunities for you and for your buyers. Just remember—the first urgency must be yours.

TACTIC #10
EXPAND THE OPTIONS –
CREATIVE FINANCING

Money talks and often says, "Goodbye."

UNKNOWN

AFFORDABILITY DRIVES THE REAL ESTATE INDUSTRY. In fact, you might even say that affordability is the real estate industry. Buyers must be able to buy in order for sellers to be able to sell. As simplistic as this sounds, it's equally that important. Affordability is the juice that makes the market go or stop. When it's up, the market goes up. When it's down, the market goes down. If you want to know where the market is headed just check how affordable a house is. There's your thermometer and it's extremely accurate. What market you're in or headed toward is easily gauged by one thing—affordability.

When I got in the business in 1979 and interest rates topped 18 percent, about the only way you could buy or sell a home was with lots of creativity. Affordability, driven by high interest rates, was unraveling and making sales tough to come by. Making any sale work was a challenge and we engaged daily in a game of "how can we make this deal work?" It was game-like in that it rewarded those who thought competitively and strategically. Like a mystery to sort out, a riddle to solve, or a code to decipher. Those who solved the riddle could then transact business, while everyone else watched from the sidelines. In a shift, finding creative ways to help buyers afford to buy and sellers afford to sell is the game you must learn to play and win—or buying and selling literally slows down to a crawl.

CREATIVE FINANCING

This is the term we use to describe creative ways to resolve affordability challenges. Every buyer is unique and every seller is unique. Every lender is unique. And then along comes the economy and the market itself, creating the unique environment in which these three parties must do business. All of this means one thing—if the conditions warrant creative deals but you aren't able to put these deals together then you could be done doing many deals.

Unfortunately, creative financing isn't well understood by most and as a result, sometimes gets a bad rap. But it's far too valuable a vehicle to abandon just because a few misbehaving individuals have misused this critical real estate consulting tool. In a shifting market you will often need all the legal, sound, historically proven financing solutions at your disposal to get some tough transactions closed. As a real estate sales consultant, your buyers and sellers expect you to educate them about all the financial options they might have to create the best win-win transaction possible. So, when the market shifts it's time to bring out the creative financial ideas and expand everyone's opportunities.

Sometimes a buyer easily falls within the standard guidelines of traditional home financing and sometimes they don't. When they do, it means they have the necessary down payment and income qualifications for a loan at the current interest rates and lending programs being offered. And if it happens to be a sellers' market, then the burden is usually completely on the buyer to figure out a way to buy a house. Houses in an upward shift usually sell without any need for creativity from anyone.

A shift can change all of this. In a shift downward not many houses are selling, so if sellers still want to sell they may have to employ creative financing. If a buyer falls outside of the standard guidelines of down payment and

FHA, VA, rural loans, and down payment grants are back—it is time to re-educate ourselves and our clients.

Ben Kinney, Bellingham, WA

qualifications for traditional financing programs then it's time to bring in the creativity to see if there is some way to help the buyer and seller put a sale together.

To make creative financing work you will do three things. First, you'll have to be clear about what buyers, sellers, and lenders want. Specifically, what each individually wants, and generally, what each of them always wants. Second, you'll want to be well-versed on what each of them can do creatively to put a sale together. Each one has a time-proven list of options they can consider to make the sale work. And last, you'll need to be creative in making all of this work at one time. Creative financing is a combination of knowledge and skill. To find success you must understand each party's motives, learn the choices available to each, and then you must creatively suggest solutions.

THE THREE AREAS OF CREATIVE FINANCING

Think of creative financing as getting outside the box to create more choices when more choices are necessary. At its most basic level creative financing is looking at more options than are used in typical financing and transactions. It is actually a checklist to consider with additional things to mull over before declaring a deal dead. It's really a combination of thinking outside the box and inside the deal.

In any creative transaction there are essentially three players who can participate: the seller who owns the house, the buyer who wants to buy it, and the lender who approves the necessary loan on the transaction. To give everyone a fighting chance to do business, you can discuss with each player the creative financing solutions that any one of them can bring to the table to get the deal done.

THE THREE AREAS OF CREATIVE FINANCING

Creative Things Sellers Can Do to Sell Their House	**Creative Things Buyers Can Do to Purchase a Home**	**Creative Things Lenders Can Do to Finance a Transaction**
1. Seller Contributions 2. Seller-Funded Permanent Buydown 3. Seller-Funded Temporary Buydown 4. Owner Financing 5. Contract for Deed 6. Seller Second 7. Lease Option and Lease Purchase 8. Wraparound and Assumable Mortgage	1. Gift Funding 2. Selling and Refinancing Existing Assets 3. Non-Occupant Co-Borrowers 4. Using a 401(k) 5. Temporary IRA Transfer 6. Pledged Asset Mortgage 7. Equity Transfer and Bridge Loan 8. Employer-Assisted Mortgage	1. Lender-Funded Buydown 2. Fannie Mae's "MyCommunityMortgage" 3. Running Scenarios with Automated Underwriting Systems 4. Adjusting Amortization Period to Lower Payment 5. Adjusting Interest Rates to Cover Closing Costs 6. State, Province, and Local Grant or Bond Programs 7. Mortgage Credit Certificate 8. Private Lending

FIGURE 50 All three players—the seller, buyer, and lender—can bring creative solutions to the table to get a house sold.

The basic financial terms of any real estate transaction are the offer amount, down payment, loan amount, interest rate, and length (or term) of the mortgage loan. Since the very first real estate transaction ever, creative individuals have been tinkering with these variables to get houses sold and closed. The twenty-four options presented in Figure 50 may be the most common, but they barely scratch the surface of what's possible. A seller buydown could be combined with a buyer's gift fund along with a bond program offered through the lender to sell a house. A buyer using a non-occupant co-borrower could negotiate a seller second in addition to an owner-financed primary loan or a conventional loan. At the end of the day, you can put together just about any combination so long as the terms are legal, all three parties agree, and everything is properly disclosed. The greater your awareness of the viable options, the more creative solutions you can offer to make the transaction work.

Creative financing begins with simply knowing where the bottom line sits for seller, buyer, or lender. You must first know what everyone wants before you can suggest creative ways to get there. What is each party most interested in accomplishing in any given transaction? Sellers are most often driven by price: *What will I net on this sale?* Buyers are most likely to be interested in terms: *How much will I have to put down, pay per month, and pay over the life of the loan?* And lenders always keep their eye on managing risk and achieving returns: *How can I structure a loan that both minimizes the chances of default and maximizes our interest rate?* With this general insight, plus a clear understanding of each party's specific needs you're ready to explore the creative financing solutions that might work and meet the needs of everyone involved in a particular transaction.

1) CREATIVE THINGS SELLERS CAN DO TO SELL THEIR HOUSE

Motivated sellers have several cards to play if they truly want to sell their houses in a slow market. David Reed, a long-time mortgage professional and author[6], teaches that "Sellers need to remember that buyers have to overcome three essential barriers to buy a house: they have to have the income, the assets, and the credit to qualify for a mortgage in a lending environment with increased standards and scrutiny. Sellers can assist with all three." In other words, sellers have the ability to help buyers who don't have the income to qualify for a loan amount, who don't have enough down payment funds available, or who may have less than perfect credit. And the dollar amount sellers would be willing to reduce their sales price by might actually translate to a greater buyer incentive when offered as a creative financing solution. It's always worth considering. The conversation alone will validate you in the eyes of any seller.

AREA ONE: CREATIVE THINGS SELLERS CAN DO TO SELL THEIR HOUSE

1. Seller Contributions
2. Seller-Funded Permanent Buydown
3. Seller-Funded Temporary Buydown
4. Owner Financing
5. Contract for Deed
6. Seller Second
7. Lease Option and Lease Purchase
8. Wraparound and Assumable Mortgage

FIGURE 51 Get together with your financing team and get familiar with these creative financing solutions for sellers.

Probably the most common solution comes in the form of seller contributions. Sometimes called "seller concessions," these can include paying for buyer closing costs or even conveying personal items in the transaction (from leaving the media room fully equipped to passing along kitchen appliances). When we were researching *The Millionaire Real Estate Investor* we heard a story about a seller who couldn't get a refurbished starter home sold until he included his old BMW. A clever ad with the

---

[6] David Reed is the author of several books on financing including *An Agent's Guide to Financing Solutions: 29 Legal, Proven Ways to Get the Deal Closed in a Shifted Market* (Keller Williams University, 2008).

tag line "shelter and transportation for one low price" got him the offer he was after. More commonly, your seller will either advertise they are willing to pay some or all of the closing costs or agree to a buyer's request for it in negotiations. One may attract an offer and the other might make an offer turn into a sale. Either way works.

Most lenders limit seller closing-cost contributions to between 3 percent and 9 percent of the sales price depending on how much the buyer pays as a down payment; however, just be aware that if a seller pays more than 6 percent, it could likely effect the appraisal. Also, as a side note, remember that anytime a buyer adds any dollars to the sales price which increases the mortgage amount they are also increasing their monthly payment. Here's how the math works.

SELLER CONTRIBUTION VS. SELLER PRICE REDUCTION

	Pay $5,000 of Closing Costs	Reduce Price by $5,000
Sales Price	$250,000	$245,000
Down Payment 5%	$12,500	$12,250
Closing Costs	$0	$5,000
Total Out of Pocket	$12,500	$17,250
Net to Seller	$245,000	$245,000
Loan Amount	$237,500	$232,750
Monthly Payment (30 years at 6.5%)	$1,501	$1,471

FIGURE 52 While the seller nets the same amount, the buyer is trading a $30 per month increase in payments for $5,000 in closing costs. They are essentially financing part or all of their closing costs.

Saving enough money to buy a home is a challenge for most home buyers, so seller contributions to closing costs can make a home purchase more achievable. Even if the buyer can afford to pay the whole amount the savings allows them to make immediate improvements to the home instead of waiting and saving for them. The price for that convenience in this example is thirty dollars a month. This could be a source of money a buyer never thought of and might consider.

Next on the list is the seller buydown. This is where the seller buys down the interest rate on the buyer's mortgage loan for the life of the loan (a permanent buydown) or for the first few years (a temporary buydown). When interest rates are low, this tactic is too often overlooked. Nevertheless buydowns can be effective tools for closing the deal. For example, a seller could pay about $5,000 to permanently buy down a 30-year note on a $250,000 loan from 6 percent to 5.5 percent (that's two points—two percent of the loan amount). While that only translates to about $70 in savings on the monthly principal and interest payments, it can save a buyer much more in interest paid over the life of the loan. In this example, a $5,000 buydown translates to almost $30,000 in interest savings over the 30-year life of the loan.

We launched our real estate business in the late 80's and early 90's with creative financing. The opportunity of those strategies has returned.

Don and Ryan Zeleznak, Phoenix, AZ

Marketing the buydown can be tricky. Do you market it as an interest rate buydown or on the total savings? It's your call. A word of caution—be very careful whenever marketing something like this. Work with a loan officer to verify your numbers based on their current rates and an expected offer price and down payment. And always follow all disclosure laws that apply to such advertising. You may find this doesn't have to be a way to advertise or market the property as much as an idea you suggest and work through with buyers and their agents should they show interest in your seller's house.

If the sellers own their home free and clear they have another excellent option—owner financing. Sellers with no mortgage can consider turning their equity into a monthly check using the house as collateral. This was very common when I got started in real estate. At that time any sales professional worth their salt could structure a solid owner-financed contract. The key is to make sure the sellers exercise their proper due diligence. For various reasons many potential buyers suffer from less-than-perfect credit. The seller simply has to determine the facts on why their credit suffered. Others may have unverified income from a personal business that isn't established enough to count towards a conventional loan (lenders usually require a two- to three-year track record). These buyers will see owner financing as a big incentive to buy. And, they might even consider it a reason to pay a higher price.

The sellers can benefit as well. Not only can they sell their house and literally move on with their lives, but they can also earn a solid return on their loan. Most private loans carry higher interest rates to offset the risk. And if the seller thinks they will need the money in a few years they can require that the buyer refinance the loan in order to pay off the seller's note. A good deal structured around a two, three or five-year balloon private mortgage will get the buyers in, earn the sellers extra income, and facilitate the buyer eventually qualifying for a conventional loan when the note comes due.

Contract for deed works just like owner financing with one extremely important exception—ownership doesn't change hands until the entire sales price is paid in full. With a conventional home purchase or in an owner financing deal, title gets conveyed up-front. Contract for deed is more like an automobile loan where the car belongs to the buyer only after all payments have been made. It was a contract for deed that helped put my sisters and me through Baylor University.

My father had bought a second house with some land across the road from my aunt and grandmother in Lake Conroe outside Houston, Texas. When it came time to sell, dad sold it on a contract for deed with very little down and monthly payments. A few years later the buyer defaulted and abandoned the property. Real estate prices had gone up quite a bit in that period of time so my father was actually okay with getting it back. So he raised the price considerably and soon sold it again using a contract for deed. Well, a few years later this buyer also defaulted and left the property. Real estate prices had continued to skyrocket so dad wasn't at all unhappy about having to take the property back. Once again, he raised the price significantly and sold it on another contract for deed. And believe it or not, this buyer soon defaulted as well. By this point, my father told me, he was feeling really bad for this buyer and so they simply worked the payments out so they could keep the property and Dad could be paid.

Another avenue of creative financing is the seller second. This is shorthand for a secondary or "subordinate" loan made by the seller. The primary loan (conventional or private) sits first in line for repayment in the event of a default, which increases the risk. But like any second loan, the interest rates are usually higher to compensate for the increased risk. These are often called a "seller carryback." Seller seconds are invaluable. Properly disclosed seller seconds can help buyers avoid private mortgage interest (PMI). Seller seconds can also benefit the buyer by allowing for a smaller down payment, lower monthly payments, or even avoiding higher interest rates on a jumbo loan. Let's take a closer look at how a seller second can help a buyer avoid PMI and lower their monthly payment.

A CLOSER LOOK AT SELLER SECONDS

	5% Down No Seller Seconds	5% Down 15% Seller Second
Sales Price	$400,000	$400,000
Down Payment 5%	$20,000	$20,000
Primary Loan Amount	$380,000 (95% LTV)	$320,000 (80% LTV)
Primary Loan Payment (30 years at 6.5%)	$2,401	$2,022
PMI Payment	$160	$0
Seller Second Loan Amount	$0	$60,000
Seller Second Payment (30 years at 7.5%)	$0	$419
Total Payment	$2,561	$2,441

FIGURE 53 To avoid PMI the buyer would have to bring a much larger down payment to the table; the seller second solves this problem and also lowers the total monthly payment.

Today, conforming loans max out at $417,000 and any loan amount above that qualifies as a "jumbo" loan. For buyers the difference is significant, since jumbo loans are considered riskier by lenders and can therefore carry a higher interest rate (often a full percentage point or more). And that can make for a much higher monthly payment. For example, a conventional 30-year loan on $417,000 might carry 6.5 percent interest rate, while a 30-year loan for $418,000 might carry a 7.5 percent interest rate. The buyer is only financing an additional $1,000 but their monthly payment would soar from $2,635 to $2, 922—that's $287 a month! So, for a seller's house that falls in the "just barely jumbo" arena, their offer to carry back a second loan could save the buyer hundreds of dollars each month (and thousands over the life of the loan) and might just be the difference to get the house sold.

Some other methods of creative financing include lease options and lease purchases, which are not as common as they once were. The difference between a lease option and a lease purchase is simple. In a lease option a buyer would rent the home for a certain period of time, after which the buyer would have the exclusive "option" to purchase the home at an agreed upon price. A lease purchase simply stipulates that the buyer will buy the home at the end of the term for an agreed upon price. When potential buyers cannot qualify any other way, these become creative ways to get the seller out from underneath the house payment and potentially sell the house if they used a lease option and definitely sell the house if they used a lease purchase. Things to look out for—document how the sellers set the rent or even pay for a formal rent survey; make sure all parties are represented by their own attorney; and, finally, if prices fall during the term of the agreement you may run into trouble getting an appraisal which means a larger down payment from the buyer.

Assemble a team of mortgage professionals that know every nook and cranny of the mortgage market. I can't tell you how often I've found financing for a buyer who had been turned down by a loan officer when all that was needed was a little more effort. If you don't have a seasoned mortgage team, you're losing money.

David Reed, Austin, TX

Finally, wrap-around mortgages (wraps) and assumable mortgages sit at the bottom of the list for a good reason—the "due on sale" clause. While both are highly effective, the advent of the due-on-sale clause (meaning the amount owed on a mortgage is due to the lender upon sale of a property) in most mortgages has made them exceedingly rare. A wrap is a situation where the owner offers you a new loan while keeping and paying down their original loan (the new loan "wraps" the original). Some lenders will allow a wrap if it is disclosed. Jay Papasan successfully used a fully disclosed wrap to purchase, subdivide, and later sell some land, all within about 14 months. The mortgage banker was involved from start to finish and agreed to it due to the short-term nature of the transaction. Don't rule wraps out without investigating the circumstances. Every now and then a wrap will be the solution that saves a sale.

Have the seller pay the buyer's closing costs. We've done this for years – in every type of market. By getting the seller to pay it, the buyer can then use their funds toward necessary upgrades, repairs or remodeling.

Rae Wayne, Los Angeles, CA

In an assumable mortgage, the buyer takes responsibility for the seller's mortgage when allowed by the seller's mortgage lender. Some government loans (like FHA and VA) are assumable, but again, these are very rare and normally the new buyer must qualify and everything must be disclosed. High mortgage interest rates can make assumable loans more attractive, so the buyer can enjoy the favorable rates of the preexisting loan. But there is little motivation for the lender to agree, since the new buyers will pay less interest and enjoy a shorter loan term. The main reason some of these loans were designed to be assumable, particularly the VA, was to protect sellers who may no longer be able to afford their home. In this case, the logic was that it was better to let the loan be assumed than force a veteran into foreclosure.

Sellers should know what their options are so once you've visited with the seller and studied the property, you can then analyze its potential for creative financing. Laws and regulations vary from state to state and from province to province, so you'd be wise to run any potential strategy by your office manager or broker before you commit pen to paper. In particular, lease options, lease purchases, and contract for deeds are subject to many local laws and restrictions, mostly enacted to protect buyers from unscrupulous sellers. Any time there is an agreement in play other than the offer contract (and this includes owner financing) make sure all parties are represented by their own attorney for everyone's protection and that you always disclose and disclaim.

2) CREATIVE THINGS BUYERS CAN DO TO PURCHASE A HOME

There are probably few things worse then being a buyer who is unable buy in a buyers' market. The market shifts and home ownership suddenly looks like a possibility for a buyer until they discover that there are mortgage challenges to overcome. When buyers have difficulty qualifying for a mortgage loan it's usually because of the CIA. I'm referring to Credit, Income, and Assets, not the other CIA. In a shift, lenders tend to tighten their lending standards, so knowing proven work-arounds for all three can become essential for some buyers.

FIGURE 54 When buyers can't qualify, they usually have challenges with the credit, income, or assets—the CIA.

Good credit is necessary for a loan. As obvious as this sounds, it always amazes me how many buyers don't grasp this. A damaged credit score can be raised, but it takes time to repair, often with the help of some sage advice from a great lender or a certified credit counselor. If your buyers have credit issues that can't be quickly remedied, then you're probably back to appealing to the seller for owner financing, a contract for deed, a lease option or a lease purchase.

Income is the second category. If your buyers have an income challenge (they don't earn enough qualifying income or the lender won't recognize it), you might suggest the buyer find a non-occupant co-borrower or, again, appeal to the seller for help.

Finally, the most common obstacle for buyers is coming up with the down payment and closing costs. Some potential home buyers simply haven't saved enough or have saved nothing at all. If the seller isn't willing to make a contribution towards the buyer's costs, you will have to find your buyer another viable source of funds. Most of the creative things buyers can do relate to coming up with the assets for a down payment.

AREA TWO: CREATIVE THINGS BUYERS CAN DO TO PURCHASE A HOME

1. Gift Funds
2. Selling or Refinancing Existing Assets
3. Non-Occupant Co-Borrowers
4. Using a 401(k)
5. Temporary IRA Transfers
6. Pledged Asset Mortgages
7. Equity Transfers and Bridge Loans
8. Employer-Assisted Mortgages

FIGURE 55 Familiarize yourself with these proven creative financing solutions for buyers, so you can get the job done when your competitors cannot.

The first place a buyer should look for assistance with purchasing a home is family. A close family member is traditionally the most common option for obtaining down payment and closing cost funds. Gift letters and documentation must be in place, but all-in-all, it's a straightforward answer to finding purchase funds. In my experience, parents and grandparents with the financial capability to help are often proud to play a part in a child's or grandchild's transition into homeownership. Along with family, there are only a handful of approved sources for financial gifts to buy real estate. Other sources for down payment funds or closing costs are available including accredited non-profit agencies, government grants, churches, domestic partners, and trade unions.

APPROVED SOURCES FOR FINANCIAL GIFTS TO PURCHASE REAL ESTATE

1. Family Members
- Parents
- Siblings
- Grandparents

2. Non-Profit Agencies

3. Non-Occupant Co-Borrowers

4. Local, State, and Provincial Agencies

5. Domestic Partners

6. Trade Unions

FIGURE 56 Any gift funds buyers bring to the closing table will need to be documented according to the lender's guidelines.

Many forward-thinking engaged couples are taking advantage of creative ideas like requesting that down payment funds be gifted in lieu of traditional registry items. When enough wedding guests offer funds instead of place settings, it can add up to a substantial portion, if not all, of the down payment. Make sure your buyers know about options like this because it may apply to them.

Another creative avenue available to buyers is selling or refinancing another asset. It's not uncommon for buyers to sell some of their stuff (boats, cars, stock options, stamp collections) to raise money to buy a home. Remember, when a buyer is truly motivated, they may surprise you with their own creative solutions. All you have to do is prompt them a little and get their creative juices flowing. Remember that the lender will want to verify the source of the money used for the down payment. You'll need to have receipts and third-party appraisals to confirm that the painting your buyer sold was really worth $3,500. Explain to the buyer that they must keep a paper trail and understand the lender will likely do an independent verification, as well.

With the lending market challenges, the opportunity for creative financing is perfect for sellers to provide more options to buyers and open the door for many more possibilities.
Chris Cormack, Ashburn, VA

Buyers can also find money and change their loan-worthiness by paying off or refinancing existing debt. I actually refinanced my beige four-door Honda Accord when I purchased my first home. The car had held its value and I had paid enough of it off so there was room to put a new loan on it and pull some money out. So I did just that and used the money for my down payment and closing costs. Even with the new car payments on my credit statement I qualified for the mortgage.

There are numerous other solutions to help buyers from non-occupant co-borrowing (where mom and dad buy the house with a son or daughter) to borrowing against 401(k) and IRA funds. With Pledged Asset Mortgages buyers can pledge assets such as CDs, stocks, or bonds that they prefer not to liquidate or borrow against. Equity transfers and bridge loans are options when the assets the buyers can't or are unwilling to sell are in the form of real property. Most lenders can help you navigate that transaction, which can be common for buyers who are trading up or down. And finally, some corporations have established employee down payment assistance programs. If your buyer works for a large corporation get them to inquire with their human resources department to check on availability.

Your awareness of these options and how to take advantage of them is the key to converting more buyers into homeowners in a shifting market. These creative financing ideas expand the number of buyers who can buy and therefore sellers who can sell. Everyone wins.

One note to buyers: Whether it's a temporary IRA transfer or the sale of an asset, many of the creative things buyers can do may have tax ramifications. Since you are not a financial adviser or a certified public accountant, leave any true decision-making advice to qualified professionals. Recommend professionals you trust and require your buyers seek their own counsel. It protects you, your buyers, and innocent sellers from unexpected and unpleasant outcomes.

3) CREATIVE THINGS LENDERS CAN DO TO FINANCE A TRANSACTION

The final player in a creative home purchase transaction is the lender. A knowledgeable loan officer could possibly help your buyer tap into a conventional loan program that may have been overlooked or forgotten in recent years. A great loan officer should also be able to offer guidance and insight into the financing solutions being considered by your buyers and sellers, as well as provide specialized assistance if necessary.

AREA THREE: CREATIVE THINGS LENDERS CAN DO TO FINANCE A TRANSACTION

1. Lender-Funded Buydowns
2. Fannie Mae's "MyCommunityMortgage"
3. Running Scenarios with Automated Underwriting Systems
4. Adjusting Amortization Periods to Lower Payments
5. Adjusting Interest Rates to Cover Closing Costs
6. State, Province, and Local Grant or Bond Programs
7. Mortgage Credit Certificates
8. Private Lending

FIGURE 57 A great mortgage professional can offer a lot of proven solutions. Run this list by your preferred mortgage vendors to see which ones they offer and what else they can do to help.

At the top of the list is a lender-funded buydown. The goal here is to help a buyer stretch their debt ratios in order to qualify for a mortgage, temporarily offsetting a current drop in income or provide permanent relief because income isn't anticipated to be higher in the future.

Let's say you have a buyer who wants to buy now but who won't be fully vested in his pay structure for another two years. The house he wants to buy costs $200,000 and he has just enough for a 10 percent down payment ($20,000). The interest rate on a 30-year note is 6.5 percent, which translates to a $1,137 monthly payment on the $180,000 financed. Unfortunately, your buyer doesn't yet make enough money to qualify for that monthly payment and neither he nor the seller has the ability to pay for an interest rate buydown to lower the payments. In this instance, you might ask the lender to pay for a 2-1 buydown, lowering the interest rate for the first two years and therefore lowering the monthly payments enough for your buyer to qualify. You may be wondering why any lender would agree to pay for a buydown. The truth is the lender doesn't actually pay for it—the buyer does.

Here's how it works. The 2-1 buydown would normally lower the base interest rate 2 percentage points in the first year and 1 percentage point in the second. In this example, a 2-1 buydown would translate to a 4.5 percent rate in year one, a 5.5 percent rate in year two, and a 6.5 percent rate for the duration of the mortgage. The lender calculates how much interest income would be lost from the original rate (6.5 percent) in the first two years (at 4.5 percent and then 5.5 percent) and then, to fund the buydown, the lender adjusts those rates back up a tiny bit. The first step is to figure the total annual payments at each interest rate.

Monthly Payment at 6.5% (30 years on $180,000)	$1,137	X 12 months =	$13,644
Monthly Payment at 5.5% (30 years on $180,000)	$1,022	X 12 months =	$12,264
Monthly Payment at 4.5% (30 years on $180,000)	$912	X 12 months =	$10,944

FIGURE 58 The first step is to figure the annual amount paid for each rate.

Next, the lender calculates how much would be "lost" in the first two years. Two years at 6.5 percent is $27,288. One year at 4.5 percent and one year at 5.5 percent equals $23,208. The difference is the amount of interest lost or $4,080 in this example. That translates to 2.3 discount points ($4,080 divided by $180,000 = 0.023) or the amount the lender will raise rates to recover the lost income. Hang with me, we're almost there.

Generally speaking, each discount point paid adjusts the mortgage interest rate down 0.25 percent. In this example, the lender will adjust the rates up by two discount points (or 0.5 percent) to recover the lost interest income. This allows your buyer to borrow $180,000 at 5 percent the first year, 6 percent the second, and 7 percent for the remainder. By the way, the difference in a monthly payment at 6.5 percent and 7 percent is only about $60 per month. So while your buyer may pay slightly more for the bulk of the loan term, the lower payments in year one and year two will enable him to actually qualify for the home.

YEARS	LOAN AMOUNT	INTEREST RATE	MONTHLY PAYMENT	THE 2-1 BUYDOWN DIFFERENCE
1	$180,000	5%	$966	-$171
2	$180,000	6%	$1,079	-$58
3-30	$180,000	7%	$1,197	+$60

FIGURE 59 The lender buydown offers nice savings in the first years from the original loan payments of $1,137. The buyer makes up for this on the back end of the mortgage loan with higher payments for the remaining years.

Next on the list is Fannie Mae's "MyCommunityMortgage" which serves as a placeholder for classic, reliable loan programs (such as FHA and VA) that are sometimes overlooked or underused. "MyCommunity-Mortgage" is a lesser-known program designed to help buyers overcome credit, income, and asset challenges. It is available to any non-investor who makes less than the median income for a specific area as defined by the Department of Housing and Urban Development (HUD). All these government-funded or bonded programs are specifically designed to help targeted buyers into homeownership. Now may be the time to rediscover them!

A great mortgage professional can help in other ways too. They can submit and resubmit loan applications through automated underwriting programs, "tweaking the criteria" until they figure out just what a buyer needs to do in order to qualify for a loan. For example, they might run an application with and without a car payment in order to see if a loan might be approved contingent on the car being paid off.

A little extra effort from the mortgage professional assisting in the transaction can go a long way toward getting it done. Lenders can also adjust amortization periods to lower payments. Buyers and their agents tend to believe 15- and 30-year loans are all that are available—but they are merely the most prevalent. Lenders will typically amortize the loan in increments of five years starting at ten and going all the way to 50 years in some cases. The longer the term of the mortgage the lower the monthly payment will be. Just make sure buyers are aware that a longer term also means it will take longer to build equity through debt pay down to the moment they can afford it. You should point out that if they go this route, they might consider making an extra payment or more each year to greatly reduce the amount of money and time it takes to pay off this mortgage. Honestly, this is a great strategy no matter which way a buyer finances their home and should be a regular part of your discussions with buyers.

Lenders will also adjust interest rates up to cover closing costs. This can be highly effective when monthly payments aren't the issue, but bringing cash to the table is. Good mortgage lenders will typically be familiar with local or regional grants available to first-time, low-income buyers as well as programs related to specific professions. If you are working with a public servant whether a teacher, a tax assessor, a police officer, or firefighter, ask your lender if there is a special program for buyers in this category.

Interestingly, lenders can factor in the tax savings associated with home ownership and count it as qualifying income with a Mortgage Credit Certificate. Only first-time homebuyers can qualify and they must make less than the median income. Nevertheless, for buyers who make almost enough to qualify for the home they want, this program can make all the difference.

When all else fails your lender may be able to recommend reputable private lenders who might finance the home purchase. These work like owner financing and usually involve short-term balloon financing. If your buyers go this route, make sure they have an attorney and, most important, a solid plan for refinancing when the note comes due. Making timely payments on a mortgage is a great way for buyers to heal a damaged credit score and prepare them for a conventional loan.

The lending landscape is inherently diverse and always subject to change. It seems new lending programs pop up each year and lending standards are in constant flux. It is therefore imperative that you seek out and partner with the best mortgage professionals in your area. You're looking for knowledge, experience, creativity, and integrity. They must be flexible and responsive to both you and your clients.

YOUR FINANCING TEAM

So how does a real estate agent add "master creative financing" to their ever growing list of important tasks to do? They don't. You only need to have a clear understanding of the market, the players, and their options. With this knowledge you can effectively expand the choices for your buyers and sellers and leave the details to your financing specialist.

Meet separately with your top two loan officers every week. These meetings should be on your calendar for the entire year. The goal of each of these brief meetings is to brainstorm the issues you and the market are facing. Ask them to put all the financing options on the table that might work in the market for each of your buyers and sellers. With that list in hand, you can then set the expectation that these same lenders will take ownership of the forms, the timelines, and the processes needed to put these ideas into action on each loan they get. You should also include your accountant, attorney, and title officer into your financing team to handle the work that falls outside the job description of a loan officer (such as offering tax advice or drafting legal or closing documents.)

Finally and most important, involve your manager. Good ethics and good business sense demand it. Your company is implicitly involved in all of your transactions. I've seen real estate agents lose their licenses, face lawsuits, and charges of loan fraud when a little caution could have prevented it all. Likewise, I've seen great offices with wonderful risk management practices in place face lawsuits, increased errors and omissions insurance premiums, and even the loss of their errors and omissions protection altogether. Just because a document is drawn up by an attorney doesn't necessarily mean that document is legal. I've been privileged to work with amazing leadership in my real estate businesses. They work tirelessly with their agents to find proven, legal, and win-win solutions for their customers. It may slow down the process to double-check and triple-check things, but in the end it is the professional way to do business.

DISCLOSE AND DISCLAIM

The last words of every creative financing transaction are disclose and disclaim. Your mantra must always be: "Disclose! Disclose! Disclose! Disclaim! Disclaim! Disclaim!" If you can't disclose it to everyone and put it on a closing statement, it probably isn't legal. And if you can't disclaim your liability from it that usually means someone is intending to hold you liable. So disclose what you're doing and disclaim responsibility for it. Always add a disclosure and disclaimer where all parties acknowledge what they're doing and agree not to hold you responsible or liable for what has been decided and done. This puts everyone on notice for what they've done and that you're not in the lawsuit loop on it. Disclosing and disclaiming it also gives your office leadership a chance to "check your math" and "watch your back." Check with them early in the process and often to ensure the financing solutions you offer won't put yourself or any of your business partners at risk. It's the right thing to do.

To succeed to your highest level in a shift you will need to become proficient at creative financing. Make sure you have a clear understanding of the current options available to your buyers and sellers and meet with your finance team weekly to work out options and solutions for them. It takes commitment, effort, and a weekly slot on your calendar. Don't let your calendar convict you on this one. Your financial success and the financial future of your buyers and sellers may depend on it. Make a date with finance and keep it all year, every year. It's one more way you'll take luck out of play and make the most of your career.

TACTIC #11
MASTER THE MARKET OF THE MOMENT – SHORT SALES, FORECLOSURES, AND REOs

The game of life is not so much in holding a good hand
as playing a poor hand well.

H.T. LESLIE

EVERY MARKET BRINGS ITS OWN RHYTHM and its own rhyme. Niches and unique opportunities that show up in one market disappear in another. While some market factors remain the same no matter the market, other factors will change in every market. Each shift has its own unique characteristics with possibilities and prospects that are specific to that market. The instant these "markets of the moment" appear make sure you take notice. Don't hesitate—there is a definite advantage that goes to those who move first. The sooner you get involved the better. Whether you completely dive into these new opportunities or not, they are worth studying and mastering.

Lenders want people to borrow money when they buy a home. Responsible lending is good business. Conversely, irresponsible lending is bad business. You would expect the first and not much of the second, but inevitably, we sometimes experience a lot of the second, which can create opportunities. Some people get in over their heads financially and this is especially true when a shift occurs. Now, done within reason, prudent borrowing is a smart thing to do. But borrowing ahead of one's income can create serious problems.

Inevitably, when a market drops it brings some people down and can even turn a few upside down. A number of people get in a financial bind and then are unable to weather the trying times. In those situations, the individual in trouble will certainly need you now more than ever. But they may be so unaware of the current market conditions as it relates to their own circumstances that they don't realize how much they need your expertise.

You are uniquely positioned in a downward shift to help both borrower and lender work out their problems, together or separately. These sellers and lenders will need you at all stages during this troubled time. Before foreclosure, during foreclosure, or after foreclosure you can help both seller and lender. From selling a house that's become a burden to helping plot a path back to creditworthiness to minimizing financial losses, you can provide a variety of services and support that can change lives—for individuals, for families, and even for institutions.

Tough times for one person usually turn into tough times for many people. A shift can turn the life of a real estate professional on its head. Previous customers as well as current vendor partners are probably experiencing some of the same challenges. Many homeowners will owe more than they can get on a house they can no longer afford to own and face a looming foreclosure. At the same time, many institutions will have foreclosed on homes they can't afford to own and will themselves be facing a fiscal crisis. Because both of these sellers (individual and institutional) must sell, home prices can become attractive enough to draw serious interest from bargain hunters and investors. Three distinct markets show up during a shift.

THREE MARKETS OF THE MOMENT

1. **SHORT SALES** Individuals or families trying to avoid foreclosure
2. **FORECLOSURES** Bargain hunters and investors seeking to buy value
3. **REOs** Financial institutions with an above average number of foreclosures to sell

In the midst of your own shift-induced financial challenges, these trying times present you with new opportunities to offer much-needed assistance and earn much-needed income in the form of short sales, foreclosures, and REOs—they are now the "market of the moment."

While there are always a small percentage of homes that go into default or foreclosure[7], during a shift distressed properties can flood the market and begin to impact the marketplace. That's why we call this the "market of the moment." These homes tend to hit the market abruptly and can grow so numerous as to dominate the overall market, driving down prices even further and thereby creating a second wave of defaults and foreclosures. This downward cycle of foreclosures and falling prices can eventually feed on itself, building momentum until bargain hunters and investors are attracted back into the market.

[7]Typically less than 1 percent during any single quarter according to RealtyTrac Inc.

THE MARKET SHIFTS

More REOs Hit the Market

Less Buyers and More Sellers

Average Home Prices Fall

Foreclosures Increase

THE DOWNWARD CYCLE OF DEFAULTS AND HOME PRICES

Sellers Get "Upside-Down" Short Sales and Defaults

More Sellers Get "Upside-Down" More Defaults

Foreclosures Increase

Average Home Prices Fall Further

REOs Hit the Market

FIGURE 60 When homeowners go into default, it can cause home prices to continue to spiral down. This makes it harder for other homeowners to avoid default. The cycle gets broken when prices become attractive enough that buyer reluctance turns into buyer urgency.

This shift presents you with both challenges as well as opportunities. Dealing with homes in default requires you to be organized and persistent. Forms, processes, and procedures are required to work from one end of this type of transaction to the other. On the other hand, there are three distinct prospects for business that arise. First, there are many individuals who now need short sale and pre-foreclosure services. If you can help them out you will earn customers for life and numerous referrals. Second, if you serve the institutions who now own foreclosed properties they need to sell (REOs or "real estate owned"), you can receive groups of listings at one time and an on-going stream of potentially well-priced houses to sell. And third, this is one of the most opportune times to provide services to bargain hunters and investors. While working with these buyers requires some special knowledge and skills, they tend to purchase multiple properties both at one time and over time, making them prospective volume customers. Since these three distinct groups of customers—individuals, institutions, and investors—show up at different times in the market cycle, I find it helpful to break down the foreclosure process into its three stages: default, foreclosure, and REO.

STAGE ONE: DEFAULT

One of the great tragedies of a shift is that when homeowners get behind on their mortgage payments they are often "upside down" on the house. They simply can't sell it for the amount of money they still owe on their mortgage loan. That leaves them with few options and in great need of assistance. They will likely need a professional real estate agent to help them sell their home quickly, negotiate a short sale on their behalf, or get the lender to renegotiate the terms of loan. Negotiating a short sale (where the lender agrees to accept less than is owed on the property) is one of the greatest services you can provide to a struggling seller. For many agents it becomes a personal mission to save as many people as possible from foreclosure.

Having a professional short sale negotiator to work with the lenders and build relationships has made a huge difference in our short sale success.

Kristina Arias, Mesa, AZ

Notices of default are made public soon after a homeowner gets behind on the mortgage payments. How long a lender will allow the owner to not make payments or make only partial payments varies. In general, the deeper you are in a downshifted market the longer the default period becomes. Local governments post public notices in the newspapers, at the courthouse, or online. There are even companies dedicated to assembling this information and reselling it. Some homeowners attempt to sell their homes themselves to "save money on commissions." So in a shifted market a "For Sale by Owner" sign can sometimes be a cry for help. You'll also uncover them in your listing presentations when you ask the critical seller prequalification question in a shifted market: "Are you current on your mortgage payments?" Understand that while all of the above are sources for finding owners in distress, they also attract the attention of others.

Owners in default can quickly find themselves confronted with a dizzying assault of offers to "help" them. Some are legitimate offers from ethical investors, but there are also illegitimate offers made by those who are more predatory in their motivation. The worst stories involve quitclaim deeds slipped into paperwork whereby the owner unintentionally deeds the property over for next to nothing.

Know the steps in the process of a short sale. Be able to document to the lender an honest attempt to get enough to pay off the note. Show that the market will not support that price. Document the hardship.

Gary Leogrande, White Plains, NY

You'll have to cut through this noise, get the sellers' attention, and differentiate yourself as a fiduciary who can help them and protect them.

The good news is that in a shifted market most lenders are much more willing to discuss potential workouts. Lenders might forgive late payments or roll them into the existing mortgage. They might even negotiate short sales. Lenders are facing a tsunami of foreclosures which can be quite costly. In April of 2007, the Joint Economic Committee of Congress asserted that the average foreclosure costs a lender approximately $50,000. Multiply that times thousands of foreclosures and you can begin to understand their lender's incentive to negotiate. If the homeowner can document hardship and is willing to cooperate, you will have significant leverage to negotiate a short sale.

One last warning—be sure your seller is for real. Unfortunately, I've seen a lot of agents spend significant time and effort trying to help someone who simply doesn't care enough to help themselves. The seller must be honest with you. If they have other assets they could sell to cover the difference the short sale is usually no longer an option. Require a current credit report from the seller that shows any other properties they own. Being thorough on the front end will save everyone time throughout the process. By making efficient use of your time you will be able to assist more clients.

Once you have a qualified, cooperative homeowner, working the problems out is a straightforward process. Contact the lender. It can sometimes be a struggle just to figure out who actually holds the note, so be patient and persistent. Most of the time you'll begin with the company who services the loan before you work your way to the actual lender. They will require a letter of authorization for you to negotiate on the seller's behalf, so have one ready.

WHAT TO INCLUDE IN THE LETTER OF AUTHORIZATION

1. A short letter authorizing you to negotiate on the homeowner's behalf
2. Loan reference number or owner's account number
3. The date
4. Property address

5.   Owner's full name and signature

6.   Owner's contact information

7.   Agent's name and contact information

Check and double-check for accuracy. With the high volume of short sales, lenders will prioritize applications that are neat and complete.

Once you've found the actual lender and are authorized to have a conversation, you'll begin negotiations with someone in their loss mitigation department. If your sellers would prefer to rework the loan (forbearance or refinancing) and keep the home, then you will begin that process with the lender. You will need to know all of the documentation they require and the qualifying parameters for their willingness to do this. If a rework of the loan does not seem possible or your sellers do not even want to consider this option, then a short sale is what you will need to seek.

While the lender will usually not consider approving a short sale until there is a legitimate offer the loss mitigation officer will supply you with a short sales packet and you'll be able to get down to work. Remember the clock is ticking toward foreclosure. Opening the communication lines can buy you and the homeowner a few months to sell the house or negotiate a workout with the lender. The lenders packet will include instructions and forms for you to document the homeowner's hardship and make your case for a workout.

THE HARDSHIP LETTER AND DOCUMENTATION

1.   Letter from owner—document the financial facts that led
     to the short sale request.

2.   Proof of income and assets

     • Bank statements

     • Pay stubs

     • Disclose and document all assets

          – Investment accounts [401(k), IRA, etc.]

          – Stocks

          – Certificates of deposit

          – Any interest in other real property or businesses

3.   Proof of hardship

     • Bills

     • Unemployment records

     • Death certificates

     • Divorce decrees

4.   Preliminary net sheet—Reflect the sales price you expect
     to get and any other fees that will be due on sale,
     including your commission.

     • Include CMA with analysis of current actives, pendings,
       and solds.

Lenders can have a heart. They will often be sympathetic with
homeowners who face true hardships that make them unable to
stay current on payments or sell the home for more than is owed.

It's a lengthy process so persistence and patience are critical to your success. It may require many contacts, several callbacks, and even long periods on hold. Remember that lenders are probably feeling overloaded and you are probably one of many files. Keep your cool—patience isn't always easy in the face of bureaucracy. And always be accurate—verify and double-check all your facts. Persistence, a cool head and credibility are vital to short sales success.

By making a commitment to help individuals through short sales or refer them to trusted agents who do, you will reap long-term goodwill. You could save the bank thousands of dollars and rescue a homeowner from financial catastrophe.

WORKOUTS AND SHORT SALES: A QUICK OVERVIEW

1. Seller typically must be 60 days behind on payments to qualify.

2. Be sure your seller is for real.

    • Ask for a credit report.

    • Search for any other properties titled in their name.

3. Contact the lender and submit a letter of authorization.

    • Who is servicing the loan? This is usually your first stop.

    • Who holds the note? Ask for a representative from the loss mitigation department authorized to negotiate a workout.

4. Document the hardship.

    • Be accurate—confirm everything in the hardship letter.

and documentation. Reliability is golden.

- Provide full and accurate financial disclosure.

- Submit a preliminary net sheet with a comprehensive market analysis.

5. Negotiate a workout.

- Ask the lender for forbearance—to suspend, roll back, forgive, or add to mortgage or reduce payments.

- Ask the lender to refinance the note with more favorable terms.

- Ask for a short sale. If you receive an offer on the home, check it for accuracy and submit it to the lender as a short sale. This is most likely when the lender will share the terms they'll accept on the house.

6. Don't buck the system.

- Follow the lender's workout systems.

- Be persistent, patient, and even-tempered.

- Be available and respond to any communications promptly.

STAGE TWO: FORECLOSURE

Once a home goes to foreclosure, your opportunities now shift. Some agents work with investors and home buyers who want to purchase homes at auctions. Others may continue to work with the former seller as the buyer (for whom financial assistance arrived too late to prevent foreclosure) to repurchase the home at auction or during the redemption period. Understand that foreclosure auctions are fraught with risk. All properties are sold "as is," you must pay with cash or "good as cash" funds and you may not have the opportunity to inspect them before purchase. These foreclosed properties could have significant damage or even carry secondary liens.

Seasoned investors with available cash are pros at working these auctions, so they can become very competitive. Just because it's an auction doesn't mean every property is a deal. If you've ever purchased something at an auction then you understand how easy it is to get caught up in the action and over-pay. Study the pre-auction list, do as much due diligence as possible, and visit the properties to determine the maximum price you or your buyer should be willing to pay. Then don't go over that limit.

I came to the REO and short sale arena kicking and screaming—now we have our own REO department on our team and I'm actually singing.

Jackie Ellis, Boynton Beach, FL

In good times foreclosure properties can be synonymous with substandard, abandoned properties. (But not always. Many years ago a former neighbor's home, which was in great shape, sold for tax liens on the courthouse steps for $100,000 in cash. At the time it was easily worth three times that amount.) After a shift, the less-than-ideal-property dynamic changes radically. Because of the dramatically increased volume, foreclosures can begin to reflect the market in general with good and even great value properties showing up in many price ranges. When that happens more and more non-investors will start asking about foreclosures, which is shorthand for "good deals."

Agents who specialize in these properties assemble their own teams of foreclosure specialists. These teams include vendor partners to help with tax, title, and mortgage issues, contractors to help with repairs, and property managers to handle the houses for the long term. With a support team in place, they promote "foreclosure best investment lists." Much like a "best buy" list we discussed in *Tactic #9: Creating Buyer Urgency,* this is a way to tap into a buyers' desire to get a great deal in a buyers' market. Whether you're actually helping buyers purchase homes at foreclosure or post-foreclosure REOs, you'll need to invest time and energy into understanding the unique challenges these properties can present. Above all else, you will need to be precise when determining the value of a property—what it's worth, what it will take to rehab it, and what it will sell for. It is very similar to doing buy-and-sell investing[8].

I have become the workout specialist for my sellers. I provide direction to the seller to work through the minefield of requests from their lender.

Betty Bezemer, Houston, TX

STAGE THREE: REO

REOs get their name from a line item in a lenders balance sheet (real estate owned). Interestingly, it's listed as a liability rather than an asset and this makes perfect sense. Lenders are in the business of loaning (not owning) so mortgages, not real property, are the assets they want to hold. With a house unsold at auction now marring their balance sheet and cost-

[8]You may want to get a copy of our book *FLIP* and become knowledgeable about all aspects of this process.

ing them money to manage and maintain, lenders have sound financial reasons to liquidate these liabilities and move on. If this happens often, banks become the dominant listing force in a particular neighborhood or even an entire city.

This presents you with two substantial opportunities—to serve as an REO seller representative or become an REO buyer representative. These roles are no different from real estate sales in general except the seller is a financial institution. It is similar in scope to the procedures for selling absentee-owner vacation properties or handling builder and developer listings.

THE TWO OPPORTUNITIES OF REOS

1. **REO Seller Representative**—listing agents who market their services to financial institutions needing to sell REO properties.
2. **REO Buyer Representative**—buyer agents who market their services to REO seller representatives and handle the buyer leads from those properties.

First, you can work with a lender, serving as their REO seller representative, to list and sell their properties. This can be a volume-listing enterprise (literally dozens if not hundreds of listings) and therefore it's a big financial opportunity for your business. Be sure you understand that these sellers are looking for two key services from their listings agents—ongoing property preservation and immediate property sales.

Making contacts, networking with lender executives, and being persistent are the keys to getting your foot in the REO door. Before you get the opportunity to list a lender's properties, you'll probably be asked to first do a number of other jobs related to preserving the properties. Vacant properties may attract squatters, vandals, and thieves. Common tasks in working REOs include rekeying the house, overseeing an eviction or "cash for keys," inspecting the property for damage, changing over utilities, and managing maintenance and repairs. Whatever your circumstances, be responsive, thorough, and accurate. You are being tested. If you do well, you've earned the right to ask for and receive their listing business.

Focus on your relationship with the asset manager, just as you would any high-priority seller. Much of your time with them will be checking off on assigned tasks and offering broker price opinions (BPOs) on the properties. Many agents have told us that by executing property preservation-related tasks they got their foot in the door. Delivering accurate and timely BPOs earned them the listings. In other words, doing BPOs can get you REOs!

I realized that it was my job to bring REO business to my team. So I set out to find key contacts and lead generate to the banks. Now, 50 percent of our listings and over 70 percent of our sales come from these REO properties.
Carol Royse, Tempe, AZ

Almost everything else can be delegated to your administrative team or your trusted service providers. Our interviews with top REO agents indicated that one full-time, talented assistant with the proper systems can handle the work on about fifty properties.

The lenders' asset managers often work with hundreds of properties at a time, so the better equipped an agent is to do volume business, the less complicated the asset managers' lives become. That can make you very valuable to them—perhaps irreplaceable. For the asset manager, having just five listing agents for 500 properties is a much better proposition than trying to manage fifty agent relationships on those same properties. The fewer contacts they have to make the easier their job. They love the concept of "single point of contact" and are looking for agents with systems and stamina who can be that point person for them.

Those agents who have already proven themselves up to the task (possibly because they got into the game before the shift) will likely already be on a lender's go-to list. You'll have to earn the right to be on that go-to list if you want to get a share of the business. But don't let this discourage you. During a shift the volume of REOs can soar, extending beyond the capabilities of the agent specialists already in the game. The moment an existing agent's performance and work standards falter, the lender's staff will be looking for someone else. This natural selection process can create opportunities for you and your business. Be ready to step in and deliver. You will likely get one chance to show them how good you are.

The second opportunity REOs present for you is in servicing the buyers these listings can generate—to serve as an REO buyer representative. Interestingly, most agents who focus on listing REOs tend to be specialists. They rarely build teams to effectively service the buyer side and instead tend to refer those leads out. In some cases, they are not even doing much to respond—to capture and convert those leads. There could be a lot of lost leads being generated around a successful REO listing business. If you can bring a high degree of service and follow-through to the buyer side, you have the chance to win this business. Remember REO agents earn their reputation by getting the properties sold. If you help them do that, you then become a very valuable and respected part of their business. Our research shows that some offices organize teams of designated REO buyer agents to service leads generated by REOs and provide leverage for the REO listing specialists. That is a win-win scenario.

THE MOMENT OF TRUTH

A market shift can be a moment of truth for your career. You will be faced with the decision to go after homes in default, foreclosure, and REOs—or not. All three areas can be as challenging as they are rewarding, and focusing on the market of the moment shouldn't be a spur-of-the-moment decision.

It has been said that "luck is when preparation meets opportunity." I agree with that sentiment. Fortune usually favors the prepared. This becomes obvious when some agents decide to take on a specialized area of real estate. For instance, I have seen residential agents become enamored by the potential commissions of huge commercial transactions. Although they acknowledge it is a complex transaction, all they're seeing is the big commission. After weeks or months of work if it falls through or they make a mistake and lose their place in the deal they are usually devastated. I have a lot of empathy for them, but not

Be willing to give your all when working the short sale, foreclosure, and REO market. The process is very time-consuming, but rewarding in the end.

Michelle Edwards, Raleigh, NC

so much sympathy. They made the mistake of thinking they could play in a game they hadn't trained for. They essentially made light of the demands of the business. At the professional level, almost no one can "play for pay" without putting in the time, study, and work it takes to master the game. Especially the complex business games that have guidelines, rules, and very experienced players.

Short sales, foreclosures, and REOs are this kind of a game. They are successfully played by experienced real estate professionals. Lending institutions can tell if an agent understands renegotiating a loan, negotiating a short sale, or taking an REO listing. And they won't give you much time if they don't think you know what you're doing. Agents who naively believe these transactions are easily profitable and require a minimum of preparation find themselves waiting on hold or embarrassed by their inability to answer questions they are asked by their colleagues.

Just as we seek people who are "able, ready, and willing" to do business, so do short sale sellers and REO lenders. That trio of qualifying words falls on any real estate agent who desires to participate in this "market of the moment." Don't just be ready because you see the opportunity and don't just be willing to take the risk because you think you have nothing to lose. Seek the business because you've studied it, learned it, and can successfully do the work—seek the business because you're able.

So, before you put too much time and effort toward pursuing these opportunities, before you take time and effort away from lead generation and conversion of traditional real estate sales be sure you know what you're doing. Take the courses, read the books, and talk with those who are experts in the business. Once you have the knowledge and know the realities of the short sale, foreclosure, and REO business, opportunities will abound. By being prepared luck will now be on your side. So, on your mark . . . get able . . . get ready . . . get willing . . . go! Go get the "market of the moment."

TACTIC #12
BULLETPROOF THE TRANSACTION –
ISSUES AND SOLUTIONS

If I had eight hours to chop down a tree, I'd spend six sharpening my ax.
ABRAHAM LINCOLN

SHIFTS CAN BE MADDENING. Just when everything seems to be going right, something goes wrong. Typical transactions are now atypical. Anything settled can quickly become unsettled. With more unusual than usual, the expected and unexpected frequently turn up together. It just feels like the only thing you can count on is not counting on anything. Nothing works like it once did. Nothing goes like it used to go.

Real estate transactions aren't particularly trouble free in any market, but when a shift happens few sales are easy and almost all closings a challenge. It's a strenuous and trying time that requires all the attention and effort you can command. You truly work for every sale and its successful close. What makes this market especially tough is the apparent willingness of buyers to walk away at any point in the sale.

When everyone believes the market is headed up, buyers are afraid of missing out. When everyone believes the market is headed down, buyers are afraid of sinking with the ship. Both markets are driven by the fear of making a mistake. But while one drives buyers to hold deals together at almost any cost, the other drives buyers to allow deals to fall apart for almost any reason. It can almost seem like buyers are actually seeking a way to undo the deal. In a shift, this often makes closing any sale demanding and difficult.

Reluctance and concern usually don't go away just because a contract is signed. When the market shifts buyer concerns often linger to some degree all the way to closing and possibly for months afterwards. Buyers are simply more open to any opportunity to rethink, renegotiate, or even break their contract. As they listen to the media, fellow coworkers, friends, and family, buyers are likely to question their own judgment. Then they begin to look for any crack in the contract or opening in the process to walk away. Many start to wonder if there is a better buy elsewhere or if there is still a way to make their buy a better deal. And to complicate things further, if there isn't an obvious and natural route to unravel the sale, some might create an exit strategy. In other words, no sale is safe until it's sealed at closing with everyone's signatures.

BULLETPROOF THE TRANSACTION

I remember when I really learned my lesson about getting contracts to close. It was my first year in the business. After selling six homes and closing five of them my very first month, I then went five straight months with no closings at all. I made sales during that period, in fact, at least two a month, but none of them closed. The market had shifted down and my selling skills hadn't scaled up. I had assumed that all buyers and sellers truly needed was an honest real estate agent with integrity who was willing to provide them the absolute best services possible. And I was absolutely right. I had just overlooked one important detail—they also needed a "salesperson." I had been a real estate agent, but I had also needed to be a real estate salesperson.

This was one of the biggest aha's of my young career. I realized with total clarity that I not only had to master the transaction, but also the sales skills that went with a successful transaction. I understood one but not the other and found myself in a shift without the necessary skills to pull me through. So I backed up, thought through the transaction, and decided how I'd handle each key point where something might go wrong. I got clear on what might happen and how to handle it and began to see ways to anticipate problems and head them off in advance. I wasn't going to get caught unprepared again and let my buyers and sellers down. In fact, I was going to be over prepared and ready for anything. And things changed. Those events that were previously unforeseen, I learned to see coming and to handle them. Those people I assumed were getting the job done now had me checking on them. I learned that any transaction that can come together can also come apart. I learned to bulletproof the transaction.

The number one challenge we all face is the level of the sales skills of the co-op agent. Don't underestimate how much of their work you'll have to do to make a sale happen.
Dianna Kokoszka, Austin, TX

I believe this is when I actually became a true professional real estate salesperson. I was now using lead generation skills for my career and selling skills for my customers' well-being. As a result, not only did my year change, but my career changed forever. In that seventh month I started keeping deals together, finished with a flurry, and before my twelfth month had hit all my first year financial goals. I rewarded myself with some well-earned time off.

HEADS UP

As determined as I was to succeed, that string of disappointments taught me the serious financial and emotional costs that I – and my customers – would pay when deals fell through. I also learned that no one else is going to do your due diligence for you. It's entirely up to you to oversee your contracts from start to finish. You have to be good at both ends of the sale—making it and closing it. The key is to remember this simple truth: You do your deals heads down, but you save your deals heads up.

Heads up is about seeing what's coming. It's about being vigilant and prepared to act. In my experience, there are four ways you can think about what might happen in any professional endeavor: nothing will go wrong, anything could go wrong, something will go wrong, or everything will go wrong. Interestingly enough, it's not about whether any of these approaches is right or wrong; nor is it about predicting the future. It's about being prepared to deal with whatever the future might bring.

Educate your clients. Tell your buyers or sellers what to expect. It keeps the drama out of the deal.

Doris Carlin, Joplin, MO

Many agents, like me in my first few months, who naively think nothing will go wrong are very surprised, and often disappointed, when something does. And, they usually aren't ready to deal with it quickly. So for them what goes wrong usually stops the sale from closing. Those who understand that anything could go wrong or even that something will go wrong are better prepared to handle unpleasant surprises. But, because of this approach, they may not be ready to take care of them.

Sometimes things work out okay and sometimes they don't. Over time they will learn from experience but along the way they will still have a fair amount of sales that don't close.

In my experience, it is best to prepare as if everything will go wrong. I know that sounds pessimistic, but it really isn't. It's the one way to be sure that you will be ready to deal with whatever happens. You'll be positioned to not only respond effectively to things when and if they go wrong, but you will stand a great chance of preventing them from happening in the first place. My coauthors Dave and Jay often comment that I am "the most black-hatted optimist they know." What they mean is that I believe anything is possible in any direction. I strive for the possible, I go after what I want to have happen, but I prepare for the worst and am ready should things go wrong. I don't know that they will go wrong, but I'm prepared if they do. It's why I have insurance. It's why I bulletproof transactions.

Problems may or may not come at any particular time, but over time they will come. They just do. In a shift, they come more often than not. So, when it comes to bulletproofing the transaction, take the everything-will-go-wrong approach. And keep your head up. Remember, you can predict exactly what can happen, but you can't predict when it might happen. Assume everything will go wrong and come up with ways to possibly prevent them from happening or effectively deal with them if they do. You won't be surprised when the problems show up and you won't be surprised when they go away.

THE SIX ISSUES

Bulletproofing transactions begins with fully understanding where things can go wrong. There are six major issues in getting from contract to close. These are the "moments of truth" that put transactions at the greatest risk. Knowing these is critical, but also knowing the certain ways in which they can go wrong is equally critical. Above all others, you are the person most responsible for getting a sale to a successful closing. Think of yourself as not only the one who makes the sale, but also the one who makes sure it closes. To do this you must be aware of, ready to handle, and better yet prevent any and all mishaps that might arise.

THE SIX "BULLETPROOFING THE TRANSACTION" ISSUES AND SOLUTIONS

ISSUES	HOW THINGS GO WRONG	SOLUTIONS
1. INSPECTIONS AND REPAIRS	Unexpected findings	Seller gets pre-inspection
	Report complexity	Attend with buyer and/or seller
	Costs and who pays	Pre-negotiated limits
	Timetable for repairs	Select and supervise vendors
	Doubt about worthiness	Prepare and reassure buyer
2. APPRAISALS	Won't support the price	Provide appraiser with research
	Won't support the loan	Find additional buyer funds
	Doesn't match the CMA	Appeal the appraisal
3. LOAN APPROVAL AND FUNDING	Application delays	Select originator – get preapproval
	Documentation problems	Assist buyer with paperwork
	Buyer credit issues	Get credit counseling for buyer
	Lender failure to approve	Reapply with corrections
	Lender failure to fund	Parallel applications
	Buyer credit changes	Give preclosing credit warning
4. OTHER CONTINGENCIES	Sale of the buyers' house	Take backup offers
	Third-party approvals	Know who and communicate
	Estate, relo, short-sale approvals	Know who, how, and timetable
	Clouded title	Preliminary title search
5. CO-OP AGENT	Bad advice or communications	Clarify the messages and intentions
	Inattention to details	Own the process and communicate
	Poor vendor selection	Provide selection list and back up
6. DEADLINES	Inspections and repairs	Confirm appointments and progress
	Closing date	Build in buyer and seller flexibility
	Occupancy	Preset dates, limits, and penalties
	Approvals/Documentation	Manage the closing checklist

FIGURE 61

Getting sales to close in a shift is not always about the technical details, although being knowledgeable about them is important. It's really about what you do when issues arise. How soon you respond, how well you handle things, how well you work with everyone involved, and ultimately both parties' willingness to close, play the most significant roles in the final outcome. So often a seller, in an upshift, or the buyer, in a downshift, will use one of the technical issues – like the inspection, the loan application or a third-party approval – as reasons to get out of the sale. So underneath these six specific issues, the emotions and decision-making of all the parties are in play. Be aware of these undertones during the closing process. Later we will talk about two strategies for handling these hidden dynamics. For now, let's be clear about the six basic issues. Dealing with them effectively is a must, particularly in the turbulence of a shifting market.

1. INSPECTIONS AND REPAIRS

Inspections and repair negotiations are a standard contingency in literally all real estate sales contracts. The buyer's final acceptance of the contract is normally contingent on a satisfactory inspection and an agreed upon handling of any repairs. Recommend as short a timetable as possible for a property inspection to be done and for the repairs, if any, to be agreed upon and completed. Don't let this drag out for time is always of the essence and you want things to keep moving forward and everyone preparing for closing.

It is always wise to put repair limits or allowances in a contract. This will help keep any further repair negotiations within potentially workable boundaries. And be sure to attend the inspection, preferably with your seller or buyer. This will put you in the best position, right up front, to take the complexity and technical jargon out of the inspection report and make sure all parties get to ask their questions and receive straight answers from the inspector. For sellers, if they'd passed on doing any up-front repairs, attending the inspection could help them see the wisdom of doing any necessary repairs. For the buyers, attending the inspection will give them a first-hand look at which repairs are really necessary and quickly get an idea of the cost involved. Help the buyer understand whether the items identified raise serious doubts about the structural integrity of the home. If they do, you must then have a serious discussion about moving ahead or not with the purchase. While your focus is always on saving a sale, it is never at the expense of the right fiduciary service. Finally, make sure the tone at the inspection is assumptive towards closing and supportive regarding the purchase. Inspectors can either pave the way to closing or throw up huge road blocks simply by the language they use. Anticipate this and visit with the inspector in advance to make sure you're both on the same page.

Keeping transactions together is about managing everyone's expectations and being a person who does not throw gas on the fire.
Martin Bouma, Ann Arbor, MI

Sellers should be prepared that any buyer will most likely ask for some repairs to be done. Consider asking the seller to have their house pre-inspected so they can be forewarned of any issues and head them off before they can cause problems. Nevertheless having reduced their price, possibly made some repairs in advance, and probably made other concessions, sellers may not feel completely comfortable negotiating additional repairs. They must be mindful of the market situation they're in and carefully weigh the potential costs against the potential benefits. It could well be worth the money to not lose a sale. On the other hand, buyers should be careful not to ask for too much. Even though in a down market they usually feel in control and in a mood to ask for whatever they want; they need to be reminded that excessiveness could alienate the seller. And that just might lose them this home, which is hopefully the one they really want.

Always have pre-selected service providers available that can handle any required repairs in a timely, dependable, and cost-effective manner. This might be one contractor who can oversee all repairs or a list of subcontractors who specialize. Some sellers or buyers may choose to select their own professionals to do the work, but most will prefer your reference advice. In fact, NAR's annual survey of home buyer and sellers regularly shows that both buyers and sellers expect you to provide them this information and guidance. Vendor selection is crucial, for the right ones can ensure that things will go as smoothly as possible. When mistakes are made or errors do occur, the best service providers get them solved quickly and satisfactorily. Your assistance in selecting these parties to the transaction increases the chances that nothing will go wrong, and if it does, it will be immediately taken care of. Unknown or untested repair services can put any closing in peril.

2. APPRAISALS

In a rapidly shifting market, a house that appraises to the sale price today could in fact have all the equity sucked out of it before the first payment is made. So just as you advise sellers to price ahead of a shifted market to get the home sold, lenders are also trying to reasonably anticipate the market to manage risk for their investors. This means appraisers are usually under increased pressure from the lender to be sure that the home is not overpriced. In a shift, fewer homes will appraise and those that do will require more attention and research from the professionals in the transaction.

The best way you can help the process is to offer to provide your research to the appraiser and to let them know how you came to a professional conclusion about why the home was worth what your buyer offered. The appraisal process is, of course, intended to be very independent of you or the needs of your client. However, your detailed research can help them justify an appraisal that meets the sale price, while one done with less data would not. Even if you are representing the seller, you may want to update your own CMA of the property and provide that data to the appraiser. If there are special circumstances involved in the sale – seller contributions to closing, seller seconds or the inclusion of personal property – the appraiser may take this into account when determining market value of the property.

This is another area where mortgage company selection can make a difference. Some lenders allow you to contact the appraiser directly, while others don't. Everything else being relatively equal, you would prefer to work with a lender who allows access to the appraiser. When you know the lender and mortgage processor, it can make a big difference in how your CMA data is used and how responsive they are to an appeal of the actual appraisal.

To really protect the transaction, you may want to prepare a back-up plan if the house doesn't appraise for the sale price or loan amount.

You can guide the buyer in finding funds to use for an additional down payment that will get the Loan to Value (LTV) ratio to a place that is acceptable to the lender, given the reduced appraisal of market value. Or if you represent the seller, you can have them ready to make a contribution to closing costs or provide a seller second. In any case, it becomes very important to track the loan application, appraisal and approval process and to know what is happening every step of the way.

3. LOAN APPROVAL AND FUNDING

Encourage buyers to apply for a loan before they find a prospective home. It's simple logic—the moment they decide to buy is the moment they should submit an application to a great loan officer and lender. It's also the safest strategy to ensure they're preapproved and that you can make a qualified offer on their behalf. Often buyers make the mistake of believing they must have a specific home in mind first. That's counterproductive, counter-successful thinking. Moving through the loan application process early is the most productive and most successful. Preapproved buyers that are qualified for a certain loan amount subject only to finding a property are the ones who can move most quickly. And knowing in advance how much they can afford, these buyers don't run the risk of finding the "perfect home" only to discover it lies beyond their financial reach. So make this happen. Plus, any gift letters, contributions to closing costs, or co-signers can already be in place. These elements are paramount in a shift. Remember, if you're not out in front on this process, the buyer is already behind before ever getting it started. And the transaction is already at risk.

More than with any other vendor in the transaction, selecting the mortgage provider is critical. It begins with knowing who is good and has a proven record of performance; and better yet if that proven performance has been with you. Then you must assert yourself to be sure that they are chosen. If you are working with the buyer, explain the benefits of working with these known professionals. If they insist on using another mortgage company, get their agreement to run a parallel application—it's a move that won't cost them anything and could save them everything. Most experienced loan officers, particularly those who have worked with you, will be glad to do this for no up-front fee and will only charge if they end up originating the loan. You don't want to get to the closing and discover that the lender your buyer selected has not approved the loan, failed to fund the loan or gone out of business. In a few cases we've seen with "discount lenders" there has even been a failure to fund after closing. Don't let this happen to you. Work with your proven professional partners and if they can't be first in line to handle the business, make sure they are ready to jump in at a moment's notice.

Even if you represent the seller, you want to be assured that the buyer's lender can and will perform. You may insist on a preapproval letter or that they apply for their mortgage with a loan officer that meets with your approval. In the end, you may even ask that they also run a parallel application with someone you know and trust. Remember, it is even more catastrophic to the seller when a transaction falls out just before closing. They have had the home off the market, they may have purchased another home or even moved. Substantial, non-refundable earnest money deposits can also reduce the likelihood of a buyer walking away from the purchase contract. If you represent the seller and are providing a major concession to the buyer you may want to treat it like an option they only receive if they back it up with some additional (non-refundable) money.

In the mortgage-funding process there is one final place the buyer can inadvertently stumble—failing to keep their credit in good standing through the closing. In the excitement of purchasing their new home and with the additional things they know they will need to purchase (new furniture, draperies, artwork, lawn care equipment, etc.) they may prematurely make financial moves that impact the final credit check by the lender. They are usually shocked to find out that they no longer qualify for the loan. As their agent, you need to warn them of this and remind them what they shouldn't do. You may even want to give them "The Seven Don'ts of Mortgage Funding."

THE SEVEN DON'TS OF MORTGAGE FUNDING

1. Don't change your employment status.
2. Don't make any major purchases (cars, furniture, home theater, vacations, etc.).
3. Don't increase your credit card debt or miss any payments.
4. Don't change bank accounts or make undisclosed large deposits.
5. Don't apply for a credit card, co-sign a loan or make a credit inquiry.
6. Don't spend money you have set aside for closing—not any, not ever.
7. Don't delay in providing all paperwork asked for by the mortgage company.

SECURE THE LOAN — CLOSE ON YOUR HOME!

As you communicate with your buyer, be sure to check that there is nothing happening personally or financially that might put their closing at risk. It is too common for them, upon being approved for a loan, to think that relatively smaller financial issues won't matter. They need to be very wary of doing anything that would raise a question with their lender.

While there are numerous ways a transaction can unravel during loan approval and funding, every one of these issues can be anticipated or avoided by a proactive agent working with a motivated buyer and seller. You can absolutely keep everyone and everything moving forward toward a successful closing. Just maintain close communication with all parties and, above all, keep your head up.

4. OTHER CONTINGENCIES

Arguably any agent's two favorite words are "all cash." Transactions with no or few contingencies – all cash, as is, and not dependent on another house to selling – tend to be our easiest and our most reliable. In reality, these types of transactions are few and far between no matter the market conditions. But, the goal is to have as few contingencies as possible with short timetables for clearing them. This is why you recommend preapproved buyers and pre-inspected properties. In a buyers' market, it is also wise for the buyers to get their house sold, or at least under contract, before they make an offer to buy their next home. It puts them in a stronger position to make an offer that is attractive to the sellers.

The seller assumes a lot of risk when they take their house off the market by entering into a contract that is contingent upon the buyer selling their home, especially when homes are not selling quickly. If they do, you would likely recommend that the seller continue to market the home and accept back-up offers. You might even insist that if a back-up offer is received and the buyer is notified that there is a limited time for this contingency to be removed. Doing this can bring greater urgency to closing the transaction and protect the sellers' interests.

Often there are other people who will need to approve the transaction. Be sure you know who they are, what they need to approve, and when they need to approve it. If family members are helping fund the transaction through gifts or co-signing, be sure to meet with them as quickly as possible, preferably before the contract is signed. Any such subject-to approvals will need to be specified in the contract and

You must look ahead at every transaction and question all the steps in the transaction— what can go wrong and react before it happens! Bulletproof before the bullet hits you!
Ron Young, Bluebell, PA

have short timelines. It is even better to make them "subject to disapproval." What I mean is this: word the contract such that if approval is not provided in writing by a specific deadline, approval is legally assumed and the transaction can move forward.

In many areas, attorneys are directly involved in the closing process, usually one for the seller and one for the buyer. You will need to work directly with them and be sure that they get whatever information they need. Attorneys sometimes take a more active role in the transaction than expected, raising questions about specific language or details which may seem incidental to the transaction. No matter. Just be proactive and get any and all questions answered in a timely fashion. Even in those areas where attorneys are not regularly used, the buyer or seller may want the contract reviewed. You need to know about this and be sure it doesn't delay the closing process.

Finally, in a shifted market, there will be short sales or third party sales (relocation or estate) in which a lender, company, institution or trustee will need to approve the sale. It will be important to know who they are and how they can be contacted. Then, once again, you will need to take the initiative to be sure they are provided what they need, when they need it. You must facilitate their approval. In these cases, you will need to let the buyer know that this is happening and the realistic timetable for getting the approvals. It is always wise to set up a "key contact list" in the transaction file so that it will be easier for you to communicate with them on a planned basis.

PARTIES TO THE SALE CHECKLIST

PARTIES TO THE TRANSACTION

Buyer(s)	Closing/Escrow Company (Closing Officer, Assistant)
Seller(s)	Attorney(s)
Co-op Agent(s)	Third Parties (Loss Mitigation, Relocation, Estate, etc.)
Lender (Loan Officer, Mortgage Processor)	Referral Sources (Agents, Past Clients, Relo, etc.)

CONTACT INFORMATION

Name	Business Address
Home Address	Business Phone
Home Phone	Business Fax
Home Fax	Business Email
Personal Email	Executive/Administrative Assistant (Gatekeeper)
Cell Phone	Preferred Methods and Times of Contact

FIGURE 62

The best time to get all the names and contact information is right at the beginning. If you have an assistant (virtual or real, full-time or part-time) you can get the information to them to do the input, but it needs to be done consistently and immediately. You will be making many calls and contacts from contract to closing – and some will be urgent – so keep these names and this information with you all the time. Put a copy of your key contacts list in the transaction file and carry another with you.

5. CO-OP AGENT

Sales is inherently competitive. Individuals who work without the safety net of a salary have good reason to fight for each and every sale—their livelihood depends on it. What makes real estate sales so remarkable is how amazingly cooperative it can be. Yes, we're competitors but we see the value in working together. Our trade association, local boards, and multiple listing services have evolved into a system of cooperative competition—call it a "co-opetition." In any case, it's an interdependent industry with an amazing range of knowledge, skill, and diligence on display among brokers and agents. And you never know which agent you'll get. One day you'll work with a salesperson with thousands of sales to their credit and at the next, you'll introduce yourself to a new agent fresh out of real estate school. So in every transaction it's critical that you carefully assess who you are "co-oping" with—their experience, their communication ability, their knowledge, and yes, even their ethics. Identify their strengths and know where you might have to carry the load, and vice versa.

You are going to be working with them and through them until this transaction gets closed. So, you might just as well get things straight up front. Once you have a signed and accepted purchase contact, it's time to move from negotiating into cooperating. An initial meeting is essential to lay down the plan, agree on the key deadlines and assign accountability for each part of the process. Insist on it. This should feel very cooperative and synergistic. After all, you both have the same goals—a completed closing, earned commissions and satisfied clients. After your initial meeting you will have a good sense of who you are working with and what you will have to watch for.

If they have some misunderstanding or have given some misinformation to their clients, now or during the closing process, you will need to kindly but strongly confront the issue and get the right perspective in place. If they won't budge, you may have to talk to their broker or a top agent in their office with whom you have a good working relationship. You can not let misinformation or wrong advice persist—it could blow up in everybody's face. And, you want to take the initiative in selecting all the vendors who will support the transaction: lenders, attorneys, inspectors, closing companies, and more. Just offer to take care of it. If they want to use someone that you don't trust, express your concerns and seek vendors that meet with both of your approval.

With so many agents not sure what to do in our current market, you will often need to handle both sides of the transaction, just to get the deal closed.

Michael Williamson, Scottsdale, AZ

While you will need to be the one who is tracking the process, checking on what is getting done and when, and insisting that the right things happen, you are not trying to micromanage the other agent. They have a job to do and you respect that. But you are going to own the outcome and be accountable to things getting done as they should. On the one hand, you are going to be open, supportive and respectful. On the other hand you are going to be assertive, insistent, and determined. In the end, if they drop the ball or leave you doing most of the work, oh well, it's just part of the game. And in a shift, getting transactions closed is far more important to you and your customers.

Here's the truth: agents gain a reputation among other agents (and among vendors for that matter). That reputation will either serve them in times of need or fail them when they most need someone's help. You want to be the most trusted and respected agent in your area—the one everyone looks forward to having as a co-op agent in their deal. So all your extra work and diligence in bulletproofing and overseeing the transaction will come back to serve you in the long run. Again, it's not about one deal or one year. It's about your career.

6. DEADLINES

Deadlines are called that for a reason—cross the line and the deal is dead. Every real estate sales contract has specific language outlining the dates and times that must be met. And there's no tiptoeing around them. If you miss a deadline, you can put the transaction at risk. You'll adopt the mental set of an air traffic controller. Even if you only represent one of the parties in the deal, you will want to track all the moving parts—inspections, approvals, funding, closing, occupancy, and any other critical dates for completion. You will be the one who reminds others what they need to do and by when they need to do it even if they've already been given a copy of the contract and notified of their responsibilities.

Time is not on your side. You will bring urgency and timeliness to the process. This requires being very assertive (with consideration and respect, of course) and reminding others about the consequences of missed deadlines. You have to be on top of the process and tough-minded about the schedule. The Contract to Close Checklist (see below) will be your roadmap to staying on course and on time.

You may decide to add other items and deadlines to this checklist. There may be specific practices and procedures that are unique to your real estate market. The important point here is to have a checklist you can share, follow, and update. It allows you to set expectations with each of the parties to the sale, anticipate issues, communicate in a timely manner, and be assured that everything is moving effectively toward a successful closing.

CONTRACT TO CLOSE CHECKLIST

		Date Expected	Date Completed
1.	Contract and earnest money received		
2.	Earnest money receipted		
3.	File opened and Key Contacts added		
4.	Introduction letter sent to clients		
5.	Payoff / Assumption statement ordered		
6.	Payoff statement received		
7.	Commitment sent to lender		
8.	Commitment sent to other agent		
9.	HOA Info / Resale certificate received		
10.	Survey ordered or existing survey verified		
11.	Hazard insurance information received		
12.	Termite inspection received		
13.	Full inspection received		
14.	Repairs Addendum signed and received		
15.	Repair completed and invoice received		
16.	Home Warranty ordered		
17.	Lender docs received and verified		
18.	Closing scheduled with all vendors		
19.	Closing schedule / reminders sent to clients		
20.	HUD Statement reviewed and approved		
21.	Final Closing Package prepared		
22.	Other		

FIGURE 63

Figure 63 is available as a free download at www.MillionaireSystems.com/shift.

TWO TIMELESS STRATEGIES

You can call it "buyer's remorse" or "cold feet" or "second thoughts" or "the jitters" or any of a number of interesting euphemisms, but the reason a transaction falls apart may not be due to any one specific issue. The fact is that it all really boils down to fear. So while the six issues we've just covered comprise the critical components in any transaction, an issue may just provide a reluctant buyer an easy way to back out of the deal. Emotions often drive home-buying decisions—be they going in or getting out. In a shifted market the decision to buy is complicated by external or subconscious factors, such as negative press, the foreclosure reports, and the less informed opinions of friends and family. We've described all of this before. Your success is dependent on your ability to keep everyone (buyers, sellers, appraisers, lenders, and all vendors) on the straight and narrow path to closing.

Proactive is better than reactive. The advantage always goes to the ones who keeps their head up and anticipate where everything might go wrong. It's not just a win for you; it is a win for all those involved, particularly sellers and buyers. Going back to ground zero and starting all over again seldom serves the interests of anyone. Your job is to keep everyone's eyes on the prize—a successful, completed, and closed transaction.

There are two timeless strategies that the best professionals use to stay on track and get to the finish line: 1) proactive prevention and 2) early response. The first keeps everyone focused on the positive, intentional, adaptable, certain achievement of the goal. The second focuses the responsible players (usually the agents and the vendors) on awareness, accountability, problem solving, and the customer-sensitive handling of whatever goes wrong. These are the best tools for fighting the frequently cited law made famous in 1949 by Capt. Edward A. Murphy, an engineer at Edwards Air Force Base: "If anything can go wrong, it will." So, take Murphy out of the game and then keep everyone's head in it.

BULLETPROOFING STRATEGIES

1. **PROACTIVE PREVENTION** with buyers, sellers, vendors, and co-ops.

   A. Outcome Framing What do we want to achieve?

   B. Setting Expectations What do we realistically need to consider?

   C. Preparing Alternatives What will we do if . . . ?

   D. Reassurance We're on track, ahead of the game, and doing fine.

2. **EARLY RESPONSE** to problems and issues.

   A. Constant Communication What's happening? How are you doing?

   B. Inspecting Expectations Has it been done? What will you do now?

   C. Problem Solving What do we need to do now? How can this get done?

   D. Contract to Close Tracking What is our progress? What's next?

1) PROACTIVE PREVENTION

In a shifted market, you will have to deal with buyer remorse, seller reluctance, loan processing delays (even last minute failures to fund), tight appraisals, tough inspections, and anxiety all around. You must be the calmest person and the calming influence in the transaction. In his famous poem "If," Rudyard Kipling encourages us to "keep your head while all about you are losing theirs." It's timeless advice and perfectly applicable to the role you will play in a troubled transaction. Thorough preparation positions you to solve problems quickly, act with calm and confidence, and keep others from "losing it."

In nearly every situation, it is effective to remind people about the intended results of their decisions and actions. This is called "outcome framing" and every great salesperson uses this effective technique. It's a very powerful mental skill. "Begin with the end in mind" and then constantly keep people in touch with that picture; the anticipation of actually being in that picture—glad they did what they set out to do and enjoying the benefits of it. In times of fear, doubt or emotional reaction, that picture of the desired outcome can bring them back to sanity and reason.

PROACTIVE PREVENTION

1. **Outcome Framing** What do we want to achieve?
2. **Setting Expectations** What do we realistically need to consider?
3. **Preparing Alternatives** What will we do if . . . ?
4. **Reassurance** We're on track, ahead of the game, and doing fine.

Once the buyer makes a decision to buy a particular home and the offer has been accepted, you as their agent must help them deal with "buyer's remorse." It is an age-old malady experienced by almost everyone who makes a big purchase or financial decision. They begin to second-guess themselves, to imagine the worst possible outcomes and to pay attention to less than knowledgeable advice from friends, relatives, and colleagues. As their trusted agent, you must warn them about this and give them practical ways to handle it. Set up early warning feedback and quick-response action plans to handle the unforeseen and unexpected—which for you are actually foreseen and expected. Your buyers avoid being blindsided because you are attentive and responsive.

Keeping things as calm as possible means setting the right expectations from start to finish, with anyone and everyone in the transaction. First with buyers, you must remind them that there are only a few great deals in this market. And, they have purchased one of those. Beyond that, you want to help them realize and not forget that this home they have decided to buy fits their criteria—it meets their needs and many of their wants. It is not a home they would want to lose nor would they want to go through another long search to find one that is comparable. In fact you make it clear to them there may not be another one that is such a good fit.

While sellers may be less likely to want to pull back from a completed sales contract, they may still be emotionally reactive. Particularly if they are asked to make any additional contributions such as doing repairs, providing a repair allowance, offering additional seller concessions, or changing the closing schedule to benefit the buyers. So, you must prepare them for these possibilities ahead of time. Let them know that these changes are normal and that they may be required to get the home sold.

No obstacle is too big if we have thought our way over, around or under it. It is important that we consider all our alternatives and options if something doesn't work out. And, it is best to do this well in advance. Sometimes we do this on our own, so as not to overly concern the customer, but often we will need to engage them in this creative process. Be ready to take care of repairs, find additional funds, provide creative financing, allow for an altered timetable, or file additional paperwork. For each key issue or event in the transaction, we need to be ready to move past the obstacle.

Sincere reassurance – delivered confidently and proactively – builds trust and peace of mind for the clients. For some reason this is often a step some agents leave out. And that's a mistake. Just because things are going well and you feel great, don't assume your buyers and sellers understand that and feel great too. They need to be told. In the absence of reassurance they may start to worry and doubt. Keeping their emotions and personal sense of well-being in a good place is, in the end, your responsibility. It's as simple as letting them know that "this is normal" or "this happens more often than you'd think." It's as direct as saying "thanks for letting me know what's on your mind and I want you to know I am aware of it" or "I'm on top of it." You are just letting them know that they and their transaction matter to you, that you're paying attention to all the details and that they can ask about whatever they want whenever they want.

Even if you need to communicate some problems or prepare some backup alternatives, they need to feel your strength and know that you are moving things along toward the outcome they want. It's difficult to fake this, so the key to being reassuring is to know, in your own mind, that you are in control. When people know they can trust you – that you do what you say you'll do and that you care about them – they not only enjoy the peace of mind, but they become your enthusiastic advocates or those Seth Godin describes as "sneezers" in his paradigm of viral-marketing. In a shifted market this word-of-mouth dissemination of your name and reputation is pure gold.

2) EARLY RESPONSE

There are very few things that left on their own get better. In fact, there's a scientific law for this truth. It's called entropy, which informally says "anything left alone tends to fall apart." Scientists who defined this phenomenon surely studied real estate transactions. In a shifted market entropy is spelled with a capital "E"—natural forces work against getting to closing in a way that just isn't true in a sellers' market. So there will absolutely be times that all your proactive prevention was for naught. You anticipated the issue and did everything in your power to keep the transaction on track, but a touch issue still comes up and puts the transaction in jeopardy. The appropriate course of action is then to respond immediately. Early response is you keep things together even when they are trying their best to fall apart.

EARLY RESPONSE

1. **Constant Communication** What's happening?
   How are you doing?

2. **Inspecting Expectations** Has it been done?
   What will you do now?

3. **Problem Solving** What do we need to do now?
   How can this get done?

4. **Contract to Close Tracking** What is our progress?
   What's next?

I once heard an agent say that her motto was "constant communication creates customer confidence." That's a great way to think and act. It is important all the way through the selling and buying process, but nowhere is it more so than during the time period from contract to closing. It's a mistake to assume that the buyer or seller knows that you are working to get everything done. Communication should happen on a consistent, predetermined basis even if there are no problems to discuss or decisions to be made. "No news is good news" is never an option for a sales professional. There is always more information to glean, a relationship to be deepened and, possibly, leads to be had. The truth is that both sellers and buyers actually believe that "no news is probably bad news." Even if they just believe that no news is simply no news, they are going to feel they are being treated like a nobody. Or even worse, that you aren't really doing anything about their deal—you're just busy working with other people.

Constant, consistent communication is the way you prevent any of these negative thoughts and their troubling outcomes. This doesn't mean hours and hours of communication, just consistent, predictable communication. It's not about spending a lot of time, it's about being timely. If you call them on a regular, predictable basis they will know you are serving them. And, it will allow you to be aware of how they are doing, how they are feeling and what they might be worried about. If there is an issue, being aware of it sooner is better than hearing about it later when it is too late to do anything.

When it comes to the work of the vendors to the transaction, accountability is the key. You must inspect what you expect. They must know you are paying attention to what they are doing. And, that you care about it being done on time and right the first time. It's amazing how much faster and better work gets done when someone knows they are being watched. This is called the Hawthorne Effect and was discovered in the 1920's while studying factory worker performance. No matter what the environment, the work being done always improved when the workers were being watched. For the vendors to the transaction, you are the one watching. Try to visit with your vendors each week to catch up on what they are seeing and what they are doing about it.

You must out-skill the competition in a shift. Your success will depend upon it. It's amazing what happens to your career when you truly learn selling skills.

Tony DiCello, Austin, TX

This will provide you with an early warning system when things start to get behind or slide off track. And the benefits run both ways, you can provide extra assistance and accountability on the transactions involving your customers and they can give you insight and forewarning on new issues they are seeing in transactions with their other customers.

Problem solving is both a skill and a process. You can be a creative person in finding alternative ways to get things done and you can be a catalyst for the creativity of others. When it comes to working through a difficult issue in the transaction, you will likely need to do both. Over time, you will take the wisdom of experience and find new ways to solve old problems— creative financing, win-win negotiations, zoning approvals or low-cost repair techniques. And, you can become adept at seeking the expertise and creativity of others. You may even even engage your clients in the process, particularly if they are required to approve of the final solution. People almost always support those plans and ideas they had a hand in creating.

Finally, if you are going to do complex and exacting professional work, you'll need a checklist. Airline pilots may have flown hundreds of flights and thousands of miles, but before every takeoff they run their checklist. They may even be able to do it from memory with their eyes closed, but they read the checklist, review each item, make sure it's done and mark it off. You'll do the same thing. It prevents unforeseen accidents and it allows for the early detection of problems. The Contract to Close Checklist (Figure 63 on page 260) is a good model to use. It is based on our research with the real estate industry's top agents, administrative assistants, and transaction coordinators. Make it yours, add whatever key items fit your local market, and then use it to fly your transactions to safe landings at the closing table.

PLAYING DEFENSE

Forewarned is forearmed. The ultimate control issue hasn't changed—you must get the transaction to and through closing. You'll do it as a fiduciary service to their clients and, frankly, you'll do it to get paid. A downshifted market just complicates the challenge and cranks up the pressure. Typically, fall-throughs or DNCs (Did Not Close) can increase from under 5 percent in a sellers' market to well over 25 percent in a shifted market. So anticipate problems and proactively takes the steps that will prevent anything from sabotaging the deal.

If "finding the motivated," "getting to the table," and "creating urgency" represent playing offense in the game of real estate sales, then "bulletproofing the transaction" is about playing defense. You take charge, occasionally you will even need to be a bit pushy in protecting your clients' welfare and your transaction. If you play it right, there won't be that many surprises. You'll catch things early, even before the problems occur and certainly before they put the closing at risk. The procedures you put in place will serve you in every market; they are always the right things to do. But, in a downshifted market they make an ever bigger difference—the difference of whether or not you get paid for your work. In the long term, your professional fail-safe systems establish you as the reliable, trustworthy, competent professional that gets things done, done right, and on time. That kind of reputation means money in your pocket, a career worth having, and a business that is not only growing but absolutely worth owning.

The real estate sales business game really has a beginning and an end. Both are critical to our success. At the beginning we must lead generate for sellers and buyers, convert these leads to appointments, and then bring about a "meeting of the minds," an accepted purchase offer contract. In the end, we must get that contract and all the involved parties to a satisfactory closing. The first part is the hard, focused work of making connections and achieving agreements. It's heads down. The second part is the wide-eyed, vigilant guardianship of the transaction until it makes it to closing. It's heads up. So, forever remember this truth about our profession: We do our deals heads down but we save our deals heads up.

THE GIFT OF SHIFT

God grant me the serenity to accept the people I cannot change, the
courage to change the one I can, and the wisdom to know it's me.

UNKNOWN

SUCCESSFUL PEOPLE SHIFT. Always. Continuously. Relentlessly. Whether it is in response to the market or their own goals, high achievers are always changing. Altering and adjusting. This is what their life looks like. Successful people know that they must constantly change and adapt if they are to stay successful. They know life is too big to think small and too short to move slowly. They know there are ups and downs. They know that old endings can give way to new and better beginnings. And they know that to triumph in any situation they must always do one thing—shift.

Sometimes shifts just happen and sometimes you make them happen. They happen when you least expect them and they happen when you most want them. Sometimes it doesn't feel right and sometimes it does. Whether you suddenly find you must shift or you suddenly find that you want to shift—the issues are the same. Whether you're in a buyers' market or a sellers' market—the issues are the same. And it doesn't matter if you're trying to keep from going backward or wanting to push forward—the issues are the same. In fact, if you should find that you need to shift and don't, you'll be one shift shy of what you really need.

Hard times aren't easy. Hence the name. But you know what? Easy times aren't easy either. Life is a continuous challenge. People say hard times aren't easy and easy times aren't hard, but I'm not so sure that's true or that it serves you well to look at it that way. I believe it's fairer to say that no matter your circumstances, things can be easy or hard—depending on you. You'll decide. You can either make easy times harder than they need to be or you can make hard times as easy as they can be. You don't get to decide what the market will do, but you definitely get to decide what you will do. My preacher Doug tells a funny story that sheds some light on an agent's relationship to the market. The captain of a ship notices a light in the distance. The captain radios out and says, "We're headed straight for you, change course!" The reply comes back, "This is the harbor master—the lighthouse isn't moving." Sometimes changing course isn't an option, sometimes you shift because you have to.

Now, no one is promising that you'll make the same money no matter the market. A lot of factors go into determining that. The bottom line is that you should make the best of any situation. Unfortunately, not everyone sees it this way. Some people truly do see tough times as times filled with too many problems to handle and wish for a problem-free market. That problem-free market does not exist.

Dr. Norman Vincent Peale once told the story of a young man who came to him and said he wished he didn't have any problems. He said that life was just too tough and he really just wanted all his problems to go away. Dr. Peale replied, "I know of a place where no one has any problems whatsoever. Would you like to know where it is?" The young man excitedly said, "Yes." Dr. Peale then said, "It's Woodlawn Cemetery. You still want to go?"

The living always have problems to solve and challenges to overcome. That's life. The real difference between people is in how they deal with them. If you want to have fewer problems I suggest you learn to become comfortable with being uncomfortable. Learn to shift.

You'll be clearer if you always think of any shift as a shift of choice. You're not always getting to pick the circumstances, but you're always choosing to shift no matter what the circumstances. So if the market shifts, you're shifting. And if the market isn't shifting, you're shifting. In other words, to be your best you can't be shiftless. You're not going to rest on your past nor assume that your future is set. To reach your full potential you are going to become like a priceless diamond and always apply the necessary pressure to harden and shine. And no matter the market, you choose to enjoy the ride.

BE CAREFUL WHAT YOU WISH FOR

That comment really hit me one day while I was having lunch with my wife Mary. I shared with her that I had been wishing that I could just shut my eyes and when I opened them the shift we were currently in would have passed. I told her that as I thought about this I suddenly realized that wasn't what I really wanted. It dawned on me that if I fast-forwarded my life a few years this shift might be over, but so would a lot of other things. I would have missed so much.

Even in tough times there is much to savor. Our dog, Max was getting up in age and we were having a wonderful time with him. The shift would be over, but he might be gone. Our son John was sixteen and we loved having him with us. The shift would be over, but he'd be in college never to live at our home again. My mom was doing great, but she wasn't young anymore. The shift would be over, but she might not be doing as well. I then realized one thing. Take nothing for granted. Assume nothing. Appreciate every moment for what it is. Take the good with the bad and the bad with the good. I had been thinking that the timing of things always had to be perfect and then I understood with total clarity that any time you have is already perfect.

No, I would never wish any of this away—not for any relief from or avoidance of some difficult times. If I want all the good days, the precious times and the meaningful moments, then I'll just have to take the challenges that life brings along with them. I know I can't have one without the other. Nor can you. If you want to be your best and experience greatness in your life, you'll be experiencing both sides of it—almost always at the same time. Besides, as the old English proverb says, "a smooth sea never made a skillful mariner." The good and the bad, the hard and the easy all work together to shape the person you become. Don't wish your life away. Embrace every moment.

THE FARMER'S LUCK

Think of a shift as an opportunity. Dave Jenks often credits Price Pritchett, one of his favorite business authors, as saying "change always comes bearing gifts." I believe this is true. Change can surprise us with the benefits it can bring.

Jay Papasan brought this truth home to Dave and me by sharing this story. His children love to have him read a picture book called *Zen Shorts* about a giant panda bear that befriends three siblings, Addy, Michael, and Karl. In the book, Stillwater the bear tells Michael the story of "The Farmer's Luck," an ancient Taoist tale.

Many years ago there lived a farmer who toiled daily in his fields. One day, without warning, his prize horse—the one he relied on to work the land—ran away. When the news reached his neighbors, they arrived at his door to offer consolation.

"What bad luck," they said with concern.

"Maybe," answered the farmer.

The following morning, the farmer awoke to find his prize horse had returned, and with it, two wild horses.

Upon hearing the news, the neighbors exclaimed, "What good luck!"

"Maybe," replied the farmer.

The very next day, while trying to tame one of the wild horses, the farmer's son was thrown and badly injured his leg.

Again, the neighbors arrived quickly to offer their condolences. "Such bad luck," they said.

"Maybe," answered the farmer.

A day later, officials from the military arrived looking for young men to fight in battle. Recognizing that the farmer's son was badly injured, they did not ask him to enlist.

"Such good luck!" shouted the neighbors.

"Maybe," answered the farmer....

After hearing the story, young Michael says, "I get it. Maybe good luck and bad luck are all mixed up. You never know what will happen next."

This is true for all of us. The good and the bad happen at the same time. In fact, it can sometimes be difficult to tell one from the other. Or, as Abe Lincoln said, "Nothing is either good or bad but thinking makes it so." There can be a "gift of the shift" and perhaps even more than one. Whether we see times as full of difficulty or full of opportunity, they will most likely turn out exactly as we see them. In the end, we determine the times by our choices. Our choice will be to either try to avoid them and wish they weren't true or to embrace the opportunities they offer.

TACKLING TOUGH TIMES

By choosing to embrace opportunity you're choosing to shift. And whether a market shift forces you to choose or you simply choose to shift your business to another level, there are twelve issues you must tackle. Although we've been looking at them through the eyes of a market shift, they aren't just about that. These are, in fact, the twelve fundamentals for shifting your business, anytime and anywhere. This just may be one of your biggest aha's you get from a shift. These twelve tactics are not just timely, they are timeless.

There are times in life when the market shifts and you have to shift to react. There are other times when you'll simply need to make a shift. These twelve tactics are appropriate for when you've been shifted and for when you choose to make a shift. When you've been disrupted by the market or when you want to disrupt the competition. Master these twelve tactics and you gain utmost control over your business. Fail to master them and, at some point, a shift will put you at the whims of the market and your competition.

So, whether you are dealing with a market shift or you've decided to give your business a lift, there are twelve things you need to do.

First, get real about your situation and get right about what you're doing. Bring a greater sense of clarity, priority, and focus to your work. Look at your role and do what you do best and get paid the most for. Most likely, that will be lead generation and conversion.

Second, re-margin your business and get serious about expense management and profitability. Stop spending money on your business and start investing money in it. Lead with revenue, not expenses. Be a "budget bully" and make your money smart.

Third, learn to do more with less. Maximize your productivity. Focus on the six core competencies of a real estate sales business and hold everyone around you to high standards. Follow a clear process for hiring and firing, continually top-grade your people, and annually upgrade your systems.

Fourth, focus your lead generation on finding motivated clients. Time-block to ensure this gets done everyday. Master the tasks, skills, and scripts of your lead generation methods. Make your message match your market and always make direct and indirect offers for immediate response.

Fifth, memorize and internalize the conversion process and the scripts of lead capture, connect, and close. Make sure everyone around you does the same. Never assume you have a lead until you have an appointment.

Sixth, catch people in your Web and focus your Internet strategy on capturing contact information. Everything else it does can be important, but secondary. Offer "thin bait" to attract hits and "fat bait" to give them a reason to register. Rapid response is your standard.

Seventh, master seller pricing so your listings are always "in the market." Show sellers the financial risks of being "overpriced," missing the "window of opportunity" and "chasing the market." Build price reductions into your agreement up front.

EIGHTH, master staging strategies so your sellers always stand out from the competition. Show them how proper clean-up, repairs, and cosmetic improvements will decrease the time on the market, increase the number of offers, and gain a higher sales price.

NINTH, help buyers overcome reluctance and acquire genuine urgency. Become their "local economist of choice," help them tap into their "why," and show them the hazards of trying to "time the market." Narrow the field and provide "best buy" lists so they see the opportunities that exist in their market.

TENTH, build a creative finance team around you and put creative financing to use whenever you can. Use seller creativity (concessions, contributions, buydowns, and owner financing), buyer down payment creativity (family, specialized agencies, government grants, and retirement fund loans) and lender creativity (FHA, special federally funded and guaranteed loans, municipal and state programs, and special application procedures).

ELEVENTH, participate in the "market of the moment" to give your business bandwidth. Know the ins and outs of short sales, foreclosures and REOs. Also become a specialist in capturing and converting the leads from yours and other's REO listings.

TWELFTH, bulletproof your transactions. Take nothing for granted. Set seller and buyer expectations up front, involve yourself in the selection and supervision of all vendors, be personally involved in inspections, repairs and any final negotiations, and employ a step-by-step process to address buyer or seller "remorse."

Tackling these areas is a never-ending process. It's the real estate business. Downward shifts are more difficult on the front end. Upward shifts become more difficult on the back end. On the front end of a buyers' market you have fewer available sales and fewer available commissions per agent. And listings won't sell, which translates to seller dissatisfaction. It is negatively emotional on the down slope. Sellers are frustrated and confused, while buyers are fearful and reluctant. On the other hand, a sustained sellers' market finishes with high competition. Competitors start discounting their value and then start discounting their price. Maintaining an adequate seller listing inventory becomes a real concern.

Economic shifts come in two shapes. These twelve topics and their tactics are timeless and apply to both. Success in a buyers' market just requires you to be doing the things you should have been doing all along.

ACT YOUR WAGE

To successfully implement these twelve tactics you must act your wage. This means you must think and act the wage you want before you earn it. Average is as average does. Good is as good does. And great is as great does. What you do is who you become. A lot of people struggle with this concept. They truly don't understand that if they want to earn a certain amount of money, then they must live the calendar of a person who earns that—or they won't earn it. It's really that simple.

I believe thoughts come before actions and actions come before results. This means unless you're counting on a lot of luck, you must think and act in such a way as to realize your goals. So, which comes first, thoughts or actions? Thoughts. You think before you act. Then which comes next, actions or results? Actions. You do something then you get a result. So, in other words, its thoughts plus actions then results. In that order. Why? Because life is an inside first, outside second experience. How you think determines what you do and what you do determines the results you get.

I was visiting with a real estate agent, and as I truly got a sense of what he was capable of I made this comment, "I think you're a $50 million dollar a year producer masquerading as a $10 million dollar a year producer." He was shocked and asked what I meant and I said, "All I mean is that you appear to have amazing potential, but you're thinking and acting like a $1 million dollar producer." I told him he was underperforming because he was underacting. I said, "If you want to grow to the next level you better start acting your wage." And the same applies to you. You must think like and take the actions of the production you want or you won't ever get it. So, if you want to shift your business to the next level you better start acting your wage.

Getting what we want in life requires hard work and there are no guarantees. Someone once told me "you must put in the time before you'll see a dime" and I agree. You must put a plan in place that focuses on the actions necessary to get the results you want. And just so we're clear, if it took you longer to say it than it did to think it up—it's not a plan. Thinking and deciding is the hard work of planning; talking about it is the easy part.

Take a look at the twelve issues and based upon your business goals and current situation prioritize them by asking this question: *If I could do just one of them which would make the biggest difference in my business?* Write down the answer. That is your first priority. Then ask this question: *If I could do only one more what would it be?* Write down that answer. And keep doing this until you've written down all twelve issues in a priority list. You now have your marching orders. You know what to do and what to do first. Now, go back to each item and ask three questions: *Do I know how to do this? Do I need anything to do this? Do I need any help doing it?* The answers will give you a list of what you need to know, what you need to have, and who's support you'll need to do each priority. Now, start with your first priority and begin accomplishing your goals.

THE SPEED OF NEED

If you want to be effective (and efficient) keep things simple. Don't try to accomplish everything at once just do the few things that matter most and see what happens. I think we've put the twelve issues in the proper order in which they occur in everyone's business, but I don't think they're necessarily in the priority order for anyone in particular. Your business is your business and your priorities are yours and yours alone. You know your goals and you know where you currently stand. You also know what is holding you back. Some people will ask me what I think, but I always answer with "what do you think?" Invariably, they know the answer. Everyone, deep down, knows their answers if they'll stop long enough to ask the question and then think about it. I believe you have to slow down just for a second before you speed up. The slowing down is for asking the question and then being still long enough to hear the answer. After that, it's time to take action at the speed of your need.

Some people say they feel the need for speed, and I know what they mean. I certainly feel that. However, I think it's more instructive to acknowledge that everyone moves at the speed of their need—that we all get our actual speed from our big whys. If you're in touch with what you really want and have turned that into a need, then I believe that need now sets the pace you'll move to go get it. Velocity creates momentum. And haste driven by big motives and a prioritized plan is never a waste. So when you see an individual moving positively in the direction of their dreams you're seeing someone who is in touch with their biggest whys.

When you're clear about what you desire then you'll be clear about the speed you'll need to move to get it. If you'll then take your priorities to your calendar and time block for them based upon this way of thinking you will get the most out of yourself and your career. And your life. You'll be moving at the speed of need. Any other way will leave you wanting or waiting.

WE FAIL OUR WAY TO SUCCESS

The real estate business has always been cyclical. If you are going to be successful over the long haul you will prepare for those cycles and find opportunities in them. Your determination, your preparation, and your implementation will put you on the right path to your goals. You will consistently be in step with the consumer and ahead of your competition. Others may see things as good times and bad times. You will always see them as opportunity time.

One of the greatest myths is that you succeed your way to success. This isn't true. In fact, just the opposite is true. You fail your way to success. Everyone fails. The ones who succeed are the ones who keep going.

The ones who fail are the ones who don't. When you succeed you do an end zone dance and celebrate. When you lose you seek to find out "what happened," learn from your mistake, and push forward. Failing at something isn't failing. It's learning what didn't work and growing from the experience. Zig Ziglar was right when he said, "A big shot is a little shot that just kept shooting." Everyone falls down, but not everyone gets up. The trick in life is to get up. The world won't judge you by your failures, but by how many times you get back up. No matter the market and no matter your results, always get up and continue on with your journey. That is what we were all meant to do. That is what you must do.

Tough times are essential for top people to get ahead. Even the best need an assist by the market to gain a step on the competition. While it knocks you down it's knocking others out. So, a shift is an opportunity to get ahead or be left behind—the only question is which one will it be for you? Time tends to reward effort and resilience.

Life is still about the basics and mastering them. Two plus two still equals four. I learned this, my son learned this, and you learned this. The basics are timeless in both how they work and how important they are. They're building blocks. When you learn them everything shows up and looks like an opportunity. When you don't learn them everything shows up and looks like a problem. Think of these twelve issues as simply another way of looking at the basics because they are the basics. Don't ever get away from doing them. Then a down market won't get you totally down and an up market can lift you to new heights.

Success never comes to the chosen few, but the few who choose. These can be the worst of times; these can be the best of times. You get to choose.

APPENDIX

Figures 64 and 65 illustrate the Law of Equilibrium at work after a shift. In the fall of 2005, both the average annual sales and the number of available sides per person began a pronounced slide while the agent population was only beginning to change direction. It is these two trends that eventually push some out of the business, renewing opportunity for those who remain.

NAR MEMBERS VS. ANNUAL SALES

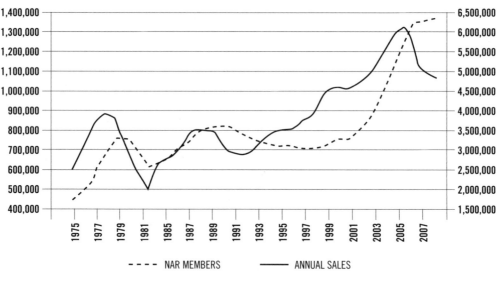

FIGURE 64

NAR MEMBERS VS. AVAILABLE SALES PER PERSON

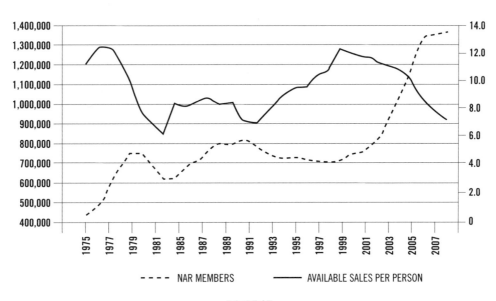

FIGURE 65

INDEX

talent scouting, steps in, 44
talent shift, steps to, 42–43
target audiences in shifted market, 65–66
target market in lead generation, 58–59
third party sales, 256
3P-2F formula for staging, 162–164
tie down close, 102
Tiffany and Co., 191
time blocking, 73–81
   defined, 73
   discipline and, 73–74
   month-at-a-glance calendar in, 76–77
   myth of, 73–74
   pencil in, 76–77
   success in, 75–79
timing
   hazards of, for market, 189
   in lead generation, 54–55
   types of buyers in regards to, 168–169
tough times, tackling, 276–279
trading up, 189–190
traffic, lead generation for, 116–121
training schedule, establishing, 42
The Traveler's Gift (Andrews), 23
trial close, 100–102
2-1 buydown, 215–216

underpricing, 145
underselling, fear of, 145–146
up markets, 31–32, 40, 194, 241
USA Today, 158

value, buyer search for, 138–139
variable expenses, 34
vendors, 39–40, 249

Walton, Sam, 27
Web metrics, 120
willingness of buyer, 176–178, 180, 194–195
Willis, Mark, 26
Willis, Rachael, 26
window of opportunity,

seller pricing, 137–139
Winters, Jonathan, 49
workouts, 232–233
wrap-around mortgages, 208–209

Yahoo!, 113
Yorke, James, 29
Young, Owen D., 36
Your First Home (Keller et al), 184–185, 286
YouTube, 113

Zen Shorts, 274
Ziglar, Zig, 24, 283

ABOUT THE AUTHORS

Authors Gary Keller, Dave Jenks, and Jay Papasan

Gary Keller and coauthors Dave Jenks and Jay Papasan have together written the national best-selling books *The Millionaire Real Estate Agent* and *The Millionaire Real Estate Investor,* and contributed to a third, *FLIP: How to Find, Fix, and Sell Houses for Profit. SHIFT* represents the latest book in this Millionaire Real Estate series. In 2008, the three collaborated on a fourth title, *Your First Home: The Proven Path to Home Ownership.*

GARY KELLER is chairman of the board of Keller Williams Realty, Inc., which he cofounded with Joe Williams in 1983. The company is one of the largest and fastest-growing real estate franchise systems in North America. In addition to helping to provide strategic direction for Keller Williams Realty, Gary maintains a busy schedule writ-

Thursday, August 16, 2007 8:49 PM

From: **Shaun Rawls**
To: Gary Keller

While I am trying to stay on top of the mortgage soap opera in order to better lead my agents, it's getting harder by the day to separate fact from fiction! I thought this memo from [a mortgage company] today would be an insightful read, and might be another piece of a 1,000 piece puzzle. I feel like I'm on chapter 2 of a novel, and I keep reading in hopes to find a happy ending.

Are there plans to address the mortgage "thing" at Mega Camp? I think people would greatly appreciate our leader's opinion of what is happening and what possible impact it could have on our industry given various outcomes (me included).

Any thoughts you have would be greatly appreciated.

Saturday, August 18, 2007 9:17 AM

From: **Gary Keller**
To: Shaun Rawls

nationally the shift appears gradual, but locally there is no such thing as a gradual shift - local shifts always come like a blunt hammer on our head - OUCH!!!

you've got the right attitude and philosophy. so:
1. cut your expenses to the bone - NOW. except training.
2. agents need to cut expenses where they can and cut dead weight – anyone not willing to put in the extra effort and time right now. their teams are shrinking and that isn't all bad. lean and mean can be very good.
3. focus on the seller issues: price/terms and condition/staging. creative financing will be making a comeback in some form.
4. focus on the buyer issue: urgency. buyers tend to think they have lots of choice now, lots of time and don't want to over pay.
5. **take care of yourself and your family** so you don't wear down during this epic battle period. i mean it.

onward.....gk

MILLIONAIRESYSTEMS.COM

Reap the benefits of thinking big and aiming high! Visit us at www.MillionaireSystems.com and expand your possibilities as part of a growing community of top performers.

- Register for training events near you.

- Explore success stories, free downloads, and business-building resources.

- Order books, audiobooks, DVDs, CDs, and more.

Plug into the energy and insights of other top-performing real estate agents, investors, and experts in the Millionaire Real Estate community. Take your sales business to its highest level possible.

ing, teaching, speaking, and consulting. His passions are golf, reading, movies, rock concerts, fly fishing, snow skiing, football, basketball, and spending as much time as possible with his family and friends. Gary lives in Austin, Texas, with his wife, Mary, their son, John, and their two dogs, Max and Grace.

DAVE JENKS served as vice president of research and development with Keller Williams Realty International from 1996 until 2008. He has trained and consulted with thousands of top real estate agents and has served as an instructor for the Dale Carnegie Institute. He loves music (especially bluegrass and guitar), travel, reading, writing, hiking, and most recently mountain biking. Dave is the father of three and grand-father of nine. He and his life partner Laurie live in Sedona, Arizona, where he continues to pursue his passion for training and consulting entrepreneurs from all walks.

JAY PAPASAN is vice president of publishing and executive editor at Keller Williams Realty International, where he oversees research, course writing, and book development. Prior to joining Keller Williams, Jay was a freelance writer for publications such as *Texas Monthly* and *Memphis Magazine*. He also spent several years as an editor at HarperCollins Publishers, where he worked on the *New York Times* best-selling books *Body for Life,* by Bill Phillips, and *Go for the Goal,* by Mia Hamm. In his free time, Jay pursues his hobbies: fly fishing, soccer, reading, writing, and the ongoing quest for the ultimate key lime pie. He resides in Austin, Texas, with his wife, Wendy, and their two children, Gus and Veronica.